1 MONTH OF
FREE
READING

at

www.ForgottenBooks.com

By purchasing this book you are eligible for one month membership to ForgottenBooks.com, giving you unlimited access to our entire collection of over 1,000,000 titles via our web site and mobile apps.

To claim your free month visit:

www.forgottenbooks.com/free821155

ISBN 978-0-364-21668-2
PIBN 10821155

This book is a reproduction of an important historical work. Forgotten Books uses
state-of-the-art technology to digitally reconstruct the work, preserving the original format
whilst repairing imperfections present in the aged copy. In rare cases, an imperfection in
the original, such as a blemish or missing page, may be replicated in our edition. We do,
however, repair the vast majority of imperfections successfully; any imperfections that
remain are intentionally left to preserve the state of such historical works.

Harding's Edition.

THE

MERRY WIVES OF WINDSOR,

COMEDY,

BY

WILLIAM SHAKSPEARE.

ACCURATELY PRINTED

FROM THE TEXT OF

Mr. STEEVENS's LAST EDITION.

Ornamented with Plates.

London:

PUBLISHED BY E. HARDING, NO. 98, PALL MALL;
J. WRIGHT, PICCADILLY; G. SAEL, STRAND;
AND VERNOR AND HOOD, POULTRY.

1798.

OBSERVATIONS.

A FEW of the incidents in this comedy might have been taken from some old translation of *Il Pecorone* by Giovanni Fiorentino. I have lately met with the same story in a very contemptible performance, intitled, *The fortunate, the deceived, and the unfortunate Lovers.* Of this book, as I am told, there are several impressions; but that in which I read it, was published in 1632, quarto. A somewhat similar story occurs in *Piacevoli Notti di Straparola*, Nott. 4ᵗ. Fav. 4ᵗ. This comedy was first entered at Stationers' Hall, Jan. 18, 1601, by John Busby. STEEVENS.

A passage in the first sketch of *The Merry Wives of Windsor* shews, I think, that it ought to be read between *the First* and *the Second Part of King Henry IV.* in the latter of which young Henry becomes king. In the last act, Falstaff says:

"Herne the hunter, quoth you? am I a ghost?
" 'Shlood, the fairies hath made a ghost of me.
" What, hunting at this time of night!
" I'le lay my life the mad *prince of Wales*
" Is stealing his father's deare."

and in this play, as it now appears, Mr. Page discountenances the addresses of Fenton to his daughter, because " he keeps company with the wild *prince*, and with Poins."

The Fishwife's Tale of Brainford in WESTWARD FOR SMELTS, a book which Shakspeare appears to have read, (having borrowed from it part of the fable of *Cymbeline*,) probably led him to lay the scene of Falstaff's love-adventures at *Windsor*. It begins thus: " In *Windsor* not long agoe dwelt a sumpterman, who had to wife a very faire but wanton creature, over whom, not without cause, he was something *jealous*; yet had he never any proof of her inconstancy. MALONE.

The adventures of *Falstaff* in this play seem to have been taken from the story of *The Lovers of Pisa*, in an old piece called "*Tarleton's Newes out of Purgatorie.*"

Mr. *Warton* observes, in a note to the last *Oxford* edition, that the play was probably not written, as we now have it, before 1607, at the earliest. I agree with my very ingenious friend in this supposition, but yet the argument here produced for it may not be conclusive. *Slender* observes to master *Page*, that his *greyhound was outrun on Cotsale*: [*Cotswold-Hills* in *Gloucestershire*]; and Mr. *Warton* thinks, that the *games* established there by Captain *Dover* in the beginning of K. *James's* reign, are alluded to.—But perhaps, though the Captain be celebrated in the *Annalia Dubrensia* as the *founder of them*, he might be the *reviver* only, or some way contribute to make them more famous; for in *The second Part of Henry IV.* 1600, Justice *Shallow* reckons among the *Swinge-bucklers* " *Will Squeele, a Cotsole man.*"

In

In the first edition of the imperfect play, *sir Hugh Evans* is called on the title page, the *Welsh Knight*; and yet there are some persons who still affect to believe, that all our author's plays were originally published by himself. FARMER.

Dr. Farmer's opinion is well supported by "An eclogue on the noble assemblies *revived* on Cotswold Hills, by Mr. Robert Dover." See Randolph's Poems, printed at Oxford, 4to. 1638, p. 114. The hills of *Cotswold*, in *Gloucestershire*, are mentioned in *K. Richard II.* Act II. sc. iii. and by Drayton, in his *Poly-olbion*, song 14. STEEVENS.

Queen Elizabeth was so well pleased with the admirable character of Falstaff in *The Two Parts of Henry IV.* that, as Mr. Rowe informs us, she commanded Shakspeare to continue it for one play more, and to shew him in love. To this command we owe *The Merry Wives of Windsor*; which Mr. Gildon says, [*Remarks* on Shakspeare's plays, 8vo. 1710,] he was very well assured our author finished in a fortnight. But this must be meant only of the first imperfect sketch of this comedy. An old quarto edition which I have seen, printed in 1602, says, in the title-page,—*As it hath been divers times acted before her majesty, and elsewhere.* This, which we have here, was altered and improved by the author almost in every speech. POPE. THEOBALD.

Mr. Gildon has likewise told us, "that our author's house at Stratford bordered on the Church-yard, and that he wrote the scene of the Ghost in *Hamlet* there." But neither for this, or the assertion that the play before us was written in a fortnight, does he quote any authority. The latter circumstance was first mentioned by Mr. Dennis. "This comedy," says he, in his Epistle Dedicatory to *The Comical Gallant*, (an alteration of the present play,) 1702, "was written at her [Queen Elizabeth's] command, and by her direction, and she was so eager to see it acted, that she commanded it to be finished in *fourteen days*; and was afterwards, as tradition tells us, very well pleased at the representation." The information, it is probable, came originally from Dryden, who from his intimacy with Sir William Davenant, had an opportunity of learning many particulars concerning our author.

At what period Shakspeare new-modelled *The Merry Wives of Windsor* is unknown. I believe it was enlarged in 1603. See some conjectures on the subject, in the *Attempt to ascertain the order of his plays.* MALONE.

It is not generally known, that the first edition of *The Merry Wives of Windsor*, in its present state, is in the valuable folio, printed 1623, from whence the quarto of the same play, dated 1630, was evidently copied. The two earlier quartos, 1602, and 1619, only exhibit this comedy as it was originally written, and are so far curious, as they contain Shakspeare's first conceptions in forming a drama, which is the most complete specimen of his comick powers. T. WARTON.

PERSONS REPRESENTED

———

Sir John Falstaff.

Fenton.

Shallow, *a country Justice.*

Slender, *cousin to* Shallow.

Mr. Ford, } *two gentlemen dwelling at* W
Mr. Page,

William Page, *a boy, son to* Mr. Page.

Sir Hugh Evans, *a Welch parson.*

Dr. Caius, *a French physician.*

Host of the Garter Inn.

Bardolph,
Pistol, } *followers of* Falstaff.
Nym,

Robin, *page to* Falstaff.

Simple, *servant to* Slender.

Rugby, *servant to* Dr. Caius.

Mrs. Ford.

Mrs. Page.

Mrs. Anne Page, *her daughter, in love* ¶

Mrs. Quickly, *servant to* Dr. Caius.

Servants to Page, Ford, /

SCENE. Windsor; *and the* ¶

ACT I. SCENE I.

WINDSOR. *Before* PAGE'S *Houſe.*

nter Juſtice SHALLOW, SLENDER, *and Sir* HUGH
EVANS.

Shallow.

SIR Hugh, perſuade me not; I will make a Star-chamber matter of it: if he were twenty ſir John Falſtaffs, he ſhall not abuſe Robert Shallow, eſquire.

Slen. In the county of Gloſter, juſtice of peace, and *coram.*

Shal. Ay, couſin Slender, and *Cuſt-alorum.*

Slen. Ay, and *ratolorum* too; and a gentleman born, maſter parſon; who writes himſelf *armigero*; in any bill, warrant, quittance, or obligation, *armigero.*

Shal. Ay, that we do; and have done any time theſe three hundred years.

Slen. All his ſucceſſors, gone before him, have done't; and all his anceſtors, that come after him, may: they may give the dozen white luces in their coat.

Shal. It is an old coat.

Eva. The dozen white louſes do become an old coat well; it agrees well, paſſant: it is a familiar beaſt to man, and ſignifies—love.

Shal.

Sbal. The luce is the freſh fiſh; the ſalt fiſh is an old coat.

Slen. I may quarter, coz ?

Sbal. You may, by marrying.

Eva. It is marring indeed, if he quarter it.

Sbal. Not a whit.

Eva. Yes, py'r-lady; if he has a quarter of your coat, there is but three ſkirts for yourſelf, in my ſimple conjec-tures; but that is all one : If ſir John Falſtaff have com-mitted diſparagements unto you, I am of the churcʰ and will be glad to do my benevolence, to make ·atoɴ ments and compromiſes between you.

Sbal. The Council ſhall hear it; it is a riot.

Eva. It is not meet the Council hear a riot; thereˢ fear of Got in a riot; the Council, look you, ſhall ⟨ to hear the fear of Got, and not to hear a riot your vizaments in that.

Sbal. Ha! o' my life, if I were young again, tʰ ſhould end it.

Eva. It is petter that friends is the ſword, a⟨ and there is alſo another device in my prain, ⟨ adventure, prings goot diſcretions with it : Th Page, which is daughter to maſter George Pag⟨ pretty virginity.

Slen. Miſtreſs Anne Page ? She has broʳ ſpeaks ſmall like a woman.

Eva. It is that fery verſon for all the 'ɩ you will deſire; and ſeven hundred pouˢ and gold, and ſilver, is her grandſire, uˢ bed (Got deliver to a joyful reſurreⴶtio ſhe is able to overtake ſeventeen years ⟨ motion, if we leave our pribbles and ⟨ a marriage between maſter Abrahaⱳ Page.

Shal. Did her grandfire leave her feven hundred pound?

Eva. Ay, and her father is make her a petter penny.

Shal. I know the young gentlewoman; fhe has good gifts.

Eva. Seven hundred pounds, and poffibilities, is good gifts.

Shal. Well, let us fee honeft mafter Page: Is Falftaff there?

Eva. Shall I tell you a lie? I do defpife a liar, as I do defpife one that is falfe; or, as I defpife one that is not true. The knight, fir John, is there; and, I befeech you, be ruled by your well-willers. I will peat the door [*knocks*] for mafter Page. What, hoa! Got plefs your houfe here!

Enter PAGE.

Page. Who's there?

Eva. Here is Got's pleffing, and your friend, and juftice Shallow: and here young mafter Slender; that, perad-ventures, fhall tell you another tale, if matters grow to your likings.

Page. I am glad to fee your worfhips well: I thank you for my venifon, mafter Shallow.

Shal. Mafter Page, I am glad to fee you; Much good do it your good heart! I wifh'd your venifon better; it was ill kill'd.—How doth good Miftrefs Page?—and I love you always with my heart, la; with my heart.

Page. Sir, I thank you.

Shal. Sir, I thank you; by yea and no, I do.

Page. I am glad to fee you, good mafter Slender.

Slen. How does your tallow greyhound, fir? I heard fay, he was out-run on Cotfale.

Page. It could not be judg'd, fir.

Slen. You'll not confefs, you'll not confefs.

Shal.

Shal. That he will not;—'tis your fault, 'tis your fault:—'Tis a good dog.

Page. A cur, fir.

Shal. Sir, he's a good dog, and a fair dog; can there be more faid? he is good, and fair.—Is fir John Falftaff here?

Page. Sir, he is within; and I would I could do a good office between you.

Eva. It is fpoke as a chriftians ought to fpeak.

Shal. He hath wrong'd me, mafter Page.

Page. Sir, he doth in fome fort confefs it.

Shal. If it be confefs'd, it is not redrefs'd; is not that fo, mafter Page? He hath wrong'd me;—indeed, he hath;—at a word, he hath;—believe me;—Robert Shallow, efquire, faith he is wrong'd.

Page. Here comes fir John.

Enter Sir JOHN FALSTAFF, BARDOLPH, NYM, *an*
PISTOL.

Fal. Now, mafter Shallow, you'll complain of *ı* the king?

Shal. Knight, you have beaten my men, kill'd m and broke open my lodge.

Fal. But not kifs'd your keeper's daughter?

Shal. Tut, a pin! this fhall be anfwer'd.

Fal. I will anfwer it ftraight;—I have done That is now anfwer'd.

Shal. The Council fhall know this.

Fal. 'Twere better for you, if it were know fel: you'll be laugh'd at.

Eva. Pauca verba, fir John; good worts.

Fal. Good worts! good cabbage.—Slen your head: What matter have you againft *ı*

Slen. Marry, fir, I have matter in my he

ı

and againſt your coney-catching raſcals, Bardolph, Nym,
and Piſtol. They carried me to the tavern, and made me
drunk, and afterwards pick'd my pocket.

Bar. You Banbury cheeſe!

Slen. Ay, it is no matter.

Piſt. How, now, Mephoſtophilus?

Slen. Ay, it is no matter.

Nym. Slice, I ſay! *pauca, pauca;* ſlice! that's my humour.

Slen. Where's Simple, my man?—Can you tell, couſin?

Eva. Peace: I pray you! Now let us underſtand:
There is three umpires in this matter, as I underſtand:
that is—maſter Page, *fidelicet,* maſter Page; and there
is myſelf, *fidelicet,* myſelf; and the three party is, laſtly
and finally, mine hoſt of the Garter.

Page. We three to hear it, and end it between them.

Eva. Fery goot: I will make a prief of it in my note-
book; and we will afterwards 'ork upon the cauſe, with
as great diſcreetly as we can.

Fal. Piſtol——

Piſt. He hears with ears.

Eva. The tevil and his tam! what phraſe is this,
He bears with ears? Why, it is affectations.

Fal. Piſtol, did you pick maſter Slender's purſe?

Slen. Ay, by theſe gloves, did he, (or I would I might
never come in mine own great chamber again elſe) of ſeven
groats in mill-ſixpences, and two Edward ſhovel-boards,
that coſt me two ſhilling and two pence a-piece of Yead
Miller, by theſe gloves.

Fal. Is this true, Piſtol?

Eva. No; it is falſe, if it is a pick-purſe.

Piſt. Ha, thou mountain-foréigner!—Sir John, and
  maſter mine,
I combat challenge of this latten bilbo:

Word

Word of denial in thy labras here;
Word of denial: froth and fcum, thou lieft.

Slen. By thefe gloves, then 'twas he.

Nym. Be avis'd, fir, and pafs good humours: I will fay, *marry-trap*, with you, if you run the nuthook's humour on me; that is the very note of it.

Slen. By this hat then, he in the red face had it: for, though I cannot remember what I did when you made me drunk, yet I am not altogether an afs.

Fal. What fay you, Scarlet and John?

Bar. Why, fir, for my part, I fay, the gentleman had drunk himfelf out of his five fentences.

Eva. It is his five fenfes: fie, what the ignorance is!

Bar. And being fap, fir, was, as they fay, cafhier'd; and fo conclufions pafs'd the careires.

Slen. Ay, you fpake in Latin then too; but 'tis no matter: I'll ne'er be drunk whilft I live again, but in honeft, civil, godly company, for this trick: if I be drunk, I'll be drunk with thofe that have the fear of God, and not with drunken knaves.

Eva. So Got 'udge me, that is a virtuous mind.

Fal. You hear all thefe matters denied, gentlemen; you hear it.

Enter Miftrefs ANNE PAGE *with wine*; *Miftrefs* FORD *and Miftrefs* PAGE *following.*

Page. Nay, daughter, carry the wine in; we'll drink within.   [*Exit* ANNE PAGE.

Slen. O heaven! this is miftrefs Anne Page.

Page. How now, miftrefs Ford?

Fal. Miftrefs Ford, by my troth, you are very well met: by your leave, good miftrefs.   [*kiffing her.*

Page. Wife, bid thefe gentlemen welcome:——Come, we

we have a hot venifon pafty to dinner ; come, gentlemen,
I hope we fhall drink down all unkindnefs.

　　[Exeunt all but SHALLOW, SLENDER, *and* EVANS.

　　Slen. I had rather than forty fhillings, I had my book
of Songs and Sonnets here.

　　　　　　　Enter SIMPLE.

How now, Simple! where have you been ? I muft wait
on myfelf, muft I ? You have not *The Book of Riddles*
about you, have you ?

　　Sim. Book of Riddles! why, did you not lend it to
Alice Shortcake upon Allhallowmas laft, a fortnight
afore Michaelmas ?

　　Shal. Come, coz ; come, coz ; we ftay for you. A
word with you, coz : marry, this, coz ; There is, as
'twere, a tender, a kind of tender, made afar off by fir
Hugh here ;—Do you underftand me ?

　　Slen. Ay, fir, you fhall find me reafonable ; if it be
fo, I fhall do that that is reafon.

　　Shal. Nay, but underftand me.

　　Slen. So I do, fir.

　　Eva. Give ear to his motions, mafter Slender : I will
defcription the matter to you, if you be capacity of it.

　　Slen. Nay, I will do as my coufin Shallow fays : I pray
you, pardon me ; he's a juftice of peace in his country,
fimple though I ftand here.

　　Eva. But that is not the queftion ; the queftion is concerning your marriage.

　　Shal. Ay, there's the point, fir.

　　Eva. Marry, is it ; the very point of it ; to miftrefs
Anne Page.

　　Slen. Why, if it be fo, I will marry her, upon any
reafonable demands.

　　　　　　　B 4　　　　　　　　　　*Eva.*

Eva. But can you affection the 'oman? Let us command to know that of your mouth, or of your lips; for divers philofophers hold, that the lips is parcel of the mouth:—Therefore, precifely, can you carry your good will to the maid?

Shal. Coufin Abraham Slender, can you love her?

Slen. I hope, fir,—I will do, as it fhall become one that would do reafon.

Eva. Nay, Got's lords and his ladies, you muft fpeak poffitable, if you can carry her your defires towards her.

Shal. That you muft: Will you, upon good dowry, marry her?

Slen. I will do a greater thing than that, upon your requeft, coufin, in any reafon.

Shal. Nay, conceive me, conceive me, fweet coz; what I do, is to pleafure you, coz: Can you love th' maid?

Slen. I will marry her, fir, at your requeft; bu there be no great love in the beginning, yet heaven decreafe it upon better acquaintance, when we are ried, and have more occafion to know one anot hope, upon familiarity will grow more contempt you fay, *marry her*, I will marry her, that I a diffolved, and diffolutely.

Eva. It is a fery difcretion anfwer; fave, (in the 'ort diffolutely: the 'ort is, according t ing, refolutely;—his meaning is good.

Shal. Ay, I think my coufin meant well.

Slen. Ay, or elfe I would I might be hy

Re-Enter ANNE PAGE.

Shal. Here comes fair miftrefs Anne.. young, for your fake, miftrefs Anne!

W.N.Gardiner del et sc

Merry Wives of Windsor.

Page. 13.

Published 1 April 1798 by Edw.ᵈ Harding Pall Mall.

Anne. The dinner is on the table; my father defires your worfhips' company.

Shal. I will wait on him, fair miftrefs Anne.

Eva. Od's pleffed will! I will not be abfence at the grace.

             [*Exeunt* SHALLOW, *and Sir* H. EVANS.

Anne. Will't pleafe your worfhip to come in, fir?

Slen. No, I thank you, forfooth, heartily; I am very well.

Anne. The dinner attends you, fir.

Slen. I am not a-hungry, I thank you, forfooth:—Go, firrah, for all you are my man, go, wait upon my coufin Shallow. [*Exit* SIMPLE.] A juftice of peace fometimes may be beholden to his friend for a man:—I keep but three men and a boy yet, till my mother be dead: But what though? yet I live like a poor gentleman born.

Anne. I may not go in without your worfhip: they will not fit till you come.

Slen. I'faith, I'll eat nothing; I thank you as much as though I did.

Anne. I pray you, fir, walk in.

Slen. I had rather walk here, I thank you: I bruis'd my fhin the other day with playing at fword and dagger with a mafter of fence, three veneys for a difh of ftew'd prunes; and, by my troth, I cannot abide the fmell of hot meat fince. Why do your dogs bark fo? be there bears i'the town?

Anne. I think there are, fir; I heard them talk'd of.

Slen. I love the fport well; but I fhall as foon quarrel at it, as any man in England:—You are afraid if you fee the bear loofe, are you not?

Anne. Ay, indeed, fir.

Slen. That's meat and drink to me, now: I have feen Sackerfon loofe twenty times; and have taken him by the

                                   chain:

came: but, I warrant you, the women have so cried and roar'd at it, that it pass'd:—but women, indeed, cannot abide 'em; they are very ill-favour'd rough things.

Re-enter PAGE.

Page. Come, gentle master Slender, come; we stay for you.

Slen. I'll eat nothing; I thank you, sir.

Page. By cock and pye, you shall not choose, sir: come, come.

Slen. Nay, pray you, lead the way.

Page. Come on, sir.

Slen. Mistress Anne, yourself shall go first.

Anne. Not I, sir; pray you keep on.

Slen. Truly, I will not go first; truly, la: I will not do you that wrong.

Anne. I pray you, sir.

Slen. I'll rather be unmannerly than troublesome: you do yourself wrong, indeed, la.   [*Exeunt.*

SCENE II.

The same.

Enter Sir HUGH EVANS *and* SIMPLE.

Eva. Go your ways, and ask of Doctor Caius' house, which is the way: and there dwells one mistress Quickly, which is in the manner of his nurse, or his dry nurse, or his cook, or his laundry, his washer, and his wringer.

Simp. Well, sir.

Eva. Nay, it is petter yet:—give her this letter; for it is a woman that altogether's acquaintance with mistress Anne Page; and the letter is, to desire and require her to

    solicit

folicit your mafter's defires to Mrs. Anne Page: I pray
you, be gone; I will make an end of my dinner; there's
pippins and cheefe to come.   [*Exeunt.*

SCENE III.

A Room in the Garter Inn.

Enter FALSTAFF, HOST, BARDOLPH, NYM, PISTOL,
and ROBIN.

Fal. Mine hoft of the Garter,—

Hoft. What fays my bully-rook? Speak fchollarly, and
wifely.

Fal. Truly, mine hoft, I muft turn away fome of my
followers.

Hoft. Difcard, bully Hercules; cafhier: let them wag;
trot, trot.

Fal. I fit at ten pounds a week.

Hoft. Thou'rt an emperor, Cæfar, Keifar, and Pheezar.
I will entertain Bardolph; he fhall draw, he fhall tap:
faid I well, bully Hector?

Fal. Do fo, good mine hoft.

Hoft. I have fpoke! let him follow: let me fee thee
froth, and lime: I am at a word, follow.   [*Exit* HOST.

Fal. Bardolph, follow him; a tapfter is a good trade:
An old cloak makes a new jerkin; a withered ferving-man
a frefh tapfter: Go; adieu.

Bard. It is a life that I have defired; I will thrive.

[*Exit* BARD.

Pift. O bafe Gongarian wight! wilt thou the fpigot
wield?

Nym. He was gotten in drink: Is not the humour con-
ceited? His mind is not heroick, and there's the humour
of it.

Fal.

Fal. I am glad I am fo acquit of this tinderbox: his thefts were too open: his filching was like an unfkilful finger, he kept not time.

Nym. The good humour is, to fteal at a minute's reft.

Pift. Convey, the wife it call: Steal! foh; a fico for the phrafe.

Fal. Well, firs, I am almoft out at heels.

Pift. Why then, let kibes enfue.

Fal. There is no remedy; I muft coney-catch; I muft fhift.

Pift. Young ravens muft have food.

Fal. Which of you know Ford, of this town?

Pift. I ken the wight; he is of fubftance good.

Fal. My honeft lads, I will tell you what I am about.

Pift. Two yards, and more.

Fal. No quips now, Piftol: Indeed I am in the waift two yards about: but I am now about no wafte; I am about thrift. Briefly, I do mean to make love to Ford's wife; I fpy entertainment in her; fhe difcourfes, fhe carves, fhe gives the leer of invitation: I can conftrue the action of her familiar ftyle; and the hardeft voice of her behaviour, to be Englifh'd rightly, is, *I am fir John Falftaff's.*

Pift. He hath ftudy'd her well, and tranflated her well; out of honefty into Englifh.

Nym. The anchor is deep: Will that humour pafs?

Fal. Now, the report goes, fhe has all the rule of her hufband's purfe; fhe hath legions of angels.

Pift. As many devils entertain; and, *To her, boy,* fay I.

Nym. The humour rifes; it is good: humour me the angels.

Fal. I have writ me here a letter to her: and here another to Page's wife; who even now gave me good eyes too, ex-amin'd my parts with moft judicious eyliads: fometimes
　　　　　　　　　　　　　　　the

the beam of her view gilded my foot, fometimes my portly belly.

Pift. Then did the fun on dung-hill fhine.

Nym. I thank thee for that humour.

Fal. O, fhe did fo courfe o'er my exteriors with fuch a greedy intention, that the appetite of her eye did feem to fcorch me up like a burning glafs! Here's another letter to her: fhe bears the purfe to; fhe is a region in Guiana, all gold and bounty. I will be cheater to them both, and they fhall be exchequers to me; they fhall be my Eaft and Weft Indies, and I will trade to them both. Go, bear thou this letter to miftrefs Page; and thou this to miftrefs Ford; we will thrive, lads, we will thrive.

Pift. Shall I fir Pandarus of Troy become,
And by my fide wear fteel? then, Lucifer, take all!

Nym. I will run no bafe humour: here, take the hu_mour letter; I will keep the 'haviour of reputation.

Fal. Hold, firrah, [*to* ROB.] bear you thefe letters tightly;
Sail like my pinnace to thefe golden fhores.—
Rogues, hence, avaunt! vanifh like hail-ftones, go;
Trudge, plod, away, o'the hoof; feek fhelter, pack!
Falftaff will learn the humour of this age,
French thrift, you rogues; myfelf, and fkirted page.

　　　　　　　[*Exeunt* FALSTAFF *and* ROBIN.

Pift. Let vultures gripe thy guts! for gourd, and fullam
　　　holds,
And high and low beguile the rich and poor:
Tefter I'll have in pouch, when thou fhalt lack,
Bafe Phrygian Turk!

Nym. I have operations in my head, which be humours of revenge.

Pift. Wilt thou revenge?

Nym. By welkin, and her ftar!

Pift. With wit, or fteel?

　　　　　　　　　　　　　　　　　Nym.

Nym. With both the humours, I :
I will difcufs the humour of this love to Page.

Pift. And I to Ford fhall eke unfold,
How Falftaff, varlet vile,
His dove will prove, his gold will hold,
And his foft couch defile.

Nym. My humour fhall not cool : I will incenfe Page
to deal with poifon; I will poffefs him with yellownefs,
for the revolt of mien is dangerous : that is my true humour.

Pift. Thou art the Mars of malcontents : I fecond thee;
troop on.   [*Exeunt.*

SCENE IV.

A Room in Dr. CAIUS's Houfe.

Enter Mrs. QUICKLY, SIMPLE, and RUGBY.

Quick. What, John Rugby!—I pray thee, go to the
cafement, and fee if you can fee my mafter, mafter Doctor
Caius, coming : if he do, i'faith, and find any body in the
houfe, here will be an old abufing of God's patience, and
the king's Englifh.

Rug. I'll go watch.   [*Exit* RUGBY.

Quick. Go; and we'll have a poffet for't foon at night,
in faith, at the latter end of a fea-coal fire. An honeft,
willing, kind fellow, as ever fervant fhall come in houfe
withal; and, I warrant you, no tell-tale, nor no breed-
bate : his worft fault is, that he is given to prayer; he is
fomething peevifh that way : but nobody but has his fault;
—but let that pafs. Peter Simple, you fay your name is?

Sim. Ay, for fault of a better.

Quick. And mafter Slender's your mafter?

Sim. Ay, forfooth.

                                       Quick.

Quick. Does he not wear a great round beard, like a glover's paring knife?

Sim. No, forsooth: he hath but a little wee face, with a little yellow beard; a Cain-colour'd beard.

Quick. A softly-sprighted man, is he not?

Sim. Ay, forsooth: but he is as tall a man of his hands, as any is between this and his head; he hath fought with a warrener.

Quick. How say you?—O, I should remember him. Does he not hold up his head, as it were? and strut in his gait?

Sim. Yes, indeed, does he.

Quick. Well, heaven send Anne Page no worse fortune! Tell master Parson Evans, I will do what I can for your master: Anne is a good girl, and I wish—

Re-enter RUGBY.

Rug. Out, alas! here comes my master.

Quick. We shall all be shent: Run in here, good young man; go into this closet. [*Shuts* Simple *in the closet.*] He will not stay long.—What, John Rugby! John, what, John, I say!—Go, John, go enquire for my master; I doubt, he be not well, that he comes not home:—*and down, down, adown-a,* &c.　　　　　　[*sings.*

Enter Doctor CAIUS.

Caius. Vat is you sing? I do not like dese toys. Pray you, go and vetch me in my closet *un boitier verd*; a box, a green-a box; Do intend vat I speak? a green-a box.

Quick. Ay, forsooth, I'll fetch it you. I am glad he went not in himself: if he had found the young man, he would have been horn-mad.　　　　　　　[*Aside.*

Caius. Fe, fe, fe, fe! ma foi, il fait fort chaud. Je m'en vais à la Cour,—la grande affaire.

　　　　　　　　　　　　　　　　Quick

Quick. Is it this, fir?

Caius. Ouy; mette le au mon pocket; *Depeche,* quickly : Vere is dat knave Rugby?

Quick. What, John Rugby! John!

Rug. Here, fir.

Caius. You are John Rugby, and you are Jack Rugby : Come, take-a your rapier, and come after my heel to de court.

Rug. 'Tis ready, fir, here in the porch.

Caius. By my trot, I tarry too long:—Od's me! *Qu'ay j'oublié?* dere is fome fimples in my clofet, dat I vill not for the varld I fhall leave behind.

Quick. Ah me! he'll find the young man there, and be mad.

Caius. O diable, diable! vat is in my clofet?—Villainy! *larron!* [*Pulling* Simple *out.*] Rugby, my rapier.

Quick. Good mafter, be content.

Caius. Verefore fhall I be content-a?

Quick. The young man is an honeft man.

Caius. Vat fhall de honeft man do in my clofet? dere is no honeft man dat fhall come in my clofet.

Quick. I befeech you, be not fo phlegmatic; hear the truth of it: He came of an errand to me from Parfon Hugh.

Caius. Vell.

Sim. Ay, forfooth, to defire her to—

Quick. Peace, I pray you.

Caius. Peace-a your tongue:—Speak-a your tale.

Sim. To defire this honeft gentlewoman, your maid, to fpeak a good word to miftrefs Anne Page for my mafter, in the way of marriage.

Quick. This is all indeed, la; but I'll ne'er put my finger in the fire, and need not.

Caius. Sir Hugh fend-a you?—Rugby, *baillez* me fome paper; tarry you a little-a while.   [*Writes.*

                                   Quick.

Quick. I am glad he is fo quiet: if he had been thoroughly moved, you fhould have heard him fo loud, and fo melancholy:—But notwithftanding, man, I'll do your mafter what good I can; and the very yea and the no is, the French doctor, my mafter.—I may call him my mafter, look you, for I keep his houfe; and I wafh, wring, brew, bake, fcour, drefs meat and drink, make the beds, and do all myfelf.

Sim. 'Tis a great charge to come under one body's hand.

Quick. Are you avis'd o'that? you fhall find it a great charge: and to be up early and down late;—but notwithftanding (to tell you in your ear, I would have no words of it;) my mafter himfelf is in love with miftrefs Anne Page: but notwithftanding that,—I know Anne's mind,—that's neither here nor there.

Caius. You jack'nape, give-a dis letter to Sir Hugh; by gar, it is a fhallenge: I vill cut his troat in de park; and I vill teach a fcurvy jack-a-nape prieft to meddle or make:—you may be gone; it is not good you tarry here: by gar, I vill cut all his two ftones; by gar, he fhall not have a ftone to trow at his dog.   [*Exit* SIMPLE.

Quick. Alas, he fpeaks but for his friend.

Caius. It is no matter-a for dat:—do not you tell-a me dat I fhall have Anne Page for myfelf?—by gar, I vill kill de Jack prieft; and I have appointed mine hoft of *de Jarterre* to meafure our weapon:—by gar, I vill myfelf have Anne Page.

Quick. Sir, the maid loves you, and all fhall be well: we muft give folks leave to prate: What, the good-jer!

Caius. Rugby, come to de court vit me;—By gar, if I have not Anne Page, I fhall turn your head out of my door:—Follow my heels, Rugby.

          [*Exeunt* CAIUS *and* RUGBY.

C   *Quick.*

Quick. You shall have An fools-head of your own. No, I know Anne's mind for that : never a woman in Windsor knows more of Anne's mind than I do; nor can do more than I do with her, I thank heaven.

Fent. [*Within.*] Who's within there? ho!

Quick. Who's there, I trow? Come near the house, I pray you.

Enter FENTON.

Fent. How now, good woman? How doft thou?

Quick. The better, that it pleafes your good worship to afk.

Fent. What news? How does pretty miftrefs Anne?

Quick. In truth, fir, and fhe is pretty, and honeft, and gentle : and one that is your friend, I can tell you that by the way; I praife heaven for it.

Fent. Shall I do any good, thinkeft thou? Shall I not lofe my fuit?

Quick. Troth, fir, all is in his hands above : but not-withftanding, mafter Fenton, I'll be fworn on a book, fhe loves you : Have not your worship a wart above your eye?

Fent. Yes, marry, have I; what of that?

Quick. Well, thereby hangs a tale;—good faith, it is fuch another Nan; but, I deteft, an honeft maid as ever broke bread : We had an hour's talk of that wart;—I shall never laugh but in that maid's company!—But, in-deed, fhe is given too much to allicholly and mufing : But for you—Well, go to.

Fent. Well, I shall fee her to-day : Hold, there's mo-ney for thee; let me have thy voice in my behalf : If thou feeft her before me, commend me—

Quick. Will I? i'faith, that we will : and I will tell

your

ir worſhip more of the wart, the next time we have
ifidence; and of other wooers.

Tent. Well, farewell; I am in great haſte now. [*Exit.*

Quick. Farewell to your worſhip.—Truly, an honeſt
itleman; but Anne loves him not; for I know Anne's
nd as well as another does:—Out upon't! what have
ɔrgot?   [*Exit.*

ACT

ACT II. SCENE I.

Before PAGE's *Houſe.*

Enter Miſtreſs PAGE, *with a letter.*

Mrs. Page. What! have I 'ſcaped love-letters in the holy-day time of my beauty, and am I now a ſubject for them? Let me ſee: [*reads.*

Aſk me no reaſon why I love you; for though love uſe reaſon for his preciſian, he admits him not for his counſel- lor. You are not young, no more am I; go to, then, there's ſympathy: you are merry, ſo am I; Ha! ha! then there's more ſympathy: you love ſack, and ſo do I; would you deſire better ſympathy? Let it ſuffice thee, miſtreſs Page, (at the leaſt, if the love of a ſoldier can ſuffice) that I love thee. I will not ſay, pity me; 'tis not a ſoldier-like phraſe; but I ſay, love me. By me,

Thine own true knight,
By day or night,
Or any kind of light,
With all his might,
For thee to fight.   John Falſtaff.

What a Herod of Jewry is this?---O wicked, wicked world!---one that is well nigh worn to pieces with age, to ſhow himſelf a young gallant! What an unweigh'd beha- viour hath this Flemiſh drunkard pick'd (with the devil's name) out of my converſation, that he dares in this man- ner aſſay me? Why, he hath not been thrice in my com- pany!---What ſhould I ſay to him?---I was then frugal of my mirth:---heaven forgive me!---Why, I'll exhibit a bill in the parliament for the putting down of men. How ſhall I be revenged on him? for revenged I will be, as ſure as his guts are made of puddings.   *Enter*

Enter Miſtreſs FORD.

Mrs. Ford. Miſtreſs Page! truſt me, I was going to your houſe.

Mrs. Page. And, truſt me, I was coming to you. You look very ill.

Mrs. Ford. Nay, I'll ne'er believe that; I have tô ſhow to the contrary.

Mrs. Page. 'Faith, but you do, in my mind.

Mrs. Ford. Well, I do then; yet, I ſay, I could ſhow you to the contrary: O, miſtreſs Page, give me ſome counſel!

Mrs. Page. What's the matter, woman?

Mrs. Ford. O woman, if it were not for one trifling reſpeċt, I could come to ſuch honour!

Mrs. Page. Hang the trifle, woman; take the honour: What is it?——diſpenſe with trifles;—what is it?

Mrs. Ford. If I would but go to hell for an eternal moment, or ſo, I could be knighted.

Mrs. Page. What?—thou lieſt!—Sir Alice Ford!—— Theſe knights will hack; and ſo thou ſhouldſt not alter the article of thy gentry.

Mrs. Ford. We burn day-light:—here, read, read;—perceive how I might be knighted.—I ſhall think the worſe of fat men, as long as I have an eye to make difference of men's liking: And yet he would not ſwear; prais'd women's modeſty; and gave ſuch orderly and well-behaved reproof to all uncomelineſs, that I would have ſworn his diſpoſition would have gone to the truth of his words: but they do no more adhere, and keep place together, than the hundredth pſalm to the tune of *Green ſleeves.* What tempeſt, I trow, threw this whale, with ſo many tuns of oil in his belly, aſhore at Windſor? How ſhall I be revenged on him? I think, the beſt way were to entertain

hið

him with hope, till the wicked fire of luft have melted
him in his own greafe.——Did you ever hear the like?

Mrs. Page. Letter for letter; but that the name of
Page and Ford differs!—To thy great comfort in this
myftery of ill opinions, here's the twin-brother of thy
letter: but let thine inherit firft; for, I proteft, mine
never fhall. I warrant, he hath a thoufand of thefe letters, writ with blank fpace for different names, (fure
more) and thefe are of the fecond edition: He will
print them out of doubt; for he cares not what he puts
into the prefs, when he would put us two. I had rather
be a giantefs, and lie under mount Pelion. Well, I
will find you twenty lafcivious turtles, ere one chafte
man.

Mrs. Ford. Why, this is the very fame; the very hand
the very words: What doth he think of us?

Mrs. Page. Nay, I know not: It makes me almoft
ready to wrangle with mine own honefty. I'll entertain
myfelf like one that I am not acquainted withal; for,
fure, unlefs he knew fome ftrain in me, that I know not
myfelf, he would never have boarded me in this fury.

Mrs. Ford. Boarding, call you it? I'll be fure to keep
him above deck.

Mrs. Page. So will I; if he come under my hatches,
I'll never to fea again. Let's be revenged on him: let's
appoint him a meeting; give him a fhow of comfort in
his fuit; and lead him on, with a fine-baited delay, till he
hath pawn'd his horfes to mine Hoft of the Garter.

Mrs. Ford. Nay, I will confent to act any villainy
againft him, that may not fully the charinefs of our honefty. O, that my hufband faw this letter! it would
give eternal food to his jealoufy.

Mrs. Page. Why, look, where he comes; and my
good man too: he's as far from jealoufy, as I am from
giving

Stothard RA del .

Birrell sc

Merry Wives of Windsor

Page 26

Publish'd 1. April 1798 by Edwd Harding Pall Mall.

giving him caufe; and that, I hope, is an unmeafurable
diftance.

Mrs. Ford. You are the happier woman.

Mrs. Page. Let's confult together againft this greafy
knight: Come hither.   {*they retire.*

Enter FORD, PISTOL, PAGE, *and* NYM.

Ford. Well, I hope it be not fo.

Pift. Hope is a curtail dog in fome affairs:
Sir John affects thy wife.

'*Ford.* Why, fir, my wife is not young.

Pift. He wooes both high and low, both rich and poor,
Both young and old, one with another, Ford;
He loves thy gally-mawfry; Ford, perpend.

Ford. Love my wife?

Pift. With liver burning hot: Prevent, or go thou,
Like Sir Actæon he, with Ring-wood at thy heels:—
O, odious is the name!

Ford. What name, fir?

Pift. The horn, I fay: Farewel.
Take heed; have open eye; for thieves do foot by night:
Take heed, ere fummer comes, or cuckoo-birds do fing.—
Away, fir corporal Nym.——
Believe it, Page; he fpeaks fenfe.   [*Exit* PISTOL.

Ford. I will be patient; I will find out this.

Nym. And this is true; [*to* Page.] I like not the humour of lying. He hath wrong'd me in fome humours:
I fhould have borne the humour'd letter to her; but I
have a fword, and it fhall bite upon my neceffity. He
loves your wife; there's the fhort and the long. My
name is corporal Nym; I fpeak, and I avouch. 'Tis
true;—my name is Nym, and Falftaff loves your wife.—
Adieu! I love not the humour of bread and cheefe; and
there's the humour of it. Adieu.   [*Exit* NYM.

Page. *The humour of it,* quoth 'a! here's a fellow frights humour out of his wits.

Ford. I will feek out Falftaff.

Page. I never heard fuch a drawling, affecting rogue.

Ford. If I do find it, well.

Page. I will not believe fuch a Cataian, though the prieft o' the town commended him for a true man.

Ford. 'Twas a good fenfible fellow : Well.

Page. How now, Meg?

Mrs. Page. Whither go you, George?—Hark you.

Mrs. Ford. How now, fweet Frank? why art thou me-lancholy?

Ford. I melancholy! I am not melancholy.—Get you home, go.

Mrs. Ford. 'Faith, thou haft fome crotchets in thy head now.—Will you go, miftrefs Page?

Mrs. Page. Have with you.—You'll come to dinner, George?—Look, who comes yonder ; fhe fhall be our mef-fenger to this paltry knight. [*Afide to Mrs.* FORD.

Enter Miftrefs QUICKLY.

Mrs. Ford. Truft me, I thought on her : fhe'll fit it.

Mrs. Page. You are come to fee my daughter Anne?

Quick. Ay, forfooth ; and, I pray, how does good mif-trefs Anne?

Mrs. Page. Go in with us, and fee ; we have an hour's talk with you.

[*Exeunt Mrs.* PAGE, *Mrs.* FORD, *and Mrs.* QUICKLY.

Page. How now, mafter Ford?

Ford. You heard what this knave told me ; did you not?

Page. Yes ; and you heard what the other told me?

Ford. Do you think there is truth in them?

Page. Hang 'em, flaves! I do not think the knight would offer it : but thefe that accufe him in his intent

towards

towards our wives, are a yoke of his difcarded men; very rogues, now they be out of fervice.

Ford. Were they his men?

Page. Marry, were they.

Ford. I like it never the better for that.—Does he lie at the Garter?

Page. Ay, marry, does he   If he fhould intend this voyage towards my wife, I would turn her loofe to him; and what he gets more of her than fharp words, let it lie on my head.

Ford. I do not mifdoubt my wife; but I would be loth to turn them together: A man may be too confident; I would have nothing lie on my head: I cannot be thus fatisfied.

Page. Look, where my ranting hoft of the Garter comes: there is either liquor in his pate, or money in his purfe, when he looks fo merrily.—How now, mine hoft?

Enter HOST, *and* SHALLOW.

Hoft. How now, bully-rook? thou'rt a gentleman: cavalero-juftice, I fay.

Sbal. I follow, mine hoft, I follow.—Good even, and twenty, good mafter Page! Mafter Page, will you go with us? we have fport in hand.

Hoft. Tell him, cavalero-juftice; tell him, bully-rook.

Sbal. Sir, there is a fray to be fought, between fir Hugh the Welch prieft, and Caius the French doctor.

Ford. Good mine hoft o' the Garter, a word with you.

Hoft. What fay'ft thou, bully-rook   [*They go afide.*

Sbal. Will you [*to* Page] go with us to behold it? My merry hoft hath had the meafuring of their weapons; and, I think, he hath appointed them contrary places: for, believe me, I hear the parfon is no jefter. Hark, I will tell you what our fport fhall be.

Hoft

Hoſt. Haſt thou no ſuit againſt my knight, my gueſt-cavalier?

Ford. None, I proteſt: but I'll give you a pottle of burnt ſack to give me recourſe to him, and tell him, my name is Brook; only for a jeſt.

Hoſt. My hand, bully: thou ſhalt have egreſs and re-greſs; ſaid I well? and thy name ſhall be Brook: It is a merry knight.—Will you go on, hearts?

Sbal. Have with you, mine hoſt.

Page. I have heard, the Frenchman hath good ſkill in his rapier.

Sbal. Tut, ſir, I could have told you more: In theſe times you ſtand on diſtance, your paſſes, ſtoccadoes, and I know not what: 'tis the heart, maſter Page; 'tis here, 'tis here. I have ſeen the time, with my long ſword, I would have made you four tall fellows ſkip like rats.

Hoſt. Here, boys, here, here! ſhall we wag?

Page. Have with you:—I had rather hear them ſcold than fight.   [*Exeunt* HOST, SHALLOW, *and* PAGE.

Ford. Though Page be a ſecure fool, and ſtands ſo firmly on his wife's frailty, yet I cannot put off my opi-nion ſo eaſily: She was in his company at Page's houſe; and what they made there, I know not. Well, I will look further into't; and I have a diſguiſe to ſound Fal-ſtaff: If I find her honeſt, I loſe not my labour; if ſhe be otherwiſe, 'tis labour well beſtow'd.   [*Exit.*

SCENE II.

A Room in the Garter Inn.

Enter FALSTAFF *and* PISTOL.

Fal. I will not lend thee a penny.

Piſt. Why, then the world's mine oyſter,

Which

Which I with·fword will open.—
I will retort the fum in equipage.

Fal. Not a penny. I have been content, fir, you
fhould lay my countenance to pawn: I have grated upon
my good friends for three reprieves for you and your
coach-fellow, Nym; or elfe you had look'd through the
grate, like a geminy of baboons. I am damn'd in hell, for
fwearing to gentlemen my friends, you were good foldiers
and tall fellows: and when miftrefs Bridget loft the handle of her fan, I took't upon mine honour thou hadft it
not.

Pift. Didft thou not fhare? hadft thou not fifteen pence?

Fal. Reafon, you rogue, reafon: Think'ft thou, I'll
endanger my foul *gratis?* At a word, hang no more about
me; 'I am no gibbet for you:—go.—A fhort knife and a
throng;—to your manor of Pickt-hatch, go.—You'll not
bear a letter for me, you rogue!—you ftand upon your
honour!—Why, thou unconfinable bafenefs, it is as much
as I can do, to keep the terms of my honour precife. I,
I, I myfelf fometimes, leaving the fear of heaven on the
left hand, and hiding mine honour in my neceffity, am
fain to fhuffle, to hedge, and to lurch; and yet you,
rogue, will enfconce your rags, your cat-a-mountain looks,
your red-lattice phrafes, and your bold-beating oaths,
under the fhelter of your honour! You will not do it, you?

Pift. I do relent: What would'ft thou more of man?

Enter ROBIN.

Rob. Sir, here's a woman would fpeak with you.

Fal. Let her approach.

Enter Mrs. QUICKLY.

Quick. Give your worfhip good-morrow.

Fal. Good-morrow, good wife.

Quick.

Quick. Not fo, an't pleafe your worſhip.

Fal. Good maid, then.

Quick. I'll be ſworn; as my mother was, the firſt hour I was born.

Fal. I do believe the ſwearer: What with me?

Quick. Shall I vouchſafe your worſhip a word or two?

Fal. Two thouſand, fair woman; and I'll vouchſafe thee the hearing.

Quick. There is one miſtreſs Ford, fir;—I pray, come a little nearer this ways:—I myſelf dwell with maſter doctor Caius.

Fal. Well, on: Miſtreſs Ford, you ſay——

Quick. Your worſhip ſays very true: I pray your wor-ſhip, come a little nearer this ways.

Fal. I warrant thee, nobody hears;—mine own people, mine own people.

Quick. Are they ſo? Heaven bleſs them, and make them his ſervants!

Fal. Well: miſtreſs Ford;—what of her?

Quick. Why, fir, ſhe's a good creature. Lord, lord! your worſhip's a wanton: Well, heaven forgive you, and all of us, I pray!

Fal. Miſtreſs Ford;—come, miſtreſs Ford,—

Quick. Marry, this is the ſhort and the long of it; you have brought her into ſuch a canaries, as 'tis wonderful. The beſt courtier of them all, when the court lay at Windſor, could never have brought her to ſuch a canary. Yet there has been knights, and lords, and gentlemen, with their coaches; I warrant you, coach after coach, letter after letter, gift after gift; ſmelling ſo ſweetly (all muſk) and ſo ruſhling, I warrant you, in ſilk and gold; and in ſuch alligant terms; and in ſuch wine and ſugar of the beſt, and the faireſt, that would have won any woman's heart; and, I warrant you, they could never get an eye-

wink

wink of her.—I had myfelf twenty angels given me this morning: but I defy all angels (in any fuch fort, as they fay) but in the way of honefty:—and, I warrant you, they could never get her fo much as fip on a cup with the proudeft of them all: and yet there has been earls, nay, which is more, penfioners; but, I warrant you, all is one with her.

Fal. But what fays fhe to me? be brief, my good fhe Mercury.

Quick. Marry, fhe hath receiv'd your letter; for the which fhe thanks you a thoufand times: and fhe gives you to notify, that her hufband will be abfence from his houfe between ten and eleven.

Fal. Ten and eleven?

Quick. Ay, forfooth; and then you may come and fee the picture, fhe fays, that you wot of;—mafter Ford, her hufband, will be from home. Alas! the fweet woman leads an ill life with him; he's a very jealoufy man; fhe leads a very frampold life with him, good heart.

Fal. Ten and eleven: Woman, commend me to her; I will not fail her.

Quick. Why you fay well: But I have another meffenger to your worfhip: Miftrefs Page hath her hearty commendations to you too;—and let me tell you in your ear, fhe's as fartuous a civil modeft wife, and one (I tell you) that will not mifs you morning nor evening prayer, as any is in Windfor, whoe'er be the other: and fhe bade me tell your worfhip, that her hufband is feldom from home; but, fhe hopes, there will come a time. I never knew a woman fo dote upon a man: furely, I think you have charms, la;·yes, in truth..

Fal. Not I, I affure thee; fetting the attraction of my good parts afide, I have no other charms.

Quick. Bleffing on your heart for't!

·Fal.

Fal. But, I pray thee, tell me this: has Ford's wife, and Page's wife, acquainted each other how they love me?

Quick. That were a jeſt, indeed!—they have not ſo little grace, I hope:—that were a trick, indeed! But miſ-treſs Page would deſire you to ſend her your little page, of all loves; her huſband has a marvellous infeĉtion to the little page: and, truly, maſter Page is an honeſt man. Never a wife in Windſor leads a better life than ſhe does; do what ſhe will, ſay what ſhe will, take all, pay all, go to bed when ſhe liſt, riſe when ſhe liſt, all is as ſhe will; and, truly, ſhe deſerves it; for if there be a kind woman in Windſor, ſhe is one. You muſt ſend her your page; no remedy.

Fal. Why, I will.

Quick. Nay, but do ſo then: and, look you, he may come and go between you both; and, in any caſe, have a nay-word, that you may know one another's mind, and the boy never need to underſtand any thing: for 'tis not good that children ſhould know any wickedneſs: old folks, you know, have diſcretion, as they ſay, and know the world.

Fal. Fare thee well: commend me to them both: there's my purſe; I am yet thy debtor.—Boy, go along with this woman.—This news diſtraĉts me!

           [*Exeunt* QUICKLY *and* ROBIN.

Piſt. This punk is one of Cupid's carriers:—
Clap on more ſails; purſue, up with your fights;
Give fire; ſhe is my prize, or ocean whelm them all!

           [*Exit* PISTOL.

Fal. Say'ſt thou ſo, old Jack? go thy ways; I'll make more of thy old body than I have done. Will they yet look after thee? Wilt thou, after the expence of ſo much money, be now a gainer? Good body, I thank thee: let them ſay, 'tis groſsly done: ſo it be fairly done, no matter.

           Enter

Enter BARDOLPH.

Bar. Sir John, there's one mafter Brook below would fain fpeak with you, and be acquainted with you; and hath fent your worfhip a morning's draught of fack.

Fal. Brook, is his name?

Bard. Ay, fir.

Fal. Call him in. [*Exit* BARDOLPH.] Such Brooks are welcome to me, that o'erflow fuch liquor. Ah! ha! miftrefs Ford and miftrefs Page, have I encompafs'd you? go to! *via!*

Re-enter BARDOLPH, *with* FORD *difguifed.*

Ford. Blefs you, fir.

Fal. And you fir: Would you fpeak with me?

Ford. I make bold, to prefs with fo little preparation upon you.

Fal. You're welcome. What's your will? Give us leave, drawer. [*Exit* BARDOLPH.

Ford. Sir, I am a gentleman that have fpent much; my name is Brook.

Fal. Good mafter Brook, I defire more acquaintance of you.

Ford. Good fir John, I fue for yours: not to charge you; for I muft let you underftand, I think myfelf in better plight for a lender than you are: the which hath fomething embolden'd me to this unfeafon'd intrufion; for they fay, if money go before, all ways do lie open.

Fal. Money is a good foldier, fir, and will on.

Ford. Troth, and I have a bag of money here troubles me: if you will help me to bear it, fir John, take all, or half, for eafing me of the carriage.

Fal. Sir, I know not how I may deferve to be your porter.

Ford.

Ford. I will tell you, fir, if you will give me the hearing.

Fal. Speak, good mafter Brook; I fhall be glad to be your fervant.

Ford. Sir, I hear you are a fcholar;—I will ·be brief with you;——and you have been a man long known to me, though I had never fo good means, as defire, to make myfelf acquainted with you. I fhall difcover a thing to you, wherein I muft very much lay open mine own imperfection : but, good fir John, as you have one eye upon my follies, as you hear them unfolded, turn another into the regifter of your own ; that I may pafs with a reproof the eafier, fith you yourfelf know, how eafy it is to be fuch an offender.

Fal. Very well, fir; proceed.

Ford. There is a gentlewoman in this town, her hufband's name is Ford.

Fal. Well, fir.

Ford. I have long loved her, and, I proteft to you, beftow'd much on her; follow'd her with a doting obfervance; engrofs'd opportunities to meet her; fee'd every flight occafion, that could but niggardly give me fight of her; not only brought many prefents to give her, but have given largely to many, to know what fhe would have given: briefly, I have purfued her, as love hath purfued me; which hath been, on the wing of all occafions. But whatfoever I have merited, either in my mind, or in my means, meed, I am fure, I have received none ; unlefs experience be a jewel: that I have purchafed at an infinite rate; and that hath taught me to fay this:

Love like a fhadow flies, when fubftance love purfues;
Purfuing that that flies, and flying what purfues.

Fal. Have you received no promife of fatisfaction at her hands ?-

Ford.

Ford. Never.

Fal. Of what quality was your love then?

Ford. Like a fair houfe, built upon another man's ground; fo that I have loft my edifice, by miftaking the place where I erected it.

Fal. To what purpofe have you unfolded this to me?

Ford. When I have told you that, I have told you all. Some fay, that, though fhe appear honeft to me, yet, in other places, fhe enlargeth her mirth fo far, that there is fhrewd conftruction made of her. Now, fir John, here is the heart of my purpofe: You are a gentleman of excellent breeding, admirable difcourfe, of great admittance, authentick in your place and perfon, generally allowed for your many war-like, court-like, and learned preparations.

Fal. O, fir!

Ford. Believe it, for you know it:—There is money; fpend it, fpend it; fpend more; fpend all I have; only give me fo much of your time in exchange of it, as to lay an amiable fiege to the honefty of this Ford's wife: ufe your art of wooing; win her to confent to you: if any man may, you may as foon as any.

Fal. Would it apply well to the vehemency of your affection, that I fhould win what you would enjoy? Methinks, you prefcribe to yourfelf very prepofte-roufly.

Ford. O, underftand my drift! fhe dwells fo fecurely on the excellency of her honour, that the folly of my foul dares not prefent itfelf; fhe is too bright to be look'd againft. Now, could I come to her with any detection in my hand, my defires had inftance and argument to commend themfelves; I could drive her then from the ward of her purity, her reputation, her marriage vow, and a thoufand other her defences, which now are too ftrongly embattled againft me: What fay you to't, fir John?

D

Fal.

Fal. Mafter Brook, I will firft make bold with your money; next, give me your hand; and laft, as I am a gentleman, you fhall, if you will, enjoy Ford's wife.

Ford. O, good fir!

Fal. Mafter Brook, I fay you fhall.

Ford. Want no money, fir John, you fhall want none.

Fal. Want no miftrefs Ford, mafter Brook, you fhall want none. I fhall be with her (I may tell you,) by her own appointment; even as you came in to me, her affiftant, or go-between, parted from me: I fay, I fhall be with her between ten and eleven; for at that time the jealous rafcally knave, her hufband, will be forth. Come you to me at night; you fhall know how I fpeed.

Ford. I am bleft in your acquaintance. Do you know Ford, fir?

Fal. Hang him, poor cuckoldly knave! I know him not:—yet I wrong him, to call him poor; they fay, the jealous wittolly knave hath maffes of money; for the which his wife feems to me well-favour'd. I will ufe her as the key of the cuckoldly rogue's coffer; and there's my harveft-home.

Ford. I would you knew Ford, fir; that you might avoid him, if you faw him.

Fal. Hang him, mechanical falt-butter rogue! I will ftare him out of his wits; I will awe him with my cud-gel: it fhall hang like a meteor o'er the cuckold's horns: mafter Brook, thou fhalt know, I will predominate over the peafant, and thou fhalt lie with his wife.——Come to me foon at night:—Ford's a knave, and I will aggravate his ftile; thou, mafter Brook, fhalt know him for knave and cuckold:——come to me foon at night.   [*Exit.*

Ford. What a damn'd Epicurean rafcal is this!—My heart is ready to crack with impatience.—Who fays, this is improvident jealoufy? My wife hath fent to him, the

5   hour

hour is fixed, the match is made.   Would any man have
thought this?—See the hell of having a falfe woman! my
bed fhall be abufed, my coffers ranfacked, my reputation
gnawn at; and I fhall not only receive this villainous
wrong, but ftand under the adoption of abominable terms,
and by him that does me this wrong.   Terms! names!—
Amaimon founds well; Lucifer, well; Barbafon, well; yet
they are devils' additions, the names of fiends: but cuckold!
wittol-cuckold!   the devil himfelf hath not fuch a name.
Page is an afs, a fecure afs; he will truft his wife, he will not
be jealous: I will rather truft a Fleming with my butter,
parfon Hugh the Welchman with my cheefe, an Irifhman
with my aqua-vitæ bottle, or a thief to walk my ambling
gelding, than my wife with herfelf: then fhe plots, then
fhe ruminates, then fhe devifes: and what they think in
their hearts they may effect, they will break their hearts
but they will effect.   Heaven be praifed for my jealoufy!—
Eleven o'clock the hour;—I will prevent this, detect my
wife, be revenged on Falftaff, and laugh at Page.   I will
about it; better three hours too foon, than a minute too
late.   Fie, fie, fie! cuckold! cuckold! cuckold! [*Exit.*

SCENE III.

Windfor Park.

Enter CAIUS *and* RUGBY.

Caius. Jack Rugby!

Rug. Sir.

Caius. Vat is de clock, Jack?

Rug. 'Tis paft the hour, fir, that fir Hugh promifed to
meet.

Caius. By gar, he has fave his foul, dat he is no come;

he

he has pray his Pible vell, dat he is no come; by gar, Jack Rugby, he is dead already, if he be come.

Rug. He is wife, fir; he knew your worfhip would kill him, if he came.

Caius. By gar, de herring is no dead, fo as I vill kill him. Take your rapier, Jack; I vill tell you how I vill kill him.

Rug. Alas, fir, I cannot fence.

Caius. Villainy, take your rapier.

Rug. Forbear, here's company.

Enter HOST, SHALLOW, SLENDER, *and* PAGE.

Hoft. 'Blefs thee, bully doctor.

Shal. 'Save you, mafter doctor Caius.

Page. Now, good mafter doctor!

Slen. Give you good morrow, fir.

Caius. Vat be all you, one, two, tree, four, come for?

Hoft. To fee thee fight, to fee thee foin, to fee thee tra-verfe, to fee thee here, to fee thee there; to fee thee pafs thy punto, thy ftock thy reverfe, thy diftance, thy montánt. Is he dead, my Ethiopian? is he dead, my Francifco? ha, bully! What fays my Æfculapius? my Galen? my heart of elder? ha! is he dead, bully Stale? is he dead?

Caius. By gar, he is de coward Jack prieft of de vorld; he is not fhow his face.

Hoft. Thou art a Caftilian king, Urinal! Hector of Greece, my boy!

Caius. I pray you, bear vitnefs dat me have ftay fix or feven, two, tree hours for him, and he is no come.

Shal. He is the wifer man, mafter doctor: he is a curer of fouls, and you a curer of bodies; if you fhould fight, you go againft the hair of your profeffions: is it not true, mafter Page?

2

Page.

Page. Mafter Shallow, you have yourfelf been a great fighter, though now a man of peace.

Sbal. Bodykins, mafter Page, though I now be old, and of the peace, if I fee a fword out, my finger itches to make one: though we are juftices, and doctors, and churchmen, mafter Page, we have fome falt of our youth in us: we are the fons of women, mafter Page.

Page. 'Tis true, mafter Shallow.

Sbal. It will be found fo, mafter Page. Mafter doctor Caius, I am come to fetch you home. I am fworn of the peace: you have fhowed yourfelf a wife phyfician, and fir Hugh hath fhown himfelf a wife and patient churchman: you muft go with me, mafter doctor.

Hoft. Pardon, gueft juftice:—A word, monfieur Muck-water.

Caius. Muck-vater! vat is dat?

Hoft. Muck-water, in our Englifh tongue, is valour, bully.

Caius. By gar, den I have as much muck-vater as de Englifhman.——Scurvy Jack-dog-prieft! by gar, me vil cut his ears.

Hoft. He will clapper-claw thee tightly, bully.

Caius. Clapper-de-claw! vat is dat.

Hoft. That is, he will make thee amends.

Caius. By gar, me do look, he fhall clapper-de-claw me; for, by gar, me vill have it.

Hoft. And I will provoke him to't, or let him wag.

Caius. Me tank you for dat.

Hoft. And moreover, bully,—But firft, mafter gueft, and mafter Page, and eke cavalero Slender, go you through the town to Frognore.　　　　[*Afide to them*.

Page. Sir Hugh is there, is he?

Hoft. He is there: fee what humour he is in; and I will bring the doctor about by the fields: will it do well?

　　　　　　　　　　　　　　Sbal.

Shal. We will do it.

Page. Shal. and *Slen.* Adieu, good mafter doctor.

[*Exeunt* PAGE, SHALLOW, *and* SLENDER.

Caius. By gar, me vill kill de prieft; for he fpeak for a jack-an-ape to Anne Page.

Hoft. Let him die: but, firft, fheath thy impatience; throw cold water on thy choler: go about the fields with me through Frogmore; I will bring thee where miftrefs Anne Page is, at a farm houfe a feafting; and thou fhalt woo her: Cry'd game, faid I well?

Caius. By gar, me tank you for dat: by gar, I love you; and I fhall procure-a you de good gueft, de earl, de knight, de lords, de gentlemen, my patients.

Hoft. For the which I will be thine adverfary toward Anne Page; faid I well?

Caius. By gar, 'tis good; vell faid.

Hoft. Let us wag then.

Caius. Come at my heels, Jack Rugby.   [*Exeunt.*

ACT

ACT III.   SCENE I.

A Field near Frogmore.

Enter Sir HUGH EVANS *and* SIMPLE.

Eva. I pray you now, good master Slender's serving-man, and friend Simple by your name, which way have you looked for master Caius, that calls himself *Doctor of Physick?*

Sim. Marry, sir, the city-ward, the park-ward, every way; old Windsor way, and every way but the town way.

Eva. I most vehemently desire you, you will also look that way.   •

Sim. I will, sir.

Eva. Pless my soul! how full of cholers I am, and trempling of mind!—I shall be glad, if he have deceived me:—how melancholies I am!—I will knog his urinals about his knave's costard, when I have good opportunities for the 'ork:—Pless my soul!   [*Sings.*

> *To shallow rivers, to whose falls*
> *Melodious birds sing madrigals;*
> *There will we make our peds of roses,*
> *And a thousand fragrant posies.*
>   *To shallow——*

'Mercy on me, I have a great dispositions to cry.

> *Melodious birds sing madrigals;——*
> *When as I sat in Pabylon,——*
> *And a thousand vagram posies*
>   *To shallow——*

                                      Sim.

Sim. Yonder he is coming, this way, fir Hugh.

Eva. He's welcome :——

　　To ſhallow rivers, to whoſe falls——

Heaven profper the right :—What weapons is he ?

Sim. No weapons, ſir : There comes my maſter, maſter Shallow, and another gentleman from Frogmore, over the ſtile, this way.

Eva. Pray you, give me my gown; or elſe keep it in your arms.

　　Enter PAGE, SHALLOW, *and* SLENDER.

Shal. How now, maſter parſon? Good-morrow, good ſir Hugh. Keep a gameſter from the dice, and a good ſtudent from his book, and it is wonderful.

Slen. Ah, ſweet Anne Page !

Page. Save you, good ſir Hugh !

Eva. 'Pleſs you from his mercy ſake, all of you !

Shal. What! the ſword and the word! do you ſtudy them both, maſter parſon ?

Page. And youthful ſtill, in your doublet and hoſe, this raw rheumatick day ?

Eva. There is reaſons and cauſes for it.

Page. We are come to you, to do a good office, maſter parſon.

Eva. Fery well, what is it ?

Page. Yonder is a moſt reverend gentleman, who be-like, having received wrong by ſome perſon, is at moſt odds with his own gravity and patience, that ever you ſaw.

Shal. I have lived fourſcore years, and upward; I ne-ver heard a man of his place, gravity, and learning, ſo wide of his own reſpect.

Eva. What is he ?

Page. I think you know him; maſter doctor Caius, the renowned French phyſician.

　　　　　　　　　　　　　　　　Eva.

Eva. Got's will, and his paffion of my heart! I had as lief you would tell me of a mefs of porridge.

Page. Why?

Eva. He has no more knowledge in Hibocrates and Galen,—and he is a knave befides; a cowardly knave, as you would defires to be acquainted withal.

Page. I warrant you, he's the man fhould fight with him.

Slen. O fweet Anne Page!

Shal. It appears fo, by his weapons:—Keep them afun-der;—here comes doctor Caius.

Enter HOST, CAIUS, *and* RUGBY.

Page. Nay, good mafter parfon, keep in your weapon.

Shal. So do you, good mafter doctor.

Hoft. Difarm them, and let them queftion; let them keep their limbs whole, and hack our Englifh.

Caius. I pray you, let-a me fpeak a word vit your ear: Verefore vill you not meet-a-me?

Eva. Pray you, ufe your patience: in good time.

Caius. Bygar, you are de coward, de Jack dog, Johnape.

Eva. Pray you, let us not be laughing ftogs to other men's humours; I defire you in friendfhip, and I will one way or other make you amends:—I will knog your urinals about your knave's cogs-comb, for miffing your meetings and appointments.

Caius. Diable!—Jack Rugby,—mine *Hoft de Jarterre*, have I not ftay for him, to kill him? have I not, at de place I did appoint?

Eva. As I am a chriftian's foul, now, look you, this is the place appointed: I'll be judgement by mine hoft of the Garter.

Hoft. Peace, I fay, Guallia and Gaul, French and Welch; foul-curer and body-curer.

Caius.

Caius. **Ay,** dat is very good! excellent!

Hoft. **Peace,** I fay; hear mine hoft of the Garter.
Am I politick? am I fubtle? am I a Machiavel? Shall
I lofe my doctor? no; he gives me the potions, and the
motions. Shall I lofe my parfon? my prieft? my fir
Hugh? no; he gives me the proverbs and the no-verbs.——
Give me thy hand, terreftrial; fo.——Give me thy hand,
celeftial; fo.——Boys of art, I have deceived you both;
I have directed you to wrong places: your hearts are
mighty, your fkins are whole, and let burnt fack be the
iffue.—Come, lay their fwords to pawn:——Follow
follow, follow, me, lad of peace; follow.

Shal. Truft me, a mad hoft:—Follow, gentlemen,
follow.

Slen. O fweet Anne Page!

[*Exeunt* SHALLOW, SLENDER, PAGE, *and* HOST.

Caius. Ha! do I perceive dat? have you make-a de
fot of us? ha, ha!

Eva. This is well; he has made us his vlouting-ftog.——
I defire you, that we may be friends; and let us knog our
prains together, to be revenge on this fame fcall, fcurvy,
cogging companion, the hoft of the Garter.

Caius. By gar, vit all my heart; he promife to bring
me vere is Anne Page: by gar, he deceive me too.

Eva. Well, I will fmite his noddles:—Pray you,
follow.   [*Exeunt.*

SCENE II.

The ftreet in Windfor.

Enter Miftrefs PAGE *and* ROBIN.

Mrs. Page. Nay, keep your way, little gallant; you
were wont to be a follower, but now you are a leader:
Whether had you rather lead mine eyes, or eye your
mafter's heels?

Rob.

Rob. I had rather, forfooth, go before you like a man, than follow him like a dwarf.

Mrs. Page. O, you are a flattering boy; now, I fee, you'll be a courtier.

Enter FORD.

Ford. Well met, miftrefs Page: Whither go you?

Mrs. Page. Truly, fir, to fee your wife: Is fhe at home?

Ford. Ay; and as idle as fhe may hang together, for want of company: I think, if your hufbands were dead, you two would marry.

Mrs. Page. Be fure of that,—two other hufbands.

Ford. Where had you this pretty weather-cock?

Mrs. Page. I cannot tell what the dickens his name is my hufband had him of: What do you call your knight's name, firrah?

Rob. Sir John Falftaff.

Ford. Sir John Falftaff!

Mrs. Page. He, he; I can never hit on's name.—There is fuch a league between my good man and he!—Is your wife at home, indeed?

Ford. Indeed, fhe is.

Mrs. Page. By your leave, fir;—I am fick till I fee her.   [*Exeunt Mrs.* PAGE *and* ROBIN.

Ford. Has Page any brains? hath he any eyes? hath he any thinking? Sure they fleep; he hath no ufe of them. Why, this boy will carry a letter twenty miles, as eafy as a cannon will fhoot point-blank twelve fcore. He pieces-out his wife's inclination; he gives her folly motion and advantage: and now fhe's going to my wife, and Falftaff's boy with her. A man may hear this fhower fing in the wind!—and Falftaff's boy with her!—Good plots!—they are laid: and our revolted wives fhare damnation together. Well; I will take him, then, torture my wife, pluck the borrowed veil of mo-

deft

desty from the so seeming mistress Page, divulge Page himself for a secure and wilful Actæon; and to these violent proceedings all my neighbours shall cry aim. [*Clock strikes.*] The clock gives me my cue, and my as- surance bids me search; there I shall find Falstaff: I shall be rather praised for this, than mocked; for it is as positive as the earth is firm, that Falstaff is there: I will go.

Enter PAGE, SHALLOW, SLENDER, HOST, *Sir* HUGH EVANS, CAIUS, *and* RUGBY.

Shal. Page, &c. Well met, master Ford.

Ford. Trust me, a good knot: I have good cheer at home; and, I pray you, all go with me.

Shal. I must excuse myself, master Ford.

Slen. And so must I, sir; we have appointed to dine with mistress Anne, and I would not break with her for more money than I'll speak of.

Shal. We have linger'd about a match between Anne Page and my cousin Slender, and this day we shall have our answer.

Slen. I hope, I have your good will, father Page.

Page. You have, master Slender; I stand wholly for you:—but my wife, master doctor, is for you altogether.

Caius. Ay, by gar; and de maid is love-a me; my nursh-a Quickly tell me so mush.

Host. What say you to young master Fenton? he ca- pers, he dances, he has eyes of youth, he writes verses, he speaks holiday, he smells April and May: he will carry't; he will carry't; 'tis in his buttons; he will carry't.

Page. Not by my consent, I promise you. The gen- tleman is of no having: he kept company with the wild prince and Poins; he is of too high a region, he knows too much. No, he shall not knit a knot in his fortunes

with

with the finger of my fubftance; if he take her, let him take her fimply; the wealth I have waits on my confent, and my confent goes not that way.

Ford. I befeech you, heartily, fome of you go home with me to dinner: befides your cheer, you fhall have fport; I will fhow you a monfter.——Mafter Doctor, you fhall go;——fo fhall you, mafter Page;——and you, Sir Hugh.

Sbal. Well, fare you well :—we fhall have the freer wooing at mafter Page's.

[*Exeunt* SHALLOW *and* SLENDER.

Caius. Go home, John Rugby ; I come anon.

[*Exit* RUGBY.

Hoft. Farewell, my hearts: I will to my honeft knight Falftaff, and drink canary with him. [*Exit* HOST.

Ford. [*Afide.*] I think, I fhall drink in pipe-wine firft with him; I'll make him dance. Will you go, gentles?

All. Have with you, to fee this monfter. [*Exeunt.*

SCENE III.

A Room in FORD'S *Houfe.*

Enter Mrs. FORD *and Mrs.* PAGE.

Mrs. Ford. What, John! what, Robert!
Mrs. Page. Quickly, quickly : Is the buck bafket—
Mrs. Ford. I warrant: What, Robin, I fay.

Enter Servants with a Bafket.

Mrs. Page. Come, come, come.
Mrs. Ford. Here, fet it down.
Mrs. Page. Give your men the charge; we muft be brief.

Mrs. Ford.

Mrs. Ford. Marry, as I told you before, John and Robert, be ready here hard by, in the brewhouse; and when
I suddenly call you, come forth, and (without any pause
or staggering,) take this basket on your shoulders: that
done, trudge with it in all haste, and carry it among the
whitsters in Datchet mead, and there empty it in the
muddy ditch, close by the Thames' side.

Mrs. Page. You will do it?

Mrs. Ford. I have told them over and over; they lack
no direction: be gone, and come when you are called.

[*Exeunt* Servants.

Mrs. Page. Here comes little Robin.

Enter ROBIN.

Mrs. Ford. How now, my eyas-musket? what news
with you?

Rob. My master, sir John, is come in at your back-door,
mistress Ford; and requests your company.

Mrs. Page. You little Jack-a-lent, have you been true
to us?

Rob. Ay, I'll be sworn: My master knows not of your
being here; and hath threaten'd to put me into everlasting
liberty if I tell you of it; for, he swears, he'll turn me
away.

Mrs. Page. Thou'rt a good boy; this secrecy of thine
shall be a tailor to thee, and shall make thee a new doublet
and hose.—I'll go hide me.

Mrs. Ford. Do so:—Go tell thy master, I am alone.
Mrs. Page, remember you your cue.   [*Exit* ROBIN.

Mrs. Page. I warrant thee; if I do not act it, hiss me.
[*Exit Mrs.* PAGE.

Mrs. Ford. Go to then; we'll use this unwholesome
humidity, this gross watry pumpion; we'll teach him to
ow turtles from jays.

Enter

Enter FALSTAFF.

Fal. Have I caught thee, my heavenly jewel? Why, now let me die, for I have lived long enough; this is the period of my ambition: O this bleſſed hour!

Mrs. Ford. O, ſweet ſir John!

Fal. Miſtreſs Ford, I cannot cog, I cannot prate, miſtreſs Ford. Now ſhall I ſin in my wiſh: I would thy huſband were dead; I'll ſpeak it before the beſt lord, I would make thee my lady.

Mrs. Ford. I your lady, ſir John! alas, I ſhould be a pitiful lady.

Fal. Let the court of France ſhew me ſuch another; I ſee how thine eye would emulate the diamond: Thou haſt the right arched bent of the brow, that becomes the ſhip-tire, the tire-valiant, or any tire of Venetian admittance.

Mrs. Ford. A plain kerchief, ſir John: my brows become nothing elſe; nor that well neither.

Fal. Thou art a traitor to ſay ſo: thou would'ſt make an abſolute courtier; and the firm fixture of thy foot would give an excellent motion to thy gait, in a ſemi-circled farthingale. I ſee what thou wert, if fortune thy foe were not; nature is thy friend: Come, thou canſt not hide it.

Mrs. Ford. Believe me, there's no ſuch thing in me.

Fal. What made me love thee? let that perſuade thee, there's ſomething extraordinary in thee. Come, I cannot cog, and ſay, thou art this and that, like a many of theſe liſping haw-thorn buds, that come like women in men's apparel, and ſmell like Buckler's-bury in ſimple-time; I cannot; but I love thee; none but thee; and thou deſerveſt it.

Mrs. Ford. Do not betray me, ſir; I fear you love miſtreſs Page.

Fal.

Fal. Thou might'ſt as well ſay, I love to walk by the Counter-gate; which is as hateful to me as the reek of a lime-kiln.

Mrs. Ford. Well, heaven knows, how I love you; and you ſhall one day find it.

Fal. Keep in that mind; I'll deſerve it.

Mrs. Ford. Nay, I muſt tell you, ſo you do; or elſe I could not be in that mind.

Rob. [*Within.*] Miſtreſs Ford, miſtreſs Ford! here's miſtreſs Page at the door, ſweating and blowing, and look-ing wildly, and would needs ſpeak with you preſently.

Fal. She ſhall not ſee me; I will enſconce me behind the arras.

Mrs. Ford. Pray you, do ſo; ſhe's a very tattling wo-man. [FALSTAFF *hides himſelf.*

Enter Miſtreſs PAGE *and* ROBIN.

What's the matter? how now?

Mrs. Page. O miſtreſs Ford, what have you done? You're ſhamed, you are overthrown, you are undone for ever.

Mrs. Ford. What's the matter, good miſtreſs Page?

Mrs. Page. O well-a-day, miſtreſs Ford! having an honeſt man to your huſband, to give him ſuch cauſe of ſuſpicion!

Mrs. Ford. What cauſe of ſuſpicion?

Mrs. Page. What cauſe of ſuſpicion?—Out upon you! how am I miſtook in you?

Mrs. Ford. Why, alas! what's the matter?

Mrs. Page Your huſband's coming hither, woman, with all the officers in Windſor, to ſearch for a gentleman, that, he ſays, is here now in the houſe, by your conſent, to take an ill advantage of his abſence: You are undone.

Mrs. Ford. Speak louder. [*aſide.*] 'Tis not ſo, I hope.

Mrs. Page.

W N Gardner del et sc

Merry Wives of Windsor

Page. 53

Published 1 April 1798 by Edw.ᵈ Harding Pall Mall.

Mrs. Page. Pray heaven it be not so, that you have such a man here; but 'tis most certain your husband's coming with half Windsor at his heels, to search for such a one. I come before to tell you: if you know yourself clear, why I am glad of it: but if you have a friend here, convey, convey him out. Be not amazed; call all your senses to you; defend your reputation, or bid farewell to your good life for ever.

Mrs. Ford. What shall I do?—There is a gentleman, my dear friend; and I fear not mine own shame, so much as his peril: I had rather than a thousand pound, he were out of the house.

Mrs. Page. For shame, never stand *you had rather*, and *you had rather*; your husband's here at hand, bethink you of some conveyance: in the house you cannot hide him.— O, how have you deceived me!—Look, here is a basket; if he be of any reasonable stature, he may creep in here; and throw foul linen upon him as if it were going to bucking: Or, it is whiting time, send him by your two men to Datchet mead.

Mrs. Ford. He's too big to go in there: What shall I do?

Re-enter FALSTAFF.

Fal. Let me see't, let me see't! O let me see't! I'll in, I'll in;—follow your friend's counsel;—I'll in.

Mrs. Page. What! sir John Falstaff! Are these your letters, knight?

Fal. I love thee, and none but thee; help me away: let me creep in here; I'll never—

[*He goes into the basket, they cover him with foul linen.*]

Mrs. Page. Help to cover your master, boy: Call your men, mistress Ford:—You dissembling knight!

E

Mrs. Ford

Mrs. Ford. What, John, Robert, John! [*Exit* Robin.
Re-enter Servants.] Go take up thefe clothes here, quickly; Where's the cowl-ftaff? look, how you drumble;
carry them to the laundrefs in Datchet mead; quickly,
come.

Enter FORD, PAGE, CAIUS, *and* Sir HUGH EVANS.

Ford. Pray you come near: if I fufpeᥱt without caufe,
why then make fport at me, then let me be your jeft; I
deferve it.—How now? whither bear you this?

Serv. To the laundrefs, forfooth.

Mrs. Ford. Why, what have you to do whither they
bear it? You were beft meddle with buck-wafhing.

Ford. Buck! I would I could wafh myfelf of the buck!
Buck, buck, buck? Ay, buck; I warrant you, buck;
and of the feafon too, it fhall appear. [*Exeunt* Servants
with the bafket.] Gentlemen, I have dream'd to-night;
I'll tell you my dream. Here, here, here be my keys;
afcend my chambers, fearch, feek, find out: I'll warrant, we'll unkennel the fox:—Let me ftop this way firft:
So now uncape.

Page. Good mafter Ford, be contented: you wrong
yourfelf too much.

Ford. True, mafter Page.—Up, gentlemen; you fhall
fee fport anon: follow me, gentlemen.   [*Exit.*

Eva. This is fery fantaftical humours, and jealoufies.

Caius. By gar, 'tis no de fafhion of France: it is not
jealous in France.

Page. Nay, follow him, gentlemen; fee the iffue of
this fearch.   [*Exeunt* EVANS, PAGE, *and* CAIUS.

Mrs. Page. Is there not a double excellency in this?

Mrs. Ford. I know not which pleafes me better, that
my hufband is deceived, or fir John.

Mrs. Page.

Mrs. Page. What a taking was he in, when your huſ-band aſk'd who was in the baſket!

Mrs. Ford. I am half afraid he will have need of waſh-ing; ſo throwing him into the water will do him a be-nefit.

Mrs. Page. Hang him, diſhoneſt raſcal! I would, all of the ſame ſtrain were in the ſame diſtreſs.

Mrs. Ford. I think, my huſband hath ſome ſpecial ſuſ-picion of Falſtaff's being here; for I never ſaw him ſo groſs in his jealouſy till now.

Mrs. Page. I will lay a plot to try that: And we will yet have more tricks with Falſtaff: his diſſolute diſeaſe will ſcarce obey this medicine.

Mrs. Ford. Shall we ſend that fooliſh carrion, miſtreſs Quickly, to him, and excuſe his throwing into the water; and give him another hope, to betray him to another pu-niſhment?

Mrs. Page. We'll do it; let him be ſent for to-morrow eight o'clock, to have amends.

Re-enter FORD, PAGE, CAIUS, *and Sir* HUGH EVANS.

Ford. I cannot find him: may be the knave bragg'd of that he could not compaſs.

Mrs. Page. Heard you that?

Mrs. Ford. Ay, ay, peace:—You uſe me well, maſter Ford, do you?

Ford. Ay, I do ſo.

Mrs. Ford. Heaven make you better than your thoughts!

Ford. Amen.

Mrs. Page. You do yourſelf mighty wrong, maſter Ford.

Ford. Ay, ay; I muſt bear it.

Eva. If there be any pody in the houſe, and in the

E 2　　　　　　　　chamber

chambers, and in the coffers, and in the preffes, heaven forgive my fins at the day of judgment!

Caius. By gar, nor I too; dere is no bodies.

Page. Fie, fie, mafter Ford! are you not afhamed? What fpirit, what devil fuggefts this imagination? I would not have your diftemper in this kind, for the wealth of Windfor Caftle.

Ford. 'Tis my fault, mafter Page: I fuffer for it.

Eva. You fuffer for a pad confcience: your wife is as honeft a'omans, as I will defires among five thoufand, and five hundred too.

Caius. By gar, I fee 'tis an honeft woman.

Ford. Well;—I promifed you a dinner:—Come, come, walk in the park: I pray you pardon me; I will hereafter make known to you why I have done this.—Come, wife; come miftrefs Page; I pray you pardon me; pray heartily, pardon me.

Page. Let's go in, gentlemen; but truft me, we'll mock him. I do invite you to-morrow morning to my houfe to breakfaft; after, we'll a birding together; I have a fine hawk for the bufh: Shall it be fo?

Ford. Any thing.

Eva. If there is one, I fhall make two in the company.

Caius. If there be one or two, I fhall make-a de turd.

Eva. In your teeth: for fhame.

Ford. Pray you go, mafter Page.

Eva. I pray you now, remembrance to-morrow on the loufy knave, mine hoft.

Caius. Dat is good; by gar, vit all my heart.

Eva. A loufy knave; to have his gibes and his mocke_
ries.   [*Exeunt.*

SCENE

SCENE IV.

A Room im PAGE's *Houfe.*

Enter FENTON *and Miftrefs* ANNE PAGE.

Fent. I fee, I cannot get thy father's love;
Therefore no more turn me to him, fweet Nan.

Anne. Alas! how then?

Fent. Why, thou muft be thyfelf.
He doth objeét, I am too great of birth;
And that, my ftate being gall'd with my expence,
I feek to heal it only by his wealth:
Befides thefe, other bars he lays before me,——
My riots paft, my wild focieties;
And tells me, 'tis a thing impoffible
I fhould love thee, but as a property.

Anne. May be, he tells you true.

Fent. No, heaven fo fpeed me in my time to come!
Albeit, I will confefs, thy father's wealth
Was the firft motive that I woo'd thee, Anne:
Yet, wooing thee, I found thee of more value
Than ftamps in gold, or fums in fealed bags;
And 'tis the very riches of thyfelf
That now I aim at.

Anne. Gentle mafter Fenton,
Yet feek my father's love; ftill feek it, fir:
If opportunity and humbleft fuit
Cannot attain it, why then,—Hark you hither.

[*They converfe apart.*

Enter SHALLOW, SLENDER, *and* Mrs. QUICKLY.

Shal. Break their talk, miftrefs Quickly; my kinfman
fhall fpeak for himfelf.

Slen. I'll make a shaft or a bolt on't: slid, 'tis but venturing.

Shal. Be not dismay'd.

Slen. No, she shall not dismay me; I care not for that, —but that I am afeard.

Quick. Hark ye; master Slender would speak a word with you.

Anne. I come to him.—This is my father's choice. O, what a world of vile ill-favour'd faults Looks handsome in three hundred pounds a year! [*Aside.*

Quick. And how does good master Fenton? Pray you a word with you.

Shal. She's coming; to her, coz. O boy, thou hadst a father!

Slen. I had a father, mistrefs Anne;—my uncle can tell you good jests of him:—Pray, you, uncle, tell mistrefs Anne the jest, how my father stole two geese out of a pen, good uncle.

Shal. Mistrefs Anne, my coufin loves you.

Slen. Ay, that I do; as well as I love any woman in Glocesterfhire.

Shal. He will maintain you like a gentlewoman.

Slen. Ay, that I will, come cut and long-tail, under the degree of a 'fquire.

Shal. He will make you a hundred and fifty pounds jointure.

Anne. Good master Shallow, let him woo for himself.

Shal. Marry, I thank you for it; thank you for that good comfort. She calls you, coz: I'll leave you.

Anne. Now, master Slender.

Slen. Now, good mistrefs Anne.

Anne. What is your will?

Slen. My will? Od's heartlings, that's a pretty jest indeed!

deed! I ne'er made my will yet, I thank heaven; I am not fuch a fickly creature, I give heaven praife.

Anne. I mean, mafter Slender, what would you with me?

Slen. Truly, for mine own part, I would little or nothing with you: Your father, and my uncle, have made motions: if it be my luck, fo; if not, happy man be his dole! They can tell you how things go, better than I can: You may afk your father; here he comes.

Enter PAGE *and Miſtreſs* PAGE.

Page. Now, mafter Slender:——Love him, daughter Anne.——
Why, how now! what does mafter Fenton here?
You wrong me, fir, thus ftill to haunt my houfe:
I told you, fir, my daughter is difpos'd of.

Fent. Nay, mafter Page, be not impatient.

Mrs. Page. Good mafter Fenton, come not to my child.

Page. She is no match for you.

Fent. Sir, will you hear me?

Page. No, good mafter Fenton.
Come, mafter Shallow; come, fon Slender; in:——
Knowing my mind, you wrong me, mafter Fenton.
　　　　[*Exeunt* PAGE, SHALLOW, *and* SLENDER.

Quick. Speak to miftrefs Page.

Fent. Good miftrefs Page, for that I love your daughter
In fuch a righteous fafhion as I do,
Perforce againft all checks, rebukes and manners,
I muft advance the colours of my love,
And not retire: Let me have your good will.

Anne. Good mother, do not marry me to 'yon fool.

Mrs. Page. I mean it not; I feek you a better hufband.

Quick. That's my mafter, mafter doctor.

　　　　　　　　　　　　　Anne.

Anne. Alas, I had rather be fet quick i'the earth,
And bowl'd to death with turnips.

Mrs. Page. Come, trouble not yourfelf: Good mafter
    Fenton,
I will not be your friend, nor enemy :
My daughter will I queftion how fhe loves you,
And as I find her, fo am I affected ;
'Till then, farewell, fir :—She muft needs go in ;
Her father will be angry.

[Exeunt Mrs. PAGE and ANNE.

Fent. Farewell, gentle miftrefs; farewell, Nan.

Quick. This is my doing now :—Nay, faid I, will you
caft away your child on a fool, and a phyfician? Look on
mafter Fenton :— this is my doing.

Fent. I thank thee ; and I pray thee, once to night
Give my fweet Nan this ring : There's for thy pains.[*Exit.*

Quick. Now heaven fend thee good fortune! A kind
heart he hath : a woman would run through fire and water for fuch a kind heart. But yet, I would my mafter
had miftrefs Anne; or I would mafter Slender had her:
or, in footh I would mafter Fenton had her; I will do
what I can for them all three; for fo I have promifed,
and I'll be as good as my word ; but fpecioufly for mafter
Fenton. Well, I muft of another errand to fir John Falftaff from my two miftreffes; What a beaft am I to flack
it ?   [*Exit.*

SCENE V.

A Room in the Garter Inn.

Enter FALSTAFF *and* BARDOLPH.

Fal. Bardolph, I fay,—
Bard. Here, fir.

Fal.

Fal. Go fetch me a quart of fack; put a toaft in't. [*Exit* BARD.] Have I lived to be carried in a bafket, like a barrow of butcher's offal; and to be thrown into the Thames? Well, if I be ferved fuch another trick, I'll have my brains ta'en out, and butter'd, and give them to a dog for a new year's gift. The rogues flighted me into the river with as little remorfe as they would have drown'd a bitch's blind puppies, fifteen i'the litter: and you may know by my fize, that I have a kind of alacrity in finking; if the bottom were as deep as hell, I fhould down. I had been drown'd, but that the fhore was fhelvy and fhallow; a death that I abhor; for the water fwells a man; and what a thing fhould I have been, when I had been fwell'd! I fhould have been a mountain of mummy.

Re-enter BARDOLPH, *with the wine.*

Bard. Here's miftrefs Quickly, fir, to fpeak with you.

Fal. Come, let me pour in fome fack to the Thames water; for my belly's as cold as if I had fwallow'd fnowballs for pills to cool the reins. Call her in.

Bard. Come in, woman.

Enter Mrs. QUICKLY.

Quick. By your leave; I cry you mercy: Give your worfhip good-morrow.

Fal. Take away thefe chalices: Go brew me a pottle of fack finely.

Bard. With eggs, fir?

Fal. Simple of itfelf; I'll no pullet-fperm in my brewage. [*Exit* BARD.]—How now?

Quick. Marry, fir, I come to your worfhip from Mrs. Ford.

Fal.

Fal. Miftrefs Ford! I have had ford enough: I was thrown into the ford; I have my belly full of ford.

Quick. Alas the day! good heart, that was not her fault: fhe does fo take on with her men; they miftook their erection.

Fal. So did I mine, to build upon a foolifh woman's promife.

Quick. Well, fhe laments, fir, for it, that it would yearn your heart to fee it. Her hufband goes this morning a birding; fhe defires you once more to come to her be-tween eight and nine: I muft carry her word quickly: fhe'll make you amends I warrant you.

Fal. Well, I will vifit her: Tell her fo; and bid her think, what a man is: let her confider his frailty, and then judge of my merit.

Quick. I will tell her.

Fal. Do fo. Between nine and ten fay'ft thou?

Quick. Eight and nine, fir.

Fal. Well, be gone: I will not mifs her.

Quick. Peace be with you, fir!   [*Exit.*

Fal. I marvel I hear not of mafter Brook; he fent me word to ftay within: I like his money well. O, here he comes.

Enter FORD.

Ford. Blefs you, fir!

Fal. Now, mafter Brook? you come to know what hath pafs'd between me and Ford's wife?

Ford. That, indeed, fir John, is my bufinefs.

Fal. Mafter Brook, I will not lie to you; I was at her houfe the hour fhe appointed me.

Ford. And how fped you, fir?

Fal. Very ill-favour'dly, mafter Brook.

Ford.

Ford. How fo, fir? Did fhe change her determination?

Fal. No, mafter Brook: but the peaking cornuto her hufband, mafter Brook, dwelling in a continual 'larum of jealoufy, comes me in the inftant of our encounter, after we had embrac'd, kifs'd, protefted, and as it were, fpoke the prologue of our comedy; and at his heels a rabble of his companions, thither provoked and inftigated by his diftemper, and, forfooth, to fearch his houfe for his wife's love.

Ford. What, while you were there?

Fal. While I was there.

Ford. And did he fearch for you, and could not find you?

Fal. You fhall hear. As good luck would have it, comes in one miftrefs Page; gives intelligence of Ford's approach; and, by her invention, and Ford's wife's diftraction, they convey'd me into a buck-bafket.

Ford. A buck-bafket!

Fal. By the Lord, a buck-bafket: ramm'd me in with foul fhirts and fmocks, focks, foul ftockings, and greafy napkins; that, mafter Brook, there was the rankeft compound of villainous fmell, that ever offended noftril.

Ford. And how long lay you there?

Fal. Nay, you fhall hear, mafter Brook, what I have fuffer'd to bring this woman to evil for your good. Being thus cramm'd in the bafket, a couple of Ford's knaves, his hinds, were call'd forth by their miftrefs, to carry me in the name of foul clothes, to Datchet-lane: they took me on their fhoulders; met the jealous knave, their mafter, in the door; who afk'd them once or twice what they had in their bafket: I quaked for fear, left the lunatic knave would have fearch'd it; but fate, ordaining he fhould be a cuckold, held his hand. Well; on went he for a fearch, and away went I for foul clothes. But mark the fequel,

mafter

mafter Brook: I fuffer'd the pangs of three feveral deaths :
firft, an intolerable fright, to be detected with a jealous
rotten bell-weather; next, to be compafs'd, like a good
bilbo, in the circumference of a peck, hilt to point, heel
to head; and then, to be ftopp'd in, like a ftrong diftil-
lation, with ftinking clothes that fretted in their own
greafe : think of that,—a man of my kidney,—think of
that ; that am as fubject to heat, as butter; a man of continual diffolution and thaw; it was a miracle to 'fcape
fuffocation.   And in the height of this bath, when I was
more than half ftew'd in greafe, like a Dutch difh, to be
thrown into the Thames, and cool'd, glowing hot, in
that furge, like a horfe-fhoe : think of that,—hiffing hot,
—think of that, mafter Brook.

Ford. In good fadnefs, fir, I am forry that for my fake
you have fuffer'd all this.   My fuit then is defperate;
you'll undertake her no more ?

Fal. Mafter Brook, I will be thrown into Ætna, as I
have into Thames, ere I will leave her thus. Her hufband
is this morning gone a birding : I have received from her
another embaffy of meeting; 'twixt eight and nine is the
hour, mafter Brook.

Ford. 'Tis paft eight already, fir.

Fal. Is it ? I will then addrefs me to my appointment.
Come to me at your convenient leifure, and you fhall
know how I fpeed; and the conclufion fhall be crown'd
with your enjoying her; Adieu. You fhall have her
mafter Brook; mafter Brook, you fhall cuckold Ford.

[*Exit.*

Ford. Hum! ha! is this a vifion ? is this a dream ? do
I fleep ? Mafter Ford, awake; awake, mafter Ford;
there's a hole made in your beft coat, mafter Ford. This
'tis to be married! this 'tis to have linen and buck-bafkets!
Well, I will proclaim myfelf what I am: I will now
take

take the lecher; he is at my houſe; he cannot 'ſcape me; 'tis impoſſible he ſhould; he cannot creep into a half-penny purſe, nor into a pepper-box; but, leſt the devil that guides him ſhould aid him, I will ſearch impoſſible places. Though what I am I cannot avoid, yet to be what I would not, ſhall not make me tame; if I have horns to make one mad, let the proverb go with me, I'll be horn mad.   [*Exit.*

ACT IV.   SCENE I.

The Street.

Enter Mrs. PAGE, *Mrs.* QUICKLY, *and* WILLIAM.

Mrs. Page. Is he at mafter Ford's already, think'ft thou ?

Quick. Sure, he is by this; or will be prefently: but truly, he is very courageous mad, about his throwing into the water.   Miftrefs Ford defires you to come fud-denly.

Mrs. Page. I'll be with her by and by; I'll but bring my young man here to fchool : Look, where his mafter comes; 'tis a playing-day, I fee.

Enter Sir HUGH EVANS.

How now, fir Hugh ? no fchool to-day ?

Eva. No; mafter Slender is let the boys leave to play.

Quick. Blefling of his heart!

Mrs. Page. Sir Hugh, my hufband fays, my fon pro-fits nothing in the world at his book; I pray you, afk him fome queftions in his accidence.

Eva. Come hither, William ; hold up your head; come.

Mrs. Page. Come on, firrah; hold up your head ; an-fwer your mafter; be not afraid.

Eva. William, how many numbers is in nouns ?

Will. Two.

Quick. Truly I thought there had been one number more; becaufe they fay, od's nouns.

Eva. Peace your tatlings.   What is *fair*, William ?

- I   Will.

Will. Pulcher.

Quick. Poulcats! there are fairer things than poulcats, sure.

Eva. You are a fery simplicity 'oman; I pray you, peace. What is *Lapis*, William?

Will. A stone.

Eva. And what is a stone, William?

Will. A pebble.

Eva. No, it is *Lapis*; I pray you remember in your prain.

Will. *Lapis.*

Eva. That is good, William. What is he, William, that does lend articles?

Will. Articles are borrowed of the pronoun; and be thus declined, *Singulariter, nominativo, bic, bæc, boc.*

Eva. Nominativo, big bag, bog;—pray you, mark: *genitivo, bujus:* Well, what is your *accufative cafe?*

Will. Accufativo, binc.

Eva. I pray you, have your remembrance, child; *Accufativo, bing, bang, bog.*

Quick. Hang hog is Latin for bacon, I warrant you.

Eva. Leave your prabbles, 'oman. What is the focative cafe, William?

Will. O—*vocativo*, O.

Eva. Remember, William; focative is, *caret.*

Quick. And that's a good root.

Eva. 'Oman, forbear.

Mrs. Page. Peace.

Eva. What is your *genitive cafe plural*, William?

Will. Genitive cafe?

Eva. Ay.

Will. Genitive,—borum, barum, borum.

Quick. 'Vengeance of *Jenny's* cafe! fie on her!—never name her, child, if she be a whore.

Eva. For shame, 'oman.

Quick.

Quick. You do ill to teach the child such words: he teaches him to hick and to hack, which they'll do fast enough of themselves: and to call horum:—fie upon you!

Eva. 'Oman, art thou lunatics? hast thou no under-standings for thy cases, and the numbers of the genders? Thou art as foolish christian creatures, as I would desires.

Mrs. Page. Pr'ythee, hold thy peace.

Eva. Shew me now, William, some declensions of your pronouns.

Will. Forsooth, I have forgot.

Eva. It is *ki, kæ, cod*; if you forget your *kies*, your *kæs*, and your *cods*, you must be preeches. Go your ways, and play, go.

Mrs. Page. He is a better scholar than I thought he was.

Eva. He is a good sprag memory.. Farewell, mistress Page.

Mrs. Page. Adieu, good sir Hugh. [*Exit Sir* HUGH.] Get you home, boy.—Come, we stay too long. [*Exeunt.*

SCENE II.

A Room in FORD'S *House.*

Enter FALSTAFF *and Mrs.* FORD.

Fal. Mistress Ford, your sorrow hath eaten up my suf-ferance: I see, you are obsequious in your love, and I profess requital to a hair's breadth; not only, mistress Ford, in the simple office of love, but in all the accoutre-ment, complement, and ceremony of it. But are you sure of your husband now?

Mrs. Ford. He's a birding, sweet sir John.

Mrs. Page. [*Within.*] What hoa, gossip Ford! what hoa!

Mrs.

Mrs. Ford. Step into the chamber, fir John.

　　　　　　　　　　[*Exit* FALSTAFF.,

　　　　　　Enter Mrs. PAGE.　　　　　.

Mrs. Page. How now, fweetheart? who's at home befides yourfelf?

Mrs. Ford. Why, none but mine own people.

Mrs. Page. Indeed?

Mrs. Ford. No, certainly :—Speak louder.　　[*Afide.*

Mrs. Page. Truly I am fo glad you have nobody here.

Mrs. Ford. Why?

Mrs. Page. Why, woman, your hufband is in his old
lunes again : he fo takes on yonder with my hufband; fo
rails againft all married mankind; fo curfes all Eve's
daughters, of what complexion foever; and fo buffets
himfelf on the forehead, crying, *Peer-out, peer-out!* that
any madnefs I have ever yet beheld, feem'd but tamenefs,
civility, and patience, to this diftemper he is in now : I
am glad the fat knight is not here.

Mrs. Ford. Why, does he talk of him?

Mrs. Page. Of none but him; and fwears he was carried out, the laft time he fearch'd for him, in a bafket;
protefts to my hufband he is now here; and hath drawn
him and the reft of their company from their fport, to
make another experiment of his fufpicion : but I am glad
the knight is not here; now he fhall fee his own foolery.

Mrs. Ford. How near is he, miftrefs Page?

Mrs. Page. Hard by; at ftreet end; he will be here
anon.

Mrs. Ford. I am undone!—the knight is here.

Mrs. Page. Why, then you are utterly fhamed, and
he's but a dead man. What a woman are you?—Away
with him, away with him; better fhame than murder.

　　　　　　　　F　　　　　　　　*Mrs.*

Mrs. Ford. Which way fhould he go? how fhould I beftow him? Shall I put him into the bafket again?

Re-enter FALSTAFF.

Fal. No, I'll come no more i' the bafket: May I not go out ere he come?

Mrs. Page. Alas, three of mafter Ford's brothers watch the door with piftols, that none fhall iffue out; otherwife you might flip away ere he came. But what make you here?

Fal. What fhall I do?—I'll creep up into the chimney.

Mrs. Ford. There they always ufe to difcharge their birding-pieces: Creep into the kiln-hole.

Fal. Where is it?

Mrs. Ford. He will feek there on my word. Neither prefs, coffer, cheft, trunk, well, vault, but he hath an ab-ftraft for the remembrance of fuch places, and goes to them by his note: There is no hiding you in the houfe.

Fal. I'll go out then.

Mrs. Page. If you go out in your own femblance, you die, fir John. Unlefs you go out difguis'd,—

Mrs. Ford. How might we difguife him?

Mrs. Page. Alas the day, I know not. There is no woman's gown big enough for him; otherwife, he might put on a hat, a muffler, and a kerchief, and fo efcape.

Fal. Good hearts, devife fomething; any extremity, rather than a mifchief.

Mrs. Ford. My maid's aunt, the fat woman of Brent-jrd, has a gown above.

Mrs. Page. On my word, it will ferve him; fhe's as big as he is; and there's her thrum'd hat, and her muf-fler too: Run up, fir John.

Mrs. Ford. Go, go, fweet fir John: miftrefs Page, and I, will look fome linen for your head.

Mrs.

Mrs. Page. Quick, quick; we'll come drefs you ftraight: put on the gown the while. [*Exit* FALSTAFF.

Mrs. Ford. I would, my hufband would meet him in this fhape: he cannot abide the old woman of Brentford; he fwears fhe's a witch, forbade her my houfe, and hath threaten'd to beat her.

Mrs. Page. Heaven guide him to thy hufband's cudgel; and the devil guide his cudgel afterwards!

Mrs. Ford. But is my hufband coming?

Mrs. Page. Ay, in good fadnefs, is he; and talks of the baſket too, howfoever he hath had intelligence.

Mrs. Ford. We'll try that; for I'll appoint my men to carry the baſket again, to meet him at the door with it, as they did laft time.

Mrs. Page. Nay, but he'll be here prefently; let's go drefs him like the witch of Brentford.

Mrs. Ford. I'll firſt direct my men, what they ſhall do with the baſket. Go up, I'll bring linen for him ftraight.
                                                                [*Exit.*

Mrs. Page. Hang him, diſhoneſt varlet! we cannot mifufe him enough.

We'll leave a proof, by that which we will do,
Wives may be merry, and yet honeſt too:
We do not act, that often jeſt and laugh;
'Tis old, but true, *Still ſwine eat all the draff.* [*Exit.*

Re-enter Mrs. FORD, *with two* Servants.

Mrs. Ford. Go, firs, take the baſket again on your ſhoulders; your maſter is hard at door; if he bid you fet it down, obey him: quickly, defpatch.   [*Exit.*

1 *Serv.* Come, come, take it up.

2 *Serv.* Pray heaven, it be not full of the knight again.

1 *Serv.* I hope not; I had as lief bear fo much lead.

Ente

Enter FORD, PAGE, SHALLOW, CAIUS, *and Sir* HUGH
EVANS.

Ford. Ay, but if it prove true, mafter Page, have you
any way then to unfool me again!—Set down the bafket,
villain:—Somebody call my wife:——You, youth in a
bafket, come out here!—O, you panderly rafcals! there's
a knot, a ging, a pack, a confpiracy, againft me: Now
fhall the devil be fhamed. What! wife, I fay! come,
come forth; behold what honeft clothes you fend forth
to bleaching.

Page. Why, this paffes! Mafter Ford, you are not to
go loofe any longer; you muft be pinion'd.

Eva. Why, this is lunatics! this is mad as a mad
dog!

Shal. Indeed, mafter Ford, this is not well; indeed.

Enter Mrs. FORD.

Ford. So fay I too, fir;—Come hither, miftrefs Ford;
miftrefs Ford, the honeft woman, the modeft wife, the
virtuous creature, that hath the jealous fool to her hufband!—I fufpect without caufe, miftrefs, do I?

Mrs. Ford. Heaven be my witnefs, you do, if you
fufpect me in any difhonefty.

Ford. Well faid, brazen-face; hold it out.——Come
forth, firrah.   [*Pulls the clothes out of the bafket.*

Page. This paffes!

Mrs. Ford. Are you not afhamed? let the clothes alone.

Ford. I fhall find you anon.

Eva. 'Tis unreafonable! Will you take up your wife's
clothes? Come away.

Ford. Empty the bafket, I fay.

Mrs. Ford. Why, man, why,—

Ford. Mafter Page, as I am a man, there was one convey'd out of my houfe yefterday in this bafket: Why may

not

not he be there again? In my houfe I am fure he is: my intelligence is true; my jealoufy is reafonable: Pluck me out all the linen.

Mrs. Ford. If you find a man there, he fhall die a flea's death.

Page. Here's no man.

Shal. By my fidelity, this is not well, mafter Ford: this wrongs you.

Eva. Mafter Ford, you muft pray, and not follow the imaginations of your own heart: this is jealoufies.

Ford. Well, he's not here I feek for.

Page. No, nor no where elfe, but in your brain.

Ford. Help to fearch my houfe this one time: if I find not what I feek, fhow no colour for my extremity, let me for ever be your table-fport; let them fay of me, As jealous as Ford, that fearch'd a hollow walnut for his wife's leman. Satisfy me once more; once more fearch with me.

Mrs. Ford. What hoa, miftrefs Page! come you and the old woman down; my hufband will come into the chamber.

Ford. Old woman! what old woman's that?

Mrs. Ford. Why, it is my maid's aunt of Brentford.

Ford. A witch, a quean, an old cozening quean! Have I not forbid her my houfe? She comes of errands, does fhe? We are fimple men; we do not know what's brought to pafs under the profeffion of fortune-telling. She works by charms, by fpells, by the figure, and fuch daubery as this is; beyond our element: we know nothing.——Come down, you witch, you hag you; come down, I fay.

Mrs. Ford. Nay, good, fweet hufband;—good gentlemen, let him not ftrike the old woman.

Enter FALSTAFF *in women's clothes, led by Mrs.* PAGE.

Mrs. Page. Come, mother Prat, come, give me your hand.   F 3   *Ford.*

Ford. I'll *pret* her;——Out of my door, you witch!
[*beats bim.*] you rag, you baggage, you polecat, you
ronyon! out! out! I'll conjure you, I'll fortune-tell you.

[*Exit* FALSTAFF.

Mrs. Page. Are you not aſhamed? I think you have
kill'd the poor woman.

Mrs. Ford. Nay, he will do it:—'Tis a goodly credit
for you.

Ford. Hang her, witch!

Eva. By yea and no, I think, the 'oman is a witch indeed: I like not when a 'oman has a great peard; I
ſpy a great peard under her muffler.

Ford. Will you follow, gentlemen? I. beſeech you,
follow; ſee but the iſſue of my jealouſy: if I cry out
thus upon no trail, never truſt me when I open again.

Page. Let's obey his humour a little further: Come, gentlemen. [*Exeunt* PAGE, FORD, SHALLOW, *and* EVANS.

Mrs. Page. Truſt me, he beat him moſt pitifully.

Mrs. Ford. Nay, by the maſs, that he did not; he beat
him moſt unpitifully, methought.

Mrs. Page. I'll have the cudgel hallow'd, and hung
o'er the altar; it hath done meritorious ſervice.

Mrs. Ford. What think you? May we, with the warrant of woman-hood, and the witneſs of a good conſcience,
purſue him with any further revenge?

Mrs. Page. The ſpirit of wantonneſs is, ſure, ſcared
out of him; if the devil have him not in fee-ſimple, with
fine and recovery, he will never, I think, in the way of
waſte, attempt us again.

Mrs. Ford. Shall we tell our huſbands how we have
ſerved him?

Mrs. Page. Yes, by all means; if it be but to ſcrape
the figures out of your huſband's brains. If they can
find in their hearts, the poor unvirtuous fat knight ſhall
be

be any further afflicted, we two will ftill be the minifters.

Mrs. Ford. I'll warrant, they'll have him publickly
fhamed: and, methinks, there would be no period to the
jeft, fhould he not be publickly fhamed.

Mrs. Page. Come, to the forge with it then, fhape it:
I would not have things cool. [*Exeunt.*

SCENE III.

A Room in the Garter Inn.

Enter HOST *and* BARDOLPH.

Bar. Sir, the Germans defire to have three of your
Horfes: the duke himfelf will be to-morrow at court, and
they are going to meet him.

Hoft. What duke fhould that be, comes fo fecretly? I
hear not of him in the court: Let me fpeak with the gentlemen; they fpeak Englifh?

Bar. Ay, fir; I'll call them to you.

Hoft. They fhall have my horfes; but I'll make them
pay, I'll fauce them: they have had my houfes a week
at command; I have turn'd away my other guefts: they
muft come off: I'll fauce them: Come. [*Exeunt.*

SCENE IV.

A Room in FORD's *Houfe.*

Enter PAGE, FORD, *Mrs.* PAGE, *Mrs.* FORD, *and* Sir
HUGH EVANS.

Eva. 'Tis one of the peft difcretions of a 'oman as ever
I did look upon.

Page. And did he fend you both thefe letters at an inftant.

Mrs.

Mrs. Page. Within a quarter of an hour.

Ford. Pardon me, wife : Henceforth do what thou wilt ;
I rather will fufpeā the fun with cold,
Than thee with wantonnefs : now doth thy honour ftand,
In him that was of late an heretick,
As firm as faith.

Page. 'Tis well, 'tis well ; no more.
Be not extreme in fubmiffion,
As in offence ;
But let our plot go forward : let our wives
Yet once again, to make us publick fport,
Appoint a meeting with this old fat fellow,
Where we may take him, and difgrace him for it.

Ford. There is no better way than that they fpoke of.

Page. How ! to fend him word they'll meet him in the
park at midnight ! fie, fie ! he'll never come.

Eva. You fay, he has been thrown into the rivers ; and
has been grievoufly peaten, as an old 'oman : methinks,
there fhould be terrors in him, that he fhould not come ;
methinks, his flefh is punifh'd, he fhall have no defires.

Page. So think I too.

Mrs. Ford. Devife but how you'll ufe him when he
     comes,
And let us two devife to bring him thither.

Mrs. Page. There is an old tale goes, that Herne the
     hunter,
Sometime a keeper here in Windfor foreft,
Doth all the winter time, at ftill midnight,
Walk round about an oak, with great ragg'd horns ;
And there he blafts the tree, and takes the cattle ;
And makes milch-kine yield blood, and fhakes a chain
In a moft hideous and dreadful manner :
You have heard of fuch a fpirit ; and well you know,
The fuperftitious idle-headed eld

Receiv'd

Receiv'd, and did deliver to our age,
This tale of Herne the hunter for a truth.

   Page. Why, yet there want not many, that do fear
In deep of night to walk by this Herne's oak :
But what of this?

   Mrs. Ford. Marry, this is our device;
That Falftaff at that oak fhall meet with us,
Difguis'd like Herne, with huge horns on his head.

   Page. Well, let it not be doubted but he'll come,
And in this fhape; When you have brought him thither,
What fhall be done with him? what is your plot?

   Mrs. Page. That likewife have we thought upon, and
       thus:
Nan Page my daughter, and my little fon,
And three or four more of their growth, we'll drefs
Like urchins, ouphes, and fairies, green and white,
With rounds of waxen tapers on their heads,
And rattles in their hands; upon a fudden,
As Falftaff, fhe and I, are newly met,
Let them from forth a faw-pit rufh at once
With fome diffufed fong; upon their fight,
We two, in great amazednefs, will fly :
Then let them all encircle him about,
And, fairy-like, to pinch the unclean knight;
And afk him, why, that hour of fairy revel,
In their fo facred paths he dares to tread,
In fhape prophane.

   Mrs. Ford. And till he tell the truth,
Let the fuppofed fairies pinch him found,
And burn him with their tapers.

   Mrs. Page. The truth being known,
We'll all prefent ourfelves; dif-horn the fpirit,
And mock him home to Windfor.

   Ford. The children muft

                            Be

Be practis'd well to this, or they'll ne'er do't.

Eva. I will teach the children their behaviours; and
I will be like a jack-an-apes also, to burn the knight with
my taber.

Ford. That will be excellent. I'll go buy them vizards.

Mrs. Page. My Nan shall be the queen of all the fairies,
finely attired in a robe of white.

Page. That silk will I go buy;—and in that time
Shall master Slender steal my Nan away,   [*Afide.*
And marry her at Eton.——Go, send to Falstaff straight.

Ford. Nay, I'll to him again in name of Brook:.
He'll tell me all his purpose: Sure, he'll come.

Mrs. Page. Fear not you that: Go, get us properties,
And tricking for our fairies..

Eva. Let us about it: It is admirable pleasures, and
fery honest knaveries. [*Exeunt* PAGE, FORD, *and* EVANS.

Mrs. Page. Go, mistress Ford,
Send Quickly to sir John, to know his mind.
                                        [*Exit Mrs.* FORD.

I'll to the doctor; he hath my good will,
And none but he, to marry with Nan Page.
That Slender, though well landed, is an ideot;,
And he my husband best of all affects:
The doctor is well money'd, and his friends
Potent at court; he, none but he, shall have her;.
Though twenty thousand worthier come to crave her:
                                        [*Exit.*

SCENE V.

A Room in the Garter Inn..

Enter Host *and* SIMPLE.

Host. What would'st thou have, boor? what, thick-
skin? speak, breathe, discuss; brief, short, quick, snap.

5   *Sim.*

Simp. Marry, fir, I come to fpeak with fir John Falftaff, from mafter Slender.

Hoft. There's his chamber, his houfe, his caftle, his ftanding-bed, and truckle-bed; 'tis painted about with the ftory of the prodigal, frefh and new : Go, knock and call; he'll fpeak like an *Anthropophaginian* unto thee : Knock, I fay.

Simp. There's an old woman, a fat woman gone up into his chamber; I'll be fo bold as ftay, fir, till fhe come down : I come to fpeak with her, indeed.

Hoft. Ha! a fat woman! the knight may be robbed; I'll call.—Bully knight! Bully fir John! fpeak from thy lungs military : Art thou there? it is thine hoft, thine Ephefian, calls.

Fal. [*above.*] How now, mine hoft?

Hoft. Here's a Bohemian Tartar tarries the coming down of thy fat woman: Let her defcend, bully, let her defcend; my chambers are honourable : Fie! privacy? fie!

Enter FALSTAFF.

Fal. There was, mine hoft, an old fat woman even now with me; but fhe's gone.

Simp. Pray you, fir, was't not the wife woman of Brentford?

Fal. Ay, marry was it, mufcle-fhell; what would you with her?

Simp. My mafter, fir, my mafter Slender, fent to her, feeing her go thorough the ftreets, to know, fir, whether one Nym, fir, that beguil'd him of a chain, had the chain, or no?

Fal. I fpake with the old woman about it.

Simp. And what fays fhe, I pray, fir?

Fal. Marry, fhe fays, that the very fame man, that beguiled mafter Slender of his chain, cozen'd him of it.

Simp

Simp. I would, I could have fpoken with the woman herfelf; I had other things to have fpoken with her too, from him.

Fal. What are they? let us know.

Hoft. Ay, come; quick.

Simp. I may not conceal them, fir.

Fal. Conceal them, or thou dieft.

Simp. Why, fir, they were nothing but about miftrefs Anne Page; to know, if it were my mafter's fortune to have her, or no.

Fal. 'Tis, 'tis his fortune.

Simp. What, fir?

Fal. To have her,—or no: Go; fay, the woman told me fo.

Simp. May I be fo bold to fay fo, fir?

Fal. Ay, fir Tike; who more bold?

Simp. I thank your worfhip: I fhall make my mafter glad with thefe tidings.   [*Exit* SIMPLE.

Hoft. Thou art clerkly, thou art clerkly, fir John: Was there a wife woman with thee?

Fal. Ay, that there was, mine hoft; one, that hath taught me more wit than ever I learn'd before in my life: and I paid nothing for it neither, but was paid for my learning.

Enter BARDOLPH.

Bard. Out, alas, fir! cozenage! meer cozenage!

Hoft. Where be my horfes? fpeak well of them, varletto.

Bard. Run away with the cozeners: for fo foon as I came beyond Eton, they threw me off, from behind one of them, in a flough of mire; and fet fpurs, and away, like three German devils, three Doctor Fauftufes.

Hoft. They are gone but to meet the duke, villain: do not fay, they be fled; Germans are honeft men.

Enter Sir HUGH EVANS.

Eva. Where is mine hoſt?

Hoſt. What is the matter, ſir?

Eva. Have a care of your entertainments: there is a friend of mine come to town, tells me, there is three couſin germans, that has cozen'd all the hoſts of Reading, of Maidenhead, of Colebrook, of horſes and money. I tell you for good-will, look you: you are wiſe, and full of gibes and vlouting-ſtogs; and 'tis not convenient you ſhould be cozen'd: Fare you well.　　　　[*Exit.*

Enter CAIUS.

Caius. Vere is mine *Hoſt de Jarterre?*

Hoſt. Here, maſter doctor, in perplexity, and doubtful dilemma.

Caius. I cannot tell vat is dat: But it is tell-a me, dat you make grand preparation for a duke *de Jarmany:* by my trot, dere is no duke, dat the court is know to come: I tell you for good vill: adieu.　　　　[*Exit.*

Hoſt. Hue and cry, villain, go:—aſſiſt me, knight; I am undone:—fly, run, hue and cry, villain! I am undone!

　　　　　　[*Exeunt* HOST *and* BARDOLPH.

Fal. I would, all the world might be cozen'd; for I have been cozen'd, and beaten too. If it ſhould come to the ear of the court, how I have been transform'd, and how my transformation hath been waſh'd and cudgel'd, they would melt me out of my fat, drop by drop, and liquor fiſhermen's boots with me; I warrant, they would whip me with their fine wits, till I were as creſt fallen as a dried pear. I never proſper'd, ſince I foreſwore myſelf at *Primero.* Well, if my wind were but long enough to ſay my prayers, I would repent.—

　　　　　　　　　　　　　　　Enter

Enter Mrs. QUICKLY.

'Now! whence come you?

Quick. From the two parties, forfooth.

Fal. The devil take one party, and his dam the other, and fo they fhall be both beftow'd! I have fuffer'd more for their fakes, more than the villainous inconftancy of man's difpofition is able to bear.

Quick. And have not they fuffer'd? Yes, I warrant; fpecioufly one of them; miftrefs Ford, good heart, is 'beaten black and blue, that you cannot fee a white fpot about her.

Fal. What tell'ft thou me of black and blue? I was beaten myfelf into all the colours of the rainbow; and I was like to be apprehended for the witch of Brentford; but that my admirable dexterity of wit, my counterfeiting the action of an old woman, deliver'd me, the knave conftable had fet me i' the ftocks, i' the common ftocks, for a witch.

Quick. Sir, let me fpeak with you in your chamber: you fhall hear how things go; and, I warrant, to your content. Here is a letter will fay fomewhat. Good hearts, what ado here is to bring you together! Sure, one of you does not ferve heaven well, that you are fo crofs'd.

Fal. Come up into my chamber.   [*Exeunt.*

SCENE VI.

Another Room in the Garter Inn.

Enter FENTON *and* HOST.

Hoft. Mafter Fenton, talk not to me; my mind is heavy, I will give over all.

Fent.

Fent. Yet hear me fpeak : Affift me in my purpofe,
And, as I am a gentleman, I'll give thee
A hundred pound in gold more than your lofs.

Hoft. I will hear you, mafter Fenton ; and I will, at
the leaft, keep your counfel.

Fent. From time to time I have acquainted you
With the dear love I bear to fair Anne Page ;
Who, mutually, hath anfwer'd my affection
(So far forth as herfelf might be her choofer,)
Even to my wifh : I have a letter from her
Of fuch contents as you will wonder at ;
The mirth whereof fo larded with my matter,
That neither, fingly, can be manifefted,
Without the fhow of both ;—wherein fat Falftaff
Hath a great fcene: the image of the jeft
                              ·[*Showing the letter*,
I'll fhow you here at large.   Hark, good mine hoft :
To-night at Herne's oak, juft 'twixt twelve and one,
Muft my fweet Nan prefent the fairy queen ;
The purpofe why, is here; in which difguife,
While other jefts are fomething rank on foot,
Her father hath commanded her to flip
Away with Slender, and with him at Eton
Immediately to marry : fhe hath confented :
Now, fir,
Her mother, even ftrong againft that match,
And firm for Doctor Caius, hath appointed
That he fhall likewife fhuffle her away,
While other fports art tafking of their minds,
And at the deanery, where a prieft attends,
Straight marry her : to this, her mother's plot,
She, feemingly obedient, likewife hath
Made promife to the doctor.—Now, thus it refts :
Her father means fhe fhall be all in white ;

                                        And

And in that habit, when Slender fees his time
To take her by the hand, and bid her go,
She fhall go with him :—Her mother hath intended,
The better to denote her to the doctor,
(For they muft all be mafk'd and vizarded,)
That, quaint in green, fhe fhall be loofe enrob'd,
With ribbands pendant, flaring 'bout her head ;
And when the doctor fpies his vantage ripe,
To pinch her by the hand, and, on that token,
The maid hath given confent to go with him.

    Hoft. Which means fhe to deceive ? father or mother ?

    Fent. Both, my good hoft, to go along with me : ·
And here it refts,—that you'll procure the vicar
To ftay for me at church, 'twixt twelve and one,
And, in the lawful name of marrying,
To give our hearts united ceremony.

    Hoft. Well, hufband your device; I'll to the vicar :
Bring you the maid, you fhall not lack a prieft.

    Fent. So fhall I evermore be bound to thee ;
Befides, I'll make a prefent recompence.   [*Exeunt.*

ACT

ACT V. SCENE I.

A Room in the Garter Inn.

Enter FALSTAFF and Miftrefs QUICKLY.

Fal. Pr'ythee, no more prattling;—go.——I'll hold: This is the third time; I hope, good luck lies in odd numbers. Away, go; they fay, there is divinity in odd numbers, either in nativity, chance, or death.—Away.

' *Quick.* I'll provide you a chain; and I'll do what I can to get you a pair of horns.

Fal. Away, I fay; time wears: hold up your head, and mince.   [*Exit Mrs.* QUICKLY.

Enter FORD.

How now, mafter Brook? Mafter Brook, the matter will be known to-night, or never. Be you in the Park about midnight, at Herne's oak, and you fhall fee wonders.

Ford. Went you not to her yefterday, fir, as you told me you had appointed?

Fal. I went to her, mafter Brook, as you fee, like a poor old man: but I came from her, mafter Brook, like a poor old woman. That fame knave, Ford her hufband, hath the finest mad devil of jealoufy in him, mafter Brook, that ever govern'd frenzy. I will tell you.—He beat me grievoufly, in the fhape of a woman; for in the fhape of a man, mafter Brook, I fear not Goliath with a weaver's beam; becaufe I know alfo, life is a fhuttle. I am in hafte; go along with me; I'll tell you all mafter Brook. Since I plucked geefe, played truant, and whipped top,

G   I knew

I knew not what it was to be beaten, till lately. Follow
me : I'll tell you ftrange things of this knave Ford ; on
whom to-night I will be revenged, and. I will deliver his
wife into your hand.—Follow : Strange things in hand,
mafter Brook! follow.   [*Exeunt.*

SCENE II.

Windfor Park.

Enter PAGE SHALLOW, *and* SLENDER.

Page. Come, come ; we'll couch i'the caftle-ditch, till
we fee the light of our fairies.—Remember, fon Slender,
my daughter.

Slen. Ay, forfooth ; I have fpoke with her, and we
have a nay-word, how to know one another. I come to
her in white, and cry *mum* ; fhe cries *budget* ; and by that
we know one another.

Shal. That's good too : but what needs either your
mum, or her *budget* ? the white will decypher her well
enough.—It hath ftruck ten o'clock.

Page. The night is dark ; light and fpirits will become
it well. Heaven profper our fport! No man means evil
but the devil, and we fhall know him by his horns. Let's
away ; follow me.   [*Exeunt.*

SCENE III.

The Street in Windfor.

Enter Mrs PAGE, *Mrs.* FORD, *and Dr.* CAIUS.

Mrs. Page. Mafter doctor, my daughter is in green :
when you fee your time, take her by the hand, away with

her

˙her to the deanery, and defpatch it quickly: Go before, into the park; we two muſt go together.

Caius. I know vat I have to do: Adieu.

Mrs. Page. Fare you well, ſir. [*Exit* CAIUS.] **My** huſband will not rejoice ſo much at the abuſe of Falſtaff, as he will chafe at the doctor's marrying my daughter: but 'tis no matter; better a little chiding, than a great deal of heart-break.

Mrs. Ford. Where is Nan now, and her troop of fairies? and the Welch devil, Hugh?

Mrs. Page. They are all couched in a pit hard by Herne's oak, with obſcured lights; which, at the very inſtant of Falſtaff's and our meeting, they will at once ·diſplay to the night.

Mrs. Ford. That cannot chooſe but amaze him.

Mrs. Page. If he be not amazed, he will be mock'd; if he be amazed, he will every way be mock'd.

Mrs. Ford. We'll betray him finely.

Mrs. Page. Againſt ſuch lewdſters, and their lechery, Thoſe that betray them do no treachery.

Mrs. Ford. The hour draws on; To the oak, to the oak !   [*Exeunt.*

SCENE IV.

Windfor Park.

Enter Sir HUGH EVANS *and Fairies.*

Eva. Trib, trib, fairies; come; and remember your parts: be pold, I pray you; follow me into the pit; and when I give the watch-'ords, do as I pid you; Come, come; trib, trib.   [*Exeunt.*

SCENE V.

Another part of the Park.

Enter FALSTAFF *difguifed, with a buck's head on.*

Fal. The Windfor bell hath ftruck twelve: the minute
draws on: Now, the hot-blooded gods affift me!—Remember, Jove, thou waft a bull for thy Europa; love fet
on thy horns.—O, powerful love! that, in fome refpect,
makes a beaft a man; in fome other, a man a beaft.—You
were alfo, Jupiter, a fwan, for the love of Leda;—O,
omnipotent love! how near the god drew to the complexion of a goofe?—A fault done firft in the form of a beaft;
—O Jove, a beaftly fault! and then another fault in the
femblance of a fowl; think on't Jove, a foul fault.—
When gods have hot backs, what fhall poor men do?
For me, I am here a Windfor ftag; and the fatteft, I think,
i'the foreft: Send me a cool rut-time, Jove, or who can
blame me to pifs my tallow? Who comes here? my doe?

Enter Mrs. FORD *and Mrs.* PAGE.

Mrs. Ford. Sir John? art thou there, my deer? my
male deer?

Fal. My doe with the black fcut;—Let the fky rain
potatoes; let it thunder to the tune of *Green Sleeves*;
hail kiffing comfits, and fnow eringoes; let there come
a tempeft of provocation, I will fhelter me here.

                             [*Embracing her.*
Mrs. Ford. Miftrefs Page is come with me, fweetheart.

Fal. Divide me like a bribe-buck, each a haunch: I
will keep my fides to myfelf, my fhoulders for the fellow
of this walk, and my horns I bequeath your hufbands.
Am I a woodman? ha! Speak I like Herne the hunter?
—Why, now is Cupid a child of confcience; he makes
reftitution. As I am a true fpirit, welcome! [*Noife within.*

Mrs. Page. Alas! what noife?   *Mrs. Ford.*

Gardiner del et sc

Merry Wives of Windsor

Page 88

Publifhd 1 April 1798 by Edwᵈ Harding Pall Mall .

Mrs. Ford. Heaven forgive our fins!

Fal. What fhould this be?

Mrs. Ford.
Mrs. Page. } Away, away.　　　[*They run off.*

Fal. I think, the devil will not have me damn'd, left the oil that is in me fhould fet hell on fire: he would never elfe crofs me thus.

Enter Sir HUGH EVANS, *like a fatyr*; *Mrs.* QUICKLY, *and* PISTOL; ANNE PAGE, *as the Fairy Queen, attended by her brother and others, dreffed like fairies, with waxen tapers on their heads.*

Quick. Fairies, black, grey, green, and white,
Ye moon-fhine revellers, and fhades of night,
You orphan-heirs of fixed deftiny,
Attend your office and your quality.——
Crier Hobgoblin, make the fairy o-yes.

Pift. Elves, lift your names; filence, you airy toys.
Cricket, to Windfor chimneys fhalt thou leap:
Where fires thou find'ft unrak'd, and hearths unfwept,
There pinch the maids as blue as bilberry:
Our radiant queen hates fluts, and fluttery.

Fal. They are fairies; he that fpeaks to them fhall die:
I'll wink and couch: No man their works muft eye.
　　　　　　　　[*Lies down upon his face.*

Eva. Where's *Bede*?—Go you, and where you find a
　　　maid,
That, ere fhe fleep has thrice her prayers faid,
Raife up the organs of her fantafy,
Sleep fhe as found as carelefs infancy;
But thofe as fleep, and think not on their fins,
Pinch them, arms, legs, backs, fhoulders, fides, and fhins.

Quick. About, about;
Search Windfor caftle, elves, within and out:

　　　　　　　　　　　　　　　　Strew

Strew good luck, ouphes, on every facred room;
That it may ftand till the perpetual doom,
In ftate as wholefome, as in ftate 'tis fit ;
Worthy the owner, and the owner it.
The feveral chairs of ordre look you fcour
With juice of balm, and every precious flower :
Each fair inftalment, coat, and feveral creft,
With loyal blazon, evermore be bleft !
And nightly, meadow-fairies, look, you fing,
Like to the Garter's compafs, in a ring :
The expreffure that it bears, green let it be,
More fertile-frefh than all the field to fee ;
And, *Hony Soit Qui Mal y Penfe*, write,
In emerald tufts, flowers purple, blue, and white ;
Like faphire, pearl, and rich embroidery, ⎫
Buckled below fair knighthood's bending knee : ⎬
Fairies ufe flowers for their charactery. ⎭
Away; difperfe : But till 'tis one o'clock,
Our dance of cuftom, round about the oak
Of Herne the hunter, let us not forget.

    Eva. Pray you, lock hand in hand; yourfelves in
       order fet :
And twenty glow-worms fhall our lanterns be,
To guide our meafure round about the tree.
But, ftay; I fmell a man of middle earth.

    Fal. Heavens defend me from that Welch fairy ! left
he transform me to a piece of cheefe !

    Pift. Vile worm, thou waft o'er-look'd even in thy birth.

    Quick. With trial-fire touch me his finger-end :
If he be chafte, the flame will back defcend,
And turn him to no pain; but if he ftart,
't is the flefh of a corrupted heart.

    Pift. A trial, come.——

    Eva. Come, will this wood take fire?

             [*They burn him with their tapers.*

                     Fal.

Fal. Oh, oh, oh!

Quick. Corrupt, corrupt, and tainted in defire!
About him, fairies; fing a fcornful rhime:
And, as you trip, ftill pinch him to your time.

Eva. It is right; indeed he is full of lecheries and
iniquity.

SONG.　*Fie on finful fantafy!*
　　　　Fie on luft and luxury!
　　　　Luft is but a bloody fire,
　　　　Kindled with unchafte defire,
　　　　Fed in heart, whofe flames afpire,
　　　　As thoughts do blow them, higher and higher.
　　　　Pinch him fairies, mutually;
　　　　Pinch him for his villainy;

Pinch him, and burn him, and turn him about,
'Till candle, and ftar-light, and moon-fhine be out.

During this fong, the fairies pinch Falftaff. *Doctor* Caius
comes one way, and fteals away a fairy in green; Slender *another way, and takes off a fairy in white; and*
Fenton *comes, and fteals away* Mrs. Anne Page. *A*
noife of hunting is made within. All the fairies run
away. Falftaff *pulls off his buck's head, and rifes.*

Enter PAGE, FORD, *Mrs.* PAGE *and Mrs.* FORD. *They*
lay hold on him.

Page. Nay, do not fly: I think, we have watch'd you
　　now;
Will none but Herne the hunter, ferve your turn?

Mrs. Page. I pray you, come; hold up the jeft no
　　higher:
Now, good fir John, how like you Windfor wives?
See you thefe, hufband? do not thefe fair yokes
Become the foreft better than the town?

Ford.

Ford. Now, fir, who's a cuckold now?—Mafter Brook, Falftaff's a knave, a cuckoldy knave; here are his horns, mafter Brook: And, mafter Brook, he hath enjoy'd nothing of Ford's but his buck-bafket, his cudgel, and twenty pounds of money; which muft be paid to mafter Brook; his horfes are arrefted for it, mafter Brook.

Mrs. Ford. Sir John, we have had ill luck; we could never meet. I will never take you for my love again, but I will always count you my deer.

Fal. I do begin to perceive, that I am made an afs.

Ford. Ay, and an ox too; both the proofs are extant.

Fal. And thefe are not fairies? I was three or four times in the thought, they were not fairies: and yet the guiltinefs of my mind, the fudden furprize of my powers, drove the grofsnefs of the foppery into a receiv'd belief, in defpite of the teeth of all rhyme and reafon, that they were fairies. See now, how wit may be made a Jack-a-lent, when 'tis upon ill employment!

Eva. Sir John Falftaff, ferve Got, and leave your defires, and fairies will not pinfe you.

Ford. Well faid, fairy Hugh.

Eva. And leave you your jealoufies too, I pray you.

Ford. I will never miftruft my wife again, till thou art able to woo her in good Englifh.

Fal. Have I lay'd my brain in the fun, and dried it, that it wants matter to prevent fo grofs o'er reaching as this? Am I ridden with a Welch goat too? Shall I have a coxcomb of frize? 'tis time I were choaked with a piece of toafted cheefe.

Eva. Seefe is not good to give putter; your pelly is all putter.

Fal. Seefe and putter! have I lived to ftand at the taunt of one that makes fritters of Englifh? This is enough to be the decay of luſt and late-walking, through the realm.

Mrs. Page. Why, ſir John, do you think, though we would have thruſt virtue out of our hearts by the head and ſhoulders, and have given ourſelves without ſcruple to hell, that ever the devil could have made you our delight ?

Ford. What, a hodge-pudding ? a bag of flax ?

Mrs. Page. A puff'd man ?

Page. Old, cold, withered, and of intolerable entrails ?

Ford And one that is as ſlanderous as Satan ?

Page. And as poor as Job ?

Ford. And as wicked as his wife ?

Eva. And given to fornications, and to taverns, and ſack, and wine, and metheglins, and to drinkings, and ſwearings, and ſtarings, pribbles and prabbles ?

Fal. Well, I am your theme; you have the ſtart of me; I am dejeɛted; I am not able to anſwer the Welch flannel; ignorance itſelf is a plummet o'er me: uſe me as you will.

Ford. Marry, ſir, we'll bring you to Windſor, to one maſter Brook, that you have cozened of money, to whom you ſhould have been a pandar : over and above that you have ſuffered, I think, to repay that money will be a biting afflietion.

Mrs. Ford. Nay, huſband, let that go to make amends: Forgive that ſum, and ſo we'll all be friends.

Ford. Well, here's my hand; all's forgiven at laſt.

Page. Yet be cheerful, knight: thou ſhalt eat a poſſet to-night at my houſe ; where I will deſire thee to laugh at my wife, that now laughs at thee: Tell her, maſter Slender hath married her daughter.

Mrs. Page. Doɛtors doubt that : If Anne Page be my daughter, ſhe is, by this, Doɛtor Caius' wife. [*Aſide.*

H Enter

Enter SLENDER.

Slen. Whoo, ho! ho! father Page!

Page. Son! how now? how now, fon? have you defpatch'd?

Slen. Defpatch'd!—I'll make the beft in Glocefterfhire know on't; would I were hanged, la, elfe.

Page. Of what, fon?

Slen. I came yonder at Eton to marry miftrefs Anne Page, and fhe's a great lubberly boy: If it had not been i'the church, I would have fwinged him, or he fhould have fwinged me. If I did not think it had been Anne Page, would I might never ftir, and 'tis a poft-mafter's boy.

Page. Upon my life then you took the wrong.

Slen. What need you tell me that? I think fo, when I took a boy for a girl: If I had been married to him, for all he was in woman's apparel, I would not have had him.

Page. Why, this is your own folly. Did not I tell you, how you fhould know my daughter by her garments?

Slen. I went to her in white, and cry'd *mum*, and fhe cry'd *budget*, as Anne and I had appointed; and yet it was not Anne, but a poft-mafter's boy.

Eva. Jefhu! mafter Slender, cannot you fee but marry boys?

Page. O, I am vex'd at heart: what fhall I do?

Mrs. Page. Good George,- be not angry; I knew of your purpofe; turned my daughter into green; and indeed, fhe is now with the doctor at the deanery, and there married.

Enter CAIUS.

Caius. Vere is miftrefs Page? By gar, I am cozened; I ha' married *un garçon*, a boy; *un paifan*, by gar, a boy; *it is not* Anne Page: by gar, I am cozened.　　　*Mrs.*

Mrs. Page. Why, did you take her in green?

Caius Ay, be gar, and 'tis a boy: be gar, I'll raife all Windfor.   [*Exit.* CAIUS.

Ford. This is ftrange: Who hath got the right Anne?

Page. My heart mifgives me: Here comes mafter Fenton.

Enter FENTON *and* ANNE PAGE.

How now, mafter Fenton?

Anne. Pardon, good father! good my mother, pardon!

Page. Now miftrefs? How chance you went not with mafter Slender?

Mrs. Page. Why went you not with mafter doctor, maid?

Fent. You do amaze her; Hear the truth of it.
You would have married her moft fhamefully,
Where there was no proportion held in love.
The truth is, fhe and I, long fince contracted,
Are now fo fure, that nothing can diffolve us.
The offence is holy, that fhe hath committed:
And this deceit lofes the name of craft,
Of difobedience, or unduteous title;
Since therein fhe doth evitate and fhun
A thoufand irreligious curfed hours,
Which forced marriage would have brought upon her.

Ford. Stand not amaz'd: here is no remedy:——
In love, the heavens themfelves do guide the ftate;
Money buys lands, and wives are fold by fate.

Fal. I am glad, though you have ta'en a fpecial ftand
to ftrike at me, that your arrow hath glanced.

Page. Well, what remedy? Fenton, heaven give thee joy!
What cannot be efchew'd, muft be embrac'd.

Fal. When night-dogs run, all forts of deer are chas'd.

2   Eva.

Eva. I will dance and eat plums at your wedding.

Mrs. Page. Well, I will muſe no further :——Maſter
      Fenton,
Heaven give you many, many merry days!—
Good huſband, let us every one go home,
And laugh this ſport o'er by a country fire ;
Sir John and all.

Ford. Let it be ſo :—Sir John,
To maſter Brook you yet ſhall hold your word ;
For he, to-night, ſhall lie with miſtreſs Ford.   [*Exeunt.*

THE END.

Thurston del   Chapman

Twelfth Night

Act 1st Sc 9th

Published by Verner and Hood, Poultry May 1 1799

Harding's Edition.

TWELFTH-NIGHT;

OR,

WHAT YOU WILL.

A

COMEDY,

BY

WILLIAM SHAKSPEARE.

ACCURATELY PRINTED

FROM THE TEXT OF

Mr. STEEVENS's LAST EDITION.

Ornamented with Plates.

London:

PUBLISHED BY E. HARDING, NO. 98, PALL-MALL;
J. WRIGHT, PICCADILLY; G. SAEL, STRAND;
AND VERNOR AND HOOD, POULTRY.

1799.

OBSERVATIONS.

THERE is great reason to believe, that the serious part of this Comedy is founded on some old translation of the seventh history in the fourth volume of *Belleforest's Histoires Tragiques.* Belleforest took the story, as usual, from Bandello. The comic scenes appear to have been entirely the production of Shakspeare. It is not impossible, however, that the circumstances of the Duke sending his Page to plead his cause with the Lady, and of the Lady's falling in love with the Page, &c. might be borrowed from the Fifth Eglog of Barnaby Googe, published with his other original Poems in 1563.

> " A worthy *Knyght* dyd love her longe,
> " And for her sake dyd feale
> " The panges of love, that happen styl
> " By frowning fortune's weale.
> " He had a *Page,* Valerius named,
> " Whom so muche he dyd truste,
> " That all the secrets of his hart
> " To hym declare he muste.
> " And made hym all the onely meanes
> " To sue for his redresse,
> " And to entreate for grace to her
> " That caused his distresse.
> " *She whan as first she saw his page*
> " *Was straight with hym in love,*
> " *That nothynge coulde Valerius face*
> " *From Claudia's mynde remove.*
> " By hym was Faustus often harde,
> " By hym his sutes toke place,
> " By hym he often dyd aspyre
> " To se his Ladyes face.

" This

" This paſſed well, tyll at the length
  " Valerius ſore did ſewe,
" With many teares beſechynge her
  " His mayſter's gryefe to rewe.
  " And tolde her that yf ſhe wolde not
    " Releaſe his mayſter's payne,
*" He never wolde attempte her more
  " Nor ſe her ones agayne," &c.

Thus alſo concludes the firſt ſcene of the third act of the Play before us :

  " And ſo adieu, good madam; never more
  " Will I my maſter's tears to you deplore," &c.

I offer no apology for the length of the foregoing extract, the book from which it is taken, being ſo uncommon, that only one copy, except that in my own poſſeſſion, has hitherto occurred. Even Dr. Farmer, the late Rev. T. Warton, Mr. Reed, and Mr. Malone, were unacquainted with this Collection of Googe's Poetry.

Auguſt 6, 1607, a Comedy called What you Will (which is the ſecond title of this play), was entered at Stationers' Hall by Tho. Thorpe. I believe, however, it was Marſton's play with that name. Ben Jonſon, who takes every opportunity to find fault with Shakſpeare, ſeems to ridicule the conduct of Twelfth-Night in his Every Man out of his Humour, at the end of Act III. ſc. vi. where he makes Mitis ſay, " That the argument of his comedy might have been of ſome other nature, as of a duke to be in love with a counteſs, and that counteſs to be in love with the duke's ſon, and the ſon in love with the lady's waiting maid: ſome ſuch craſs wooing, with a clown to their ſerving man, better than be thus near and familiarly allied to the time." STEEVENS.

I ſuppoſe this comedy to have been written in 1614. If however the foregoing paſſage was levelled at Twelfth-Night, my ſpeculation falls to the ground. MALONE.

PERSONS REPRESENTED.

ORSINO, *duke of* Illyria.
SEBASTIAN, *a young gentleman, brother to* Viola.
ANTONIO, *a sea-captain, friend to* Sebastian.
A sea-captain, friend to Viola.
VALENTINE,⎱ *Gentlemen attending on the Duke.*
CURIO, ⎰
Sir TOBY BELCH, *uncle to* Olivia.
Sir ANDREW AGUE-CHEEK.
MALVOLIO, *steward to* Olivia.
FABIAN, ⎱ *servants to* Olivia.
Clown, ⎰

OLIVIA, *a rich countess.*
VIOLA, *in love with the duke.*
MARIA, Olivia's *woman.*

Lords, Priests, Sailors, Officers, Musicians, and other Attendants.

SCENE, *a city in* Illyria; *and the sea coast near it.*

TWELFTH-NIGHT.

ACT I. SCENE I.

An Apartment in the Duke's *Palace.*

Enter DUKE, CURIO, Lords; *Muficians attending.*

Duke.

IF mufick be the food of love, play on,
 Give me excefs of it; that, furfeiting,
The appetite may ficken, and fo die.————
That ftrain again;—it had a dying fall:
O, it came o'er my ear like the fweet fouth,
That breathes upon a bank of violets,
Stealing, and giving odour.—Enough; no more;
'Tis not fo fweet now, as it was before.
O fpirit of love, how quick and frefh art thou!
Thát notwithftanding thy capacity
Receiveth as the fea, nought enters there,
Of what validity and pitch foever,
But falls into abatement and low price,
Even in a minute! fo full of fhapes is fancy,
That it alone is high-fantaftical.
 Cur. Will you go hunt, my lord?
 Duke.   What, Curio?
 Cur.   The hart.
 Duke. Why, fo I do, the nobleft that I have:
O, when mine eyes did fee Olivia firft,
Methought, fhe purg'd the air of peftilence;

That

That inftant was I turn'd into a hart;
And my defires, like fell and cruel hounds,
E'er fince purfue me.—How now? what news from her

Enter VALENTINE.

Val. So pleafe my lord, I might not be admitted,
But from her hand-maid do return this anfwer:
The element itfelf, till feven years heat,
Shall not behold her face at ample view;
But, like a cloiftrefs, fhe will veiled walk,
And water once a day her chamber round
With eye-offending brine: all this, to feafon
A brother's dead love, which fhe would keep frefh,
And lafting, in her fad remembrance.
    Duke. O, fhe, that hath a heart of that fine frame,
To pay this debt of love but to a brother,
How will fhe love, when the rich golden fhaft,
Hath kill'd the flock of all affections elfe
That live in her! when liver, brain, and heart,
Thefe fovereign thrones, are all fupply'd, and fill'd,
(Her fweet perfections,) with one felf king!—
Away before me to fweet beds of flowers;
Love-thoughts lie rich, when canopy'd with bowers.

                                        [*Exeun*

SCENE II.

The Sea-coaft.

Enter VIOLA, Captain, *and* Sailors.

Vio. What country, friends, is this?
Cap.   Illyria, lady.
Vio. And what fhould I do in Illyria?
My brother he is in Elyfium.
Perchance, he is not drown'd:—What think you, failor

                                        C

Cap. It is perchance, that you yourfelf were fav'd.

Vio. O my poor brother! and fo, perchance, may he be.

Cap. True, madam: and, to comfort you with chance,
Affure yourfelf, after our fhip did fplit,
When you, and that poor number fav'd with you,
Hung on our driving boat, I faw your brother,
Moft provident in peril, bind himfelf
(Courage and hope both teaching him the practice)
To a ftrong maft, that liv'd upon the fea;
Where, like Arion on the dolphin's back,
I faw him hold acquaintance with the waves,
So long as I could fee.

Vio.   For faying fo, there's gold:
Mine own efcape unfoldeth to my hope,
Whereto thy fpeech ferves for authority,
The like of him. Know'ft thou this country?

Cap. Ay, madam, well; for I was bred and born;
Not three hours travel from this very place.

Vio. Who governs here?

Cap. A noble duke in nature, as in name.

Vio. What is his name?

Cap. Orfino.

Vio. Orfino! I have heard my father name him:
He was a bachelor then.

Cap.   And fo is now,
Or was fo very late: for but a month
Ago I went from hence; and then 'twas frefh
In murmur, (as, you know, what great ones do,
The lefs will prattle of,) that he did feek
The love of fair Olivia.

Vio.   What's fhe?

Cap. A virtuous maid, the daughter of a count
That dy'd fome twelve-month fince; then leaving her
In the protection of his fon, her brother,
Who fhortly alfo dy'd: for whofe dear love,

They

They fay, fhe hath abjur'd the company
And fight of men.

   Vio.   O, that I ferv'd that lady;
And might not be deliver'd to the world,
Till I had made mine own occafion mellow,
What my eftate is!

   Cap.   .   That were hard to compafs;
Becaufe fhe will admit no kind of fuit,
No, not the duke's.

   Vio. There is a fair behaviour in thee, captain;
And though that nature with a beauteous wall
Doth oft clofe in pollution, yet of thee
I will believe, thou haft a mind that fuits
With this thy fair and outward character.
I pray thee, and I'll pay thee bounteoufly,
Conceal me what I am; and be my aid
For fuch difguife as, haply, fhall become
The form of my intent.   I'll ferve this duke;
Thou fhalt prefent me as an eunuch to him,
It may be worth thy pains; for I can fing,
And fpeak to him in many forts of mufick,
That will allow me very worth his fervice.
What elfe may hap, to time I will commit;
Only fhape thou thy filence to my wit.

   Cap. Be you his eunuch, and your mute I'll be:
When my tongue blabs, then let mine eyes not fee!

   Vio. I thank thee: Lead me on.   [*Exeunt.*

SCENE III.

A Room in Olivia's *houfe.*

Enter Sir Toby Belch, *and* Maria.

   Sir To. What a plague means my niece, to take the
death

death of her brother thus? I am sure, care's an enemy to life.

Mar. By my troth, Sir Toby, you must come in earlier o'nights; your cousin, my lady, takes great exceptions to your ill hours.

Sir To. Why, let her except before excepted.

Mar. Ay, but you must confine yourself within the modest limits of order.

Sir To. Confine? I'll confine myself no finer than I am: these clothes are good enough to drink in, and so be these boots too; an they be not, let them hang themselves in their own straps.

Mar. That quaffing and drinking will undo you: I heard my lady talk of it yesterday; and of a foolish knight, that you brought in one night here, to be her wooer.

Sir To. Who? Sir Andrew Ague-cheek?

Mar. Ay, he.

Sir To. He's as tall a man as any's in Illyria.

Mar. What's that to the purpose?

Sir To. Why, he has three thousand ducats a year.

Mar. Ay, but he'll have but a year in all these ducats; he's a very fool, and a prodigal.

Sir To. Fie, that you'll say so! he plays o'the viol-de-gambo, and speaks three or four languages word for word without book, and hath all the good gifts of nature.

Mar. He hath, indeed,—almost natural: for, besides that he's a fool, he's a great quarreller; and, but that he hath the gift of a coward to allay the gust he hath in quarrelling, 'tis thought among the prudent, he would quickly have the gift of a grave.

Sir To. By this hand they are scoundrels, and subtractors, that say so of him. Who are they?

Mar. They that add moreover, he's drunk nightly in your company.

B 3

Sir To.

Sir To. With drinking healths to my niece; I'll drink to her, as long as there's a paſſage in my throat and drink in Illyria: He's a coward, and a coyſtril, that will not drink to my niece, till his brains turn o'the toe like a pariſh-top. What, wench? Caſtiliano vulgo; for here comes Sir Andrew Ague-face.

Enter SIR ANDREW AGUE-CHEEK.

Sir And. Sir Toby Belch! how now, Sir Toby Belch?
Sir To. Sweet ſir Andrew!
Sir And. Bleſs you, fair ſhrew.
Mar. And you too, ſir.
Sir To. Accoſt, ſir Andrew, accoſt.
Sir And. What's that?
Sir To. My niece's chamber-maid.
Sir And. Good miſtreſs Accoſt, I deſire better acquaintance.
Mar. My name is Mary, ſir.
Sir And. Good Miſtreſs Mary Accoſt,———
Sir To. You miſtake, knight: accoſt, is, front her, board her, woo her, aſſail her.
Sir And. By my troth, I would not undertake her in this company. Is that the meaning of accoſt?
Mar. Fare you well, gentlemen.
Sir To. An thou let part ſo, ſir Andrew, 'would thou might'ſt never draw ſword again.
Sir And. An you part ſo, miſtreſs, I would I might never draw ſword again. Fair lady, do you think you have fools in hand?
Mar. Sir, I have not you by the hand.
Sir And. Marry, but you ſhall have; and here's my hand.
Mar. Now, ſir, thought is free: I pray you, bring your hand to the buttery-bar, and let it drink.

Sir And.

Sir And. Wherefore, fweet heart? what's your me-
taphor?

Mar. It's dry, fir.

Sir And. Why, I think fo; I am not fuch an afs, but
I can keep my hand dry.   But what's your jeft?

Mar. A dry jeft, fir.

Sir And. Are you full of them?

Mar. Ay, fir; I have them at my fingers' ends: marry,
now I let go your hand, I am barren.   [*Exit* MARIA.

Sir To. O knight, thou lack'ft a cup of canary:
When did I fee thee fo put down?

Sir And. Never in your life, I think; unlefs you fee
canary put me down: Methinks, fometimes I have no
more wit than a Chriftian, or an ordinary man has: but
I am a great eater of beef, and, I believe, that does harm
to my wit.

Sir To. No queftion.

Sir And. An I thought that, I'd forfwear it.   I'll ride
home to-morrow, fir Toby.

Sir To. Pourquoy, my dear knight?

Sir And. What is *pourquoy?* do, or not do?   I would I
had beftowed that time in the tongues, that I have in fenc-
ing, dancing, and bear-baiting: O, had I but follow'd
the arts!

Sir To. Then hadft thou an excellent head of hair.

Sir And. Why, would that have mended my hair?

Sir To. Paft queftion; for thou feeft, it will not curl by
nature.

Sir And. But it becomes me well enough, does't not?

Sir To. Excellent; it hangs like flax on a diftaff; and I
hope to fee a houfewife take thee between her legs, and
fpin it off.

Sir And. 'Faith, I'll home to-morrow, Sir Toby: your
niece will not be feen; or, if fhe be, it's four to one fhe'll

none of me: the count himfelf, here hard by, wooes her.

Sir To. She'll none o'the count; fhe'll not match above her degree, neither, in eftate, years, nor wit; I have heard her fwear it. Tut, there's life in't, man.

Sir And. I'll ftay a month longer. I am a fellow o'the ftrangeft mind i'the world; I delight in mafques and revels fometimes altogether.

Sir To. Art thou good at thefe kick-fhaws, knight?

Sir And. As any man in Illyria, whatfoever he be, under the degree of my betters; and yet I will not compare with an old man.

Sir To. What is thy excellence in a galliard, knight?

Sir And. 'Faith, I can cut a caper.

Sir To. And I can cut the mutton to't.

Sir And. And, I think, I have the back-trick, fimply as ftrong as any man in Illyria.

Sir To. Wherefore are thefe things hid? wherefore have thefe gifts a curtain before them? are they like to take duft, like miftrefs Mall's picture? why doft thou not go to church in a galliard, and come home in a coranto? My very walk fhould be a jig; I would not fo much as make water, but in a fink-a-pace. What doft thou mean? is it a world to hide virtues in? I did think, by the excellent conftitution of thy leg, it was form'd under the ftar of a galliard.

Sir And. Ay, 'tis ftrong, and it does indifferent well in a flame-colour'd ftock. Shall we fet about fome revels?

Sir To. What fhall we do elfe? were we not born under Taurus?

Sir And. Taurus? that's fides and heart.

Sir To. No, fir; it is legs and thighs. Let me fee thee caper: ha! higher: ha, ha!—excellent!   [*Exeunt.*

SCENE

SCENE IV.

A Room in the **Duke's** *Palace.*

Enter VALENTINE, *and* VIOLA *in man's attire.*

Val. If the duke continue thefe favours towards you,
Cefario, you are like to be much advanced; he hath
known you but three days, and already you are no ftranger.

Vio. You either fear his humour, or my negligence, that
you call in queftion the continuance of his love : Is he in-
conftant, fir, in his favours?

Val. No, believe me.

Enter DUKE, CURIO, *and Attendants.*

Vio. I thank you.   Here comes the count.
Duke. Who faw Cefario, ho?
Vio. On your attendance, my lord; here.
Duke. Stand you awhile aloof.—Cefario,
Thou know'ft no lefs but all; I have unclafp'd
To thee the book even of my fecret foul :
Therefore, good youth, addrefs thy gait unto her;
Be not deny'd accefs, ftand at her doors,
And tell them, there thy fixed foot fhall grow,
Till thou have audience.
Vio.   Sure, my noble lord,
If fhe be fo abandon'd to her forrow
As it is fpoke, fhe never will admit me.
Duke. Be clamorous, and leap all civil bounds,
Rather than make unprofited return.
Vio. Say, I do fpeak with her, my lord; What then?
Duke. O, then unfold the paffion of my love,
Surprize her with difcourfe of my dear faith :

Vt

It fhall become thee well to act my woes ;
She will attend it better in thy youth,
Than in a nuncio of more grave afpéct.

 Vio. I think not fo, my lord.

 Duke.   Dear lad, believe it ;
For they fhall yet belie thy happy years,
That fay, thou art a man : Diana's lip
Is not more fmooth, and rubious ; thy fmall pipe
Is as the maiden's organ, fhrill, and found,
And all is femblative a woman's part.
I know, thy conftellation is right apt
For this affair :—Some four, or five, attend him ;
All, if you will ; for I myfelf am beft,
When leaft in company :—Profper well in this,
And thou fhalt live as freely as thy lord,
To call his fortunes thine.

 Vio.   I'll do my beft,
To woo your lady : yet, [*Afide.*] a barrful ftrife !
Whoe'er I woo, myfelf would be his wife.   [*Exeunt.*

SCENE V.

A room in Olivia's *houfe.*

Enter MARIA, *and* CLOWN.

 Mar. Nay, either tell me where thou haft been, or I
will not open my lips, fo wide as a briftle may enter, in
way of thy excufe : my lady will hang thee for thy abfence.

 Cio. Let her hang me : he, that is well hang'd in this
world, needs to fear no colours.

 Mar. Make that good.

    He fhall fee none to fear.

     3   *Mar.*

Mar. A good lenten anſwer: I can tell thee where that ſaying was born, of, I fear no colours.

Clo. Where, good miſtreſs Mary?

Mar. In the wars; and that may you be bold to ſay in your foolery.

Clo. Well, God give them wiſdom, that have it; and thoſe that are fools, let them uſe their talents.

Mar. Yet you will be hang'd, for being ſo long abſent: or, to be turn'd away; is not that as good as a hanging to you?

Clo. Many a good hanging prevents a bad marriage; and, for turning away, let ſummer bear it out.

Mar. You are reſolute then?

Clo. Not ſo neither; but I am reſolv'd on two points.

Mar. That if one break, the other will hold; or, if both break, your gaſkins fall.

Clo. Apt, in good faith; very apt! Well, go thy way; if Sir Toby would leave drinking, thou wert as witty a piece of Eve's fleſh as any in Illyria.

Mar. Peace, you rogue, no more o'that; here comes my lady: make your excuſe wiſely, you were beſt. [*Exit*.

Enter OLIVIA, *and* MALVOLIO.

Clo. Wit, and't be thy will, put me into good fooling! Thoſe wits, that think they have thee, do very oft prove fools; and I, that am ſure I lack thee, may paſs for a wiſe man: For what ſays Quinapalus? Better a witty fool, than a fooliſh wit.——God bleſs thee, lady!

Oli. Take the fool away.

Clo. Do you not hear, fellows? Take away the lady.

Oli. Go to, you're a dry fool; I'll no more of you: beſides, you grow diſhoneſt.

Clo. Two faults, Madonna, that drink and good c

fel will amend: for give the dry fool drink, then is the fool not dry; bid the difhoneft man mend himfelf; if he mend, he is no longer difhoneft; if he cannot, let the botcher mend him: Any thing, that's mended, is but patch'd: virtue, that tranfgreffes, is but patch'd with fin; and fin, that amends, is but patch'd with virtue: If that this fim- ple fyllogifm will ferve, fo; if it will not, What remedy? As there is no true cuckold but calamity, fo beauty's a flower:—the lady bade take away the fool; therefore, I fay again, take her away.

Oli. Sir, I bade them take away you.

Clo. Mifprifion in the higheft degree!—Lady, *Cucullus non facit monachum*; that's as much as to fay, I wear not motley in my brain. Good Madonna, give me leave to prove you a fool.

Oli. Can you do it?

Clo. Dexterioufly, good Madonna.

Oli. Make your proof.

Clo. I muft catechize you for it, Madonna; Good my moufe of virtue, anfwer me.

Oli. Well, fir, for want of other idlenefs, I'll bide your proof.

Clo. Good Madonna, why mourn'ft thou?

Oli. Good fool, for my brother's death.

Clo. I think, his foul is in hell, Madonna.

Oli. I know his foul is in heaven, fool.

Clo. The more fool you, Madonna, to mourn for your brother's foul being in heaven.—Take away the fool, gentlemen?

Oli. What think you of this fool, Malvolio? doth he not mend?

Mal. Yes; and fhall do, till the pangs of death fhake him: Infirmity, that decays the wife, doth ever make the better fool.

                                                    Clo.

Clo. God fend you, fir, a fpeedy infirmity, for the better encreafing your folly! Sir Toby will be fworn, that I
am no fox; but he will not pafs his word for two-pence
that you are no fool.

Oli. How fay you to that, Malvolio?

Mal. I marvel your ladyfhip takes delight in fuch a barren rafcal; I faw him put down the other day with an
ordinary fool, that has no more brain than a ftone: Look
you now, he's out of his guard already; unlefs you laugh
and minifter occafion to him, he is gagg'd. I proteft, I
take thefe wife men, that crow fo at thefe fet kind of fools,
no better than the fools' zanies.

Oli. O, you are fick of felf-love, Malvolio, and tafte
with a diftemper'd appetite. To be generous, guiltlefs,
and of free difpofition, is to take thofe things for bird-
bolts, that you deem cannon-bullets: There is no flander
in an allow'd fool, though he do nothing but rail; nor
no railing in a known difcreet man, though he do nothing
but reprove.

Clo. Now Mercury indue thee with leafing, for thou
fpeak'ft well of fools!

Re-enter MARIA.

Mar. Madam, there is at the gate a young gentleman,
much defires to fpeak with you.

Oli. From the count Orfino, is it?

Mar. I know not, madam; 'tis a fair young man, and
well attended.

Oli. Who of my people hold him in delay?

Mar. Sir Toby, madam, your kinfman.

Oli. Fetch him off, I pray you; he fpeaks nothing but
madman: Fie on him! [*Exit* MARIA.] Go you, Malvolio: if it be a fuit from the count, I am fick, or not at
home;

home; what you will, to difmifs it. [*Exit* MALVOLIO.]
Now you fee, fir, how your fooling grows old, and people diflike it.

Clo. Thou haft fpoke for us, Madonna, as if thy eldeft
fon fhould be a fool: whofe fcull Jove cram with brains,
for here he comes, one of thy kin, has a moft weak *pia
mater*.

Enter SIR TOBY BELCH.

Oli. By mine honour, half drunk.—What is he at the
gate, coufin?

Sir To. A gentleman.

Oli. A gentleman? What gentleman?

Sir To. 'Tis a gentleman here—A plague o'thefe pickle-
herrings!—How now, fot?

Clo. Good Sir Toby,——

Oli. Coufin, coufin, how have you come fo early by
this lethargy?

Sir To. Lechery! I defy lechery: There's one at the
gate.

Oli. Ay, marry; what is he?

Sir To. Let him be the devil, an he will, I care not:
give me faith, fay I. Well, it's all one.   [*Exit*.

Oli. What's a drunken man like, fool?

Clo. Like a drown'd man, a fool, and a madman: one
draught above heat makes him a fool; the fecond mads
him; and a third drowns him.

Oli. Go thou and feek the coroner, and let him fit o'
my coz; for he's in the third degree of drink, he's drown'd:
go, look after him.

Clo. He is but mad yet, Madonna; and the fool fhall
look to the madman.   [*Exit* CLOWN.

Re-enter

Re-enter MALVOLIO.

Mal. Madam, yond young fellow fwears he will fpeak
with you.   I told him you were fick; he takes on him to
underftand fo much, and therefore comes to fpeak with
you : I told him you were afleep; he feems to have a fore-
knowledge of that too, and therefore comes to fpeak with
you.   What is to be faid to him, lady? he's fortified
againft any denial.

Oli. Tell him, he fhall not fpeak with me.

Mal. He has been told fo; and he fays, he'll ftand at
your door like a fheriff's poft, and be the fupporter to a
bench, but he'll fpeak with you.

Oli. What kind of man is he?

Mal. Why, of man kind.

Oli. What manner of man?

Mal. Of very ill manner; he'll fpeak with you, will
you, or no.

Oli. Of what perfonage, and years, is he?

Mal. Not yet old enough for a man, nor young enough
for a boy; as a fquafh is before 'tis a peafcod, or a cod-
ling when 'tis almoft an apple : 'tis with him e'en ftanding
water, between boy and man.   He is very well-favour'd,
and he fpeaks very fhrewifhly; one would think, his mother's milk were fcarce out of him.

Oli. Let him approach : Call in my gentlewoman.

Mal. Gentlewoman, my lady calls.   [*Exit.*

Re-enter MARIA.

Oli. Give me my veil : come, throw it o'er my face;
We'll once more hear Orfino's embaffy.

                                        Enter

Enter VIOLA.

Vio. The honourable lady of the houfe, which is fhe?

Oli. Speak to me, I fhall anfwer for her; Your will?

Vio. Moft radiant, exquifite, and unmatchable beauty,—
I pray you, tell me, if this be the lady of the houfe, for
I never faw her: I would be loth to caft away my fpeech;
for, befides that it is excellently well penn'd, I have taken
great pains to con it. Good beauties, let me fuftain no
fcorn; I am very comptible, even to the leaft finifter
ufage.

Oli. Whence came you, fir?

Vio. I can fay little more than I have ftudied, and that
queftion's out of my part. Good gentle one, give me
modeft affurance, if you be the lady of the houfe, that I
may proceed in my fpeech.

Oli. Are you a comedian?

Vio. No, my profound heart: and yet, by the very
fangs of malice, I fwear, I am not that I play. Are you
the lady of the houfe?

Oli. If I do not ufurp myfelf, I am.

Viol. Moft certain, if you are fhe, you do ufurp yourfelf; for what is yours to beftow, is not yours to referve.
But this is from my commiffion: I will on with my fpeech
in your praife, and then fhew you the heart of my meffage.

Oli. Come to what is important in't: I forgive you the
praife.

Vio. Alas, I took great pains to ftudy it, and 'tis poe-
tical.

Oli. It is the more like to be feign'd; I pray you, keep
it in. I heard, you were faucy at my gates; and allow'd
your approach, rather to wonder at you than to hear you.
If you be not mad, be gone; if you have reafon, be brief:

'tis

'tis not that time of moon with me, to make one in so skipping a dialogue.

Mar. Will you hoist sail, sir? here lies your way.

Vio. No, good swabber; I am to hull here a little longer.—Some mollification for your giant, sweet lady.

Oli. Tell me your mind.

Vio. I am a messenger.

Oli. Sure, you have some hideous matter to deliver, when the courtesy of it is so fearful. Speak your office.

Vio. It alone concerns your ear. I bring no overture of war, no taxation of homage; I hold the olive in my hand; my words are as full of peace as matter.

Oli. Yet you began rudely. What are you? what would you?

Vio. The rudeness, that hath appear'd in me, have I learn'd from my entertainment. What I am, and what I would, are as secret as maidenhead: to your ears, divinity; to any other's, prophanation.

Oli. Give us the place alone: we will hear this divinity. [*Exit* MARIA.] Now, sir, what is your text?

Vio. Most sweet lady,——

Oli. A comfortable doctrine, and much may be said of it. Where lies your text?

Vio. In Orsino's bosom.

Oli. In his bosom? In what chapter of his bosom?

Vio. To answer by the method, in the first of his heart.

Oli. O, I have read it; it is heresy. Have you no more to say?

Vio. Good madam, let me see your face.

Oli. Have you any commission from your lord to negotiate with my face? you are now out of your text: but we will draw the curtain, and shew you the picture. Look you, sir, such a one I was this present: Is't not well done?   [*Unveiling.*

C   *Vio.*

Vio. Excellently done, if God did all.

Oli. 'Tis in grain, fir; 'twill endure wind and weather.

Vio. 'Tis beauty truly blent, whofe red and white
Nature's own fweet and cunning hand laid on:
Lady, you are the cruel'ft fhe alive,
If you will lead thefe graces to the grave,
And leave the world no copy.

Oli. O, fir, I will not be fo hard-hearted; I will give
out divers fchedules of my beauty: It fhall be inventori-
ed; and every particle, and utenfil, label'd to my will: as,
item, two lips indifferent red; item, two grey eyes, with
lids to them; item, one neck, one chin, and fo forth.
Were you fent hither to 'praife me?

Vio. I fee you what you are: you are too proud;
But, if you were the devil, you are fair.
My lord and mafter loves you; O, fuch love
Could be but recompens'd, though you were crown'd
The non-pariel of beauty!

Oli. How does he love me?

Vio. With adorations, with fertile tears,
With groans that thunder love, with fighs of fire.

Oli. Your lord does know my mind, I cannot love
him:
Yet I fuppofe him virtuous, know him noble,
Of great eftate, of frefh and ftainlefs youth;
In voices well divulg'd, free, learn'd, and valiant,
And, in dimenfion, and the fhape of nature,
A gracious perfon: but yet I cannot love him;
He might have took his anfwer long ago.

Vio. If I did love you in my mafter's flame,
With fuch a fuffering, fuch a deadly life,
In your denial I would find no fenfe,
I would not underftand it.

Oli. Why what would you?

Vio.

Vio. Make me a willow cabin at your gate,
And call upon my foul within the houſe;
Write loyal cantons of contemned love,
And ſing them loud even in the dead of night;
Holla your name to the reverberate hills,
And make the babbling goſſip of the air
Cry out, Olivia! O, you ſhould not reſt
Between the elements of air and earth,
But you ſhould pity me.

    Oli. You might do much: What is your parentage?

    Vio. Above my fortunes, yet my ſtate is well:
I am a gentleman.

    Oli.   Get you to your lord;
I cannot love him: let him ſend no more;
Unleſs, perchance, you come to me again,
To tell me how he takes it. Fare you well:
I thank you for your pains: ſpend this for me.

    Vio. I am no fee'd poſt, lady; keep your purſe;
My maſter, not myſelf, lacks recompenſe.
Love make his heart of flint, that you ſhall love;
And let your fervour, like my maſter's, be
Plac'd in contempt! Farewel, fair cruelty.   [*Exit.*

    Oli. What is your parentage?
Above my fortunes, yet my ſtate is well:
I am a gentleman.——I'll be ſworn thou art;
Thy tongue, thy face, thy limbs, actions, and ſpirit,
Do give thee five-fold blazon:—Not too faſt:—ſoft! ſoft!
Unleſs the maſter were the man.—How now?
Even ſo quickly may one catch the plague?
Methinks, I feel this youth's perfections,
With an inviſible and ſubtle ſtealth,
To creep in at mine eyes. Well, let it be.—
What, ho, Malvolio!—

Re-enter MALVOLIO.

Mal.   Here, madam, at your service.

Oli. Run after that same peevish messenger,
The county's man: he left this ring behind him,
Would I, or not; tell him, I'll none of it.
Desire him not to flatter with his lord,
Nor hold him up with hopes; I am not for him:
If that the youth will come this way to-morrow,
I'll give him reasons for't. Hie thee, Malvolio.

Mal. Madam, I will.   [*Exit.*

Oli. I do I know not what; and fear to find
Mine eye too great a flatterer for my mind.
Fate, shew thy force: Ourselves we do not owe;
What is decreed, must be; and be this so!   [*Exit.*

ACT II.   SCENE I.

The Sea-coaft.

Enter ANTONIO *and* SEBASTIAN.

Ant. Will you ftay no longer? nor will you not, that I go with you?

Seb. By your patience, no: my ftars fhine darkly over me; the malignancy of my fate might, perhaps, diftemper yours; therefore I fhall crave of you your leave, that I may bear my evils alone: It were a bad recompenfe for your love, to lay any of them on you.

Ant. Let me yet know of you, whither you are bound.

Seb. No, 'footh, fir; my determinate voyage is mere extravagancy. But I perceive in you fo excellent a touch of modefty, that you will not extort from me what I am willing to keep in; therefore it charges me in manners the rather to exprefs myfelf. You muft know of me then, Antonio, my name is Sebaftian, which I call'd Rodorigo; my father was that Sebaftian of Meffaline, whom, I know, you have heard of: he left behind him, myfelf, and a fifter, both born in an hour: If the heavens had been pleas'd, 'would we had fo ended! but, you, fir, alter'd that; for, fome hour before you took me from the breach of the fea, was my fifter drown'd.

Ant. Alas, the day!

Seb. A lady, fir, though it was faid fhe much refembled me, was yet of many accounted beautiful: but, though I could not, with fuch eftimable wonder, over-far believe that, yet thus far I will boldly publifh her, fhe bore a

C 3   mind

mind that envy could not but call fair: fhe is drown'd
already, fir, with falt water, though I feem to drown her
remembrance again with more.

Ant. Pardon me, fir, your bad entertainment.

Seb. O, good Antonio, forgive me your trouble.

Ant. If you will not murder me for my love, let me be
your fervant.

Seb. If you will not undo what you have done, that is,
kill him whom you have recover'd, defire it not. Fare ye
well at once: my bofom is full of kindnefs; and I am
yet fo near the manners of my mother, that upon the leaft
occafion more, mine eyes will tell tales of me. I am
bound to the count Orfino's court: farewel.   [*Exit.*

Ant. The gentlenefs of all the gods go with thee!
I have many enemies in Orfino's court,
Elfe would I very fhortly fee thee there:
But, come what may, I do adore thee fo,
That danger fhall feem fport, and I will go.   [*Exit.*

SCENE II.

A Street.

Enter VIOLA; MALVOLIO *following.*

Mal. Were not you even now with the countefs Olivia?

Vio. Even now, fir; on a moderate pace I have fince
arrived but hither.

Mal. She returns this ring to you, fir; you might have
faved me my pains, to have taken it away yourfelf. She
adds moreover, that you fhould put your lord into a defperate affurance fhe will none of him: And one thing
more; that you be never fo hardy to come again in his

affairs,

affairs, unlefs it be to report your lord's taking of this.
Receive it fo.

Vio. She took the ring of me; I'll none of it.

Mal. Come, fir, you peevifhly threw it to her; and her
will is, it fhould be fo return'd: if it be worth ftooping
for, there it lies in your eye; if not, be it his that finds
it.   [*Exit.*

Vio. I left no ring with her: What means this lady?
Fortune forbid, my outfide have not charm'd her!
She made good view of me; indeed, fo much,
That, fure, methought, her eyes had loft her tongue,
For fhe did fpeak in ftarts diftractedly.
She loves me, fure; the cunning of her paffion
Invites me in this churlifh meffenger.
None of my lord's ring! why, he fent her none.
I am the man;—If it be fo, (as 'tis)
Poor lady, fhe were better love a dream.
Difguife, I fee, thou art a wickednefs,
Wherein the pregnant enemy does much.
How eafy is it, for the proper-falfe
In women's waxen hearts to fet their forms!
Alas, our frailty is the caufe, not we;
For, fuch as we are made of, fuch we be.
How will this fadge? My mafter loves her dearly;
And I, poor monfter, fond as much on him;
And fhe, miftaken, feems to dote on me:
What will become of this? As I am man,
My ftate is defperate for my mafter's love;
As I am woman, now alas the day!
What thriftlefs fighs fhall poor Olivia breathe?
O time, thou muft untangle this, not I;
It is too hard a knot for me to untie.   [*Exit.*

SCENE III.

A Room in Olivia's *Houfe.*

Enter SIR TOBY BELCH, *and* SIR ANDREW AGUE-
CHEEK.

Sir To. Approach, fir Andrew: not to be a-bed after
midnight, is to be up betimes; and *diluculo furgere,* thou
know'ft,——

Sir And. Nay, by my troth, I know not: but I know,
to be up late, is to be up late.

Sir To. A falfe conclufion; I hate it as an unfill'd can:
To be up after midnight, and to go to bed then, is early;
fo that, to go to bed after midnight, is to go to bed betimes. Do not our lives confift of the four elements?

Sir And. 'Faith, fo they fay; but, I think, it rather con-
fifts of eating and drinking.

Sir To. Thou art a fcholar; let us therefore eat and
drink.—Marian, I fay!——a ftoop of wine!

Enter Clown.

Sir And. Here comes the fool, i'faith.

Clo. How now, my hearts? Did you never fee the picture of we three?

Sir To. Welcome, afs. Now let's have a catch.

Sir And. By my troth, the fool has an excellent breaft.
I had rather than forty fhillings I had fuch a leg; and fo
fweet a breath to fing, as the fool has. In footh, thou
waft in very gracious fooling laft night, when thou fpokeft
of Pigrogromitus, of the Vapians paffing the equinoctial
of Queubus; 'twas very good, i'faith. I fent thee fix-
pence for thy leman; Hadft it?

Clo.

Twelfth Night.

Published by Vernor & Hood 31 Poultry, Septem.ʳ 1.ˢᵗ 1799.

Clo. I did impeticos thy gratillity; for Malvolio's nose is no whipstock: My lady has a white hand, and the Myrmidons are no bottle-ale houses.

Sir And. Excellent! Why, this is the best fooling, when is done. Now, a song.

Sir To. Come on; there is six-pence for you: let's have a song.

Sir And. There's a testril of me too: if one knight give a——

Clo. Would you have a love-song, or a song of good life?

Sir To. A love-song, a love-song.

Sir And. Ay, ay; I care not for good life.

SONG.

Clo. *O mistress mine, where are you roaming?*
  O, stay and hear; your true love's coming,
   That can sing both high and low:
  Trip no further, pretty sweeting;
  Journeys end in lovers' meeting,
   Every wise man's son doth know.

Sir And. Excellent good, i'faith!

Sir To. Good, good.

Clo. *What is love? 'tis not hereafter;*
  Present mirth hath present laughter;
   What's to come, is still unsure:
  In delay there lies no plenty;
  Then come kiss me, sweet and twenty,
   Youth's a stuff will not endure.

Sir And. A mellifluous voice, as I am true knight.

                                        Sir To.

Sir To. A contagious breath.

Sir And. Very fweet and contagious, i'faith.

Sir To. To hear by the nofe, it is dulcet in contagion. But fhall we make the welkin dance indeed? Shall we roufe the night-owl in a catch, that will draw three fouls out of one weaver? fhall we do that?

Sir And. An you love me, let's do't: I am dog at a catch.

Clo. By'r lady, fir, and fome dogs will catch well.

Sir And. Moft certain: let our catch be, *Thou knave.*

Clo. *Hold thy peace, thou knave,* knight? I fhall be con-ftrain'd in't to call thee knave, knight.

Sir And. 'Tis not the firft time I have conftrain'd one to call me knave. Begin, fool; it begins, *Hold thy peace.*

Clo. I fhall never begin, if I hold my peace.

Sir And. Good, i'faith! Come, begin.

[*They fing a Catch.*

Enter MARIA.

Mar. What a catterwauling do you keep here! If my lady have not call'd up her fteward, Malvolio, and bid him turn you out of doors, never truft me.

Sir To. My lady's a Cataian, we are politicians; Malvo-lio's a Peg-a-Ramfey, and *Three merry men be we.* Am not I confanguineous? am I not of her blood? Tilly-valley lady! *There dwelt a man in Babylon, lady, lady!*

[*Singing.*

Clo. Befhrew me, the knight's in admirable fooling.

Sir And. Ay, he does well enough, if he be difpos'd, and fo do I too; he does it with a better grace, but I do it more natural.

Sir To. O, *the twelfth day of December,*—   [*Singing.*

Mar. For the love o'God, peace.

[*Enter*

Enter MALVOLIO.

Mal. My masters, are you mad? or what are you? Have you no wit, manners, nor honesty, but to gabble like tinkers at this time of night? Do ye make an ale-house of my lady's house, that ye squeak out your co-ziers' catches without any mitigation or remorse of voice? Is there no respect of place, persons, nor time, in you?

Sir To. We did keep time, sir, in our catches. Sneck up!

Mal. Sir Toby, I must be round with you. My lady bade me tell you, that, though she harbours you as her kinsman, she's nothing allied to your disorders. If you can separate yourself and your misdemeanors, you are welcome to the house; if not, an it would please you to take leave of her, she is very willing to bid you farewel.

Sir To. *Farewel, dear heart, since I must needs be gone.*

Mal. Nay, good sir Toby.

Clo. *His eyes do shew his days are almost done.*

Mal. Is't even so.

Sir To. *But I will never die.*

Clo. Sir Toby, there you lie.

Mal. This is much credit to you.

Sir To. *Shall I bid him go?*   [*Singing.*

Clo. *What an if you do?*

Sir To. *Shall I bid him go, and spare not?*

Clo. *O no, no, no, no, you dare not.*

Sir To. Out o'time? sir, ye lie.—Art any more than a steward? Dost thou think, because thou art virtuous, there shall be no more cakes and ale?

Clo. Yes, by Saint Anne; and ginger shall be hot i'the mouth too.

Sir To. Thou'rt i'the right.—Go, sir, rub your chain with crums:—A stoop of wine, Maria!

Mal.

Mal. Miftrefs Mary, if you priz'd my lady's favour at any thing more than contempt, you would not give means for this uncivil rule; fhe fhall know of it, by this hand.

                                [*Exit.*

Mar. Go fhake your ears.

Sir And. ' Twere as good a deed, as to drink when a man's a hungry, to challenge him to the field; and then to break promife with him, and make a fool of him.

Sir To. Do't, knight; I'll write thee a challenge; or I'll deliver thy indignation to him by word of mouth.

Mar. Sweet fir Toby, be patient for to-night; fince the youth of the count's was to-day with my lady, fhe is much out of quiet. For monfieur Malvolio, let me alone with him: if I do not gull him into a nayword, and make him a common recreation, do not think I have wit enough to lie ftraight in my bed: I know, I can do it.

Sir To. Poffefs us, poffefs us; tell us fomething of him.

Mar. Marry, fir, fometimes he is a kind of Puritan.

Sir And. O, if I thought that, I'd beat him like a dog.

Sir To. What, for being a Puritan? thy exquifite reafon, dear knight?

Sir And. I have no exquifite reafon for't, but I have reafon good enough.

Mar. The devil a Puritan that he is, or any thing conftantly but a time-pleafer; an affection'd afs, that cons ftate without book, and utters it by great fwarths: the beft perfuaded of himfelf, fo cramm'd, as he thinks, with excellencies, that it is his ground of faith, that all, that look on him, love him; and on that vice in him will my revenge find notable caufe to work.

Sir To. What wilt thou do?

Mar. I will drop in his way fome obfcure epiftles of love; wherein, by the colour of his beard, the fhape of his leg, the manner of his gait, the expreffure of his eye,

                                forehead,

forehead, and complexion, he shall find himself most feelingly personated: I can write very like my lady, your niece; on a forgotten matter we can hardly make distinction of our hands.

Sir To. Excellent! I smell a device.

Sir And. I have't in my nose too.

Sir To. He shall think, by the letters that thou wilt drop, that they come from my niece, and that she is in love with him.

Mar. My purpose is, indeed, a horse of that colour.

Sir And. And your horse now would make him an ass.

Mar. Ass, I doubt not.

Sir And. O, 'twill be admirable.

Mar. Sport royal, I warrant you: I know, my physick will work with him. I will plant you two, and let the fool make a third, where he shall find the letter; observe his construction of it. For this night, to bed, and dream on the event. Farewel.   [*Exit.*

Sir To. Good night, Penthesilea.

Sir And. Before me, she's a good wench.

Sir To. She's a beagle, true-bred, and one that adores me; What o'that?

Sir And. I was adored once too.

Sir To. Let's to bed, knight.—Thou hadst need send for more money.

Sir And. If I cannot recover your niece, I am a foul way out.

Sir To. Send for money, knight; if thou hast her not i'the end, call me Cut.

Sir And. If I do not, never trust me, take it how you will.

Sir To. Come, come; I'll go burn some sack, 'tis too late to go to bed now: come, knight; come, knight.

                [*Exeunt.*
SCENE

SCENE IV.

A room in the Duke's *palace.*

Enter DUKE, VIOLA, CURIO, *and Others.*

Duke. Give me fome mufick :—Now, good morrow,
      friends :———
Now, good Cefario, but that piece of fong,
That old and antique fong we heard laft night ;
Methought, it did relieve my paffion much ;
More than light airs, and recollected terms,
Of thefe moft brifk and giddy-paced times :———
Come, but one verfe.

    Cur. He is not here, fo pleafe your lordfhip, that fhould
fing it.

    Duke. Who was it ?

    Cur. Fefte, the jefter, my lord ; a fool, that the lady
Olivia's father took much delight in : he is about the
houfe.

    Duke. Seek him out, and play the tune the while.

                        [*Exit* CURIO.—*Mufic.*
Come hither, boy ; If ever thou fhalt love,
In the fweet pangs of it, remember me :
For, fuch as I am, all true lovers are ;
Unftaid and fkittifh in all motions elfe,
Save, in the conftant image of the creature
That is belov'd.—How doft thou like this tune ?

    Vio. It gives a very echo to the feat
Where Love is thron'd.

    Duke. Thou doft fpeak mafterly :
My life upon't, young though thou art, thine eye
Hath ftay'd upon fome favour that it loves ;
Hath it not, boy ?

                             Vio.

Vio.   A little, by your favour.

Duke. What kind of woman is't?

Vio.   Of your complexion.

Duke. She is not worth thee then. What years, i'faith?

Vio. About your years, my lord.

Duke. Too old, by heaven; Let still the woman take
An elder than herself; so wears she to him,
So sways she level in her husband's heart.
For, boy, however we do praise ourselves,
Our fancies are more giddy and unfirm,
More longing, wavering, sooner lost and worn,
Than women's are.

Vio.   I think it well, my lord.

Duke. Then let thy love be younger than thyself,
Or thy affection cannot hold the bent:
For women are as roses; whose fair flower,
Being once display'd, doth fall that very hour.

Vio. And so they are: alas, that they are so;
To die, even when they to perfection grow!

Re-enter CURIO, *and* CLOWN.

Duke. O fellow, come, the song we had last night:——
Mark it, Cesario; it is old, and plain:
The spinsters and the knitters in the sun,
And the free maids, that weave their thread with bones,
Do use to chaunt it; it is silly sooth,
And dallies with the innocence of love,
Like the old age.

Clo. Are you ready, sir?

Duke. Ay; pr'ythee, sing.   [*Musick.*

SONG.

SONG.

Clo.   *Come away, come away, death,*
       And in sad cypress let me be laid;
         Fly away, fly away, breath;
       I am slain by a fair cruel maid.
       My shroud of white, stuck all with yew,
             O, prepare it;
       My part of death no one so true
          · *Did share it.*

       Not a flower, not a flower sweet,
     On my black coffin let there be strown;
       Not a friend, not a friend greet
     My poor corpse, where my bones shall be thrown :
     A thousand thousand sighs to save,
         Lay me, O, where
     Sad true lovers ne'er find my grave,
         To weep there.

Duke. There's for thy pains.

Clo. No pains, sir; I take pleasure in singing, sir.

Duke. I'll pay thy pleasure then.

Clo. Truly, sir, and pleasure will be paid, one time or another.

Duke. Give me now leave to leave thee.

Clo. Now, the melancholy god protect thee; and the tailor make thy doublet of changeable taffata, for thy mind is a very opal!—I would have men of such constancy put to sea, that their business might be every thing, and their intent every where; for that's it, that always makes a good voyage of nothing.—Farewel.

                 [*Exit* Clown.
                  - · *Duke.*

Duke. Let all the reft give place.——

                    [*Exeunt* CURIO *and Attendants.*

                        Once more, Cefario,

Get thee to yon' fame fovereign cruelty:
Tell her, my love, more noble than the world,
Prizes not quantity of dirty lands;
The parts that fortune hath beftow'd upon her,
Tell her, I hold as giddily as fortune;
But 'tis that miracle, and queen of gems,
That nature pranks her in, attracts my foul.

    Vio. But, if fhe cannot love you, fir?

    Duke. I cannot be fo anfwer'd.

    Vio.   'Sooth, but you muft.

Say, that fome lady, as, perhaps, there is,
Hath for your love as great a pang of heart
As you have for Olivia: you cannot love her;
You tell her fo; Muft fhe not then be anfwer'd?

    Duke. There is no woman's fides
Can bide the beating of fo ftrong a paffion
As love doth give my heart; no woman's heart
So big, to hold fo much; they lack retention.
Alas, their love may be call'd appetite,—
No motion of the liver, but the palate,—
That fuffer furfeit, cloyment, and revolt;
But mine is all as hungry as the fea,
And can digeft as much: make no compare
Between that love a woman can bear me,
And that I owe Olivia.

    Vio.   Ay, but I know,—

    Duke. What doft thou know?

    Vio. Too well what love women to men may owe:
In faith, they are as true of heart as we.
My father had a daughter lov'd a man,

               D   **As**

As it might be, perhaps, were I a woman,
I should your lordship.

 Duke.   And what's her history?

 Vio. A blank, my lord : She never told her love,
But let concealment, like a worm i'the bud,
Feed on her damask cheek : she pin'd in thought;
And, with a green and yellow melancholy,
She sat like patience on a monument,
Smiling at grief. Was not this love, indeed?
We men may say more, swear more : but, indeed,
Our shows are more than will ; for still we prove
Much in our vows, but little in our love.

 Duke. But dy'd thy sister of her love, my boy?

 Vio. I am all the daughters of my father's house,
And all the brothers too ;—and yet I know not :—
Sir, shall I to this lady?

 Duke.   Ay, that's the theme.
To her in haste ; give her this jewel; say,
My love can give no place, bide no denay. [*Exeunt.*

SCENE V.

Olivia's *Garden.*

Enter SIR TOBY BELCH, SIR ANDREW AGUE-CHEEK,
   and FABIAN.

 Sir To. Come thy ways, signior Fabian.

 Fab. Nay, I'll come ; if I lose a scruple of this sport,
let me be boil'd to death with melancholy.

 Sir To. Would'st thou not be glad to have the niggardly
rascally sheep-biter come by some notable shame?

 Fab. I would exult, man : you know, he brought me
out of favour with my lady, about a bear-baiting here.

              Sir To.

Sir To. To anger him, we'll have the bear again; and we will fool him black and blue:—Shall we not, fir Andrew?

Sir And. An we do not, it is pity of our lives.

Enter MARIA.

Sir To. Here comes the little villain:—How now, my nettle of India?

Mar. Get ye all three into the box-tree: Malvolio's coming down this walk; he has been yonder i'the fun, practifing behaviour to his own fhadow, this half hour: obferve him, for the love of mockery; for, I know, this letter will make a contemplative idiot of him. Clofe, in the name of jefting! [*The men hide themfelves.*] Lie thou there; [*throws down a letter.*] for here comes the trout that muft be caught with tickling.　　[*Exit* MARIA.

Enter MALVOLIO.

Mar. 'Tis but fortune; all is fortune. Maria once told me, fhe did affect me: and I have heard herfelf come thus near, that, fhould fhe fancy, it fhould be one of my complexion. Befides, fhe ufes me with a more exalted refpect, than any one elfe that follows her. What fhould I think on't?

Sir To. Here's an over-weening rogue!

Fab. O, peace! Contemplation makes a rare turkey-cock of him; how he jets under his advanced plumes!

Sir And. 'Slight, I could fo beat the rogue:—

Sir To. Peace, I fay.

Mal. To be count Malvolio;—

Sir To. Ah, rogue!

Sir And. Piftol him, piftol him.

Fab. A fuſtian riddle!

Sir To. Excellent wench, ſay I.

Mal. M, O, A, I, doth ſway my life.—Nay, but firſt, let me ſee,—let me ſee,—let me ſee.

Fab. What a diſh of poiſon has ſhe dreſs'd him!

Sir To. And with what wing the ſtannyel checks at it!

Mal. *I may command where I adore.* Why, ſhe may command me; I ſerve her, ſhe is my lady. Why, this is evident to any formal capacity. There is no obſtruction in this;—And the end;—What ſhould that alphabetical poſition portend? if I could make that reſemble ſomething in me,—Softly;—*M, O, A, I.*—

Sir To. O, ay! make up that:—he is now at a cold ſcent.

Fab. Sowter will cry upon't, for all this, though it be as rank as a fox.

Mal. M,—Malvolio:—*M,*—why, that begins my name.

Fab. Did not I ſay, he would work it out? the cur is excellent at faults.

Mal. M,—But then there is no conſonancy in the ſequel; that ſuffers under probation: *A* ſhould follow, but *O* does.

Fab. And *O* ſhall end, I hope.

Sir To. Ay, or I'll cudgel him, and make him cry, *O.*

Mal. And then *I* comes behind,

Fab. Ay, an you had any eye behind you, you might ſee more detraction at your heels, than fortunes before you.

Mal. M, O, A, I;—This ſimulation is not as the former:—and yet, to cruſh this a little, it would bow to me, for every one of theſe letters are in my name. Soft; here follows proſe.—*If this fall into thy hand, revolve. In my ſtars I am above thee; but be not afraid of greatneſs: Some are born great, ſome atchieve greatneſs, and ſome have great-*
neſs

*ness thrust upon them. Thy fates open their hands; let thy
blood and spirit embrace them. And, to inure thyself to what
thou art like to be, cast thy humble slough, and appear fresh.
Be opposite with a kinsman, surly with servants: let thy tongue
tang arguments of state; put thyself into the trick of singularity:
She thus advises thee, that sighs for thee. Remember who
commended thy yellow stockings; and wish'd to see thee ever
cross-garter'd: I say, remember. Go to; thou art made, if
thou desirest to be so; if not, let me see thee a steward still, the
fellow of servants, and not worthy to touch fortune's fingers.
Farewel. She, that would alter services with thee,*

The fortunate-unhappy.

Day-light and champian difcovers not more: this is open.
I will be proud, I will read politic authors, I will baffle
Sir Toby, I will wafh off grofs acquaintance, I will be
point-de-vice, the very man. I do not now fool myfelf,
to let imagination jade me; for every reafon excites to this,
that my lady loves me. She did commend my yellow
ftockings of late, fhe did praife my leg being crofs-garter'd; and in this fhe manifefts herfelf to my love, and,
with a kind of injunction, drives me to thefe habits of
her liking. I thank my ftars, I am happy. I will be
ftrange, ftout, in yellow ftockings, and crofs-garter'd,
even with the fwiftnefs of putting on. Jove, and my
ftars be praifed!—Here is yet a poftfcript. *Thou canst not
choose but know who I am. If thou entertainest my love, let it
appear in thy smiling; thy smiles become thee well: therefore in
my presence still smile, dear my sweet, I pr'ythee.*—Jove, I
thank thee.—I will fmile; I will do every thing that thou
wilt have me. [*Exit.*

Fab. I will not give my part of this fport for a penfion
of thoufands to be paid from the Sophy.

Sir To. I could marry this wench for this device:

Sir And. So could I too.

D 4

Sir To.

Sir To. And aſk no other dowry with her, but ſuch another jeſt.

Enter MARIA.

Sir And. Nor I neither.

Fab. Here comes my noble gull-catcher.

Sir To. Wilt thou ſet thy foot o'my neck ?

Sir And. Or o'mine either ?

Sir To. Shall I play my freedom at tray-trip, and be-come thy bond-ſlave ?

Sir And. I'faith, or I either ?

Sir To. Why, thou haſt put him in ſuch a dream, that, when the image of it leaves him, he muſt run mad.

Mar. Nay, but ſay true ; does it work upon him ?

Sir To. Like aqua-vitæ with a midwife.

Mar. If you will then ſee the fruits of the ſport, mark his firſt approach before my lady : he will come to her in yellow ſtockings, and 'tis a colour ſhe abhors ; and croſs-garter'd, à faſhion ſhe deteſts ; and he will ſmile upon her, which will now be ſo unſuitable to her diſpoſition, being addicted to a melancholy as ſhe is, that it cannot but turn him into a notable contempt : if you will ſee it, follow me.

Sir To. To the gates of Tartar, thou moſt excellent devil of wit !

Sir And. I'll make one too.   [*Exeunt.*

ACT

ACT III. SCENE I.

Olivia's *Garden.*

Enter VIOLA, *and* Clown, *with a tabor.*

Vio. Save thee, friend, and thy mufick : Doft thou live by thy tabor ?

Clo. No, fir, I live by the church.

Vio. Art thou a churchman ?

Clo. No fuch matter, fir; I do live by the church : for I do live at my houfe, and my houfe doth ftand by the church.

Vio. So thou may'ft fay, the king lies by a beggar, if a beggar dwell near him : or, the church ftands by thy tabor, if thy tabor ftand by the church.

Clo. You have faid, fir.—To fee this age !—A fentence is but a cheveril glove to a good wit ; How quickly the wrong fide may be turned outward !

Vio. Nay, that's certain ; they, that dally nicely with words, may quickly make them wanton.

Clo. I would therefore, my fifter had had no name, fir.

Vio. Why, man ?

Clo. Why, fir, her name's a word : and to dally with that word, might make my fifter wanton : But, indeed, words are very rafcals, fince bonds difgraced them.

Vio. Thy reafon, man ?

Clo. Troth, fir, I can yield you none without words ; and words are grown fo falfe, I am loth to prove reafon with them.

Vio. I warrant, thou are a merry fellow, and careft for nothing.

C

Clo. Not fo, fir, I do care for fomething : but in my
confcience, fir, I do not care for you ; if that be to care
for nothing, fir, I would it would make you invifible.

Vio. Art thou not the lady Olivia's fool ?

Clo. No, indeed, fir ; the lady Olivia has no folly : fhe
will keep no fool, fir, till fhe be married ; and fools are as
like hufbands, as pilchards are to herrings, the hufband's
the bigger : I am, indeed, not her fool, but her corrupter
of words.

Vio. I faw thee late at the count Orfino's.

Clo. Foolery, fir, does walk about the orb, like the
fun ; it fhines every where. I would be forry, fir, but
the fool fhould be as oft with your mafter, as with my
miftrefs : I think, I faw your wifdom there.

Vio. Nay, an thou pafs upon me, I'll no more with
thee. Hold, there's expences for thee.

Clo. Now Jove, in his next commodity of hair, fend
thee a beard !

Vio. By my troth, I'll tell thee ; I am almoft fick for
one ; though I would not have it grow on my chin. Is
thy lady within ?

Clo. Would not a pair of thefe have bred, fir ?

Vio. Yes, being kept together, and put to ufe.

Clo. I would play lord Pandarus of Phrygia, fir, to
bring a Creffida to this Troilus.

Vio. I underftand you, fir ; 'tis well begg'd.

Clo. The matter, I hope, is not great, fir, begging but
a beggar ; Creffida was a beggar. My lady is within, fir.
I will conftrue to them whence you come ; who you are,
and what you would, are out of my welkin : I might fay,
element ; but the word is over-worn.   [*Exit.*

Vio. This fellow's wife enough to play the fool ;
And, to do that well, craves a kind of wit :
He muft obferve their mood on whom he jefts,

The

The quality of perfons, and the time ;
And, like the haggard, check at every feather
That comes before his eye.   This is a practice,
As full of labour as a wife man's art :
For folly, that he wifely fhows, is fit ;
But wife men, folly-fallen, quite taint their wit.

Enter Sir Toby Belch, *and* Sir Andrew Ague-
cheek.

Sir To. Save you, gentleman.
Vio. And you, fir.
Sir And. Dieu vous garde, monfieur.
Vio. Et vous auffi; votre ferviteur.
Sir And. I hope, fir, you are; and I am yours.
Sir To. Will you encounter the houfe ? my niece is defir-
ous you fhould enter, if your trade be to her.
Vio. I am bound to your niece, fir : I mean, fhe is the
lift of my voyage.
Sir To. 'Tafte your legs, fir, put them to motion.
Vio. My legs do better underftand me, fir, than I un-
derftand what you mean by bidding me tafte my legs.
Sir To. I mean, to go, fir, to enter.
Vio. I will anfwer you with gait and entrance : But we
are prevented.

Enter Olivia *and* Maria.

Moft excellent accomplifh'd lady, the heavens rain odours
on you !
Sir And. That youth's a rare courtier! *Rain odours !*
well.
Vio. My matter hath no voice, lady, but to your own
moft pregnant and vouchfafed ear.

Sir And.

Sir And. Odours, pregnant, and *vouchsafed:*—I'll get
'em all three ready.

Oli. Let the garden door be shut, and leave me to my
hearing. [*Exeunt* Sir Toby, Sir Andrew, *and* Maria.
Give me your hand, sir.

Vio. My duty, madam, and most humble service.

Oli. What is your name?

Vio. Cesario is your servant's name, fair princess.

Oli. My servant, sir! 'Twas never merry world,
Since lowly feigning was call'd compliment:
You are servant to the count Orsino, youth.

Vio. And he is yours, and his must needs be yours;
Your servant's servant is your servant, madam.

Oli. For him, I think not on him: for his thoughts,
'Would they were blanks, rather than fill'd with me!

Vio. Madam, I come to whet your gentle thoughts
On his behalf:—

Oli.   O, by your leave, I pray you;
I bade you never speak again of him:
But, would you undertake another suit,
I had rather hear you to solicit that,
Than musick from the spheres.

Vio.   Dear lady,——

Oli. Give me leave, I beseech you: I did send,
After the last enchantment you did here,
A ring in chase of you; so did I abuse
Myself, my servant, and, I fear me, you:
Under your hard construction must I sit,
To force that on you, in a shameful cunning,
Which you knew none of yours: What might you think?
Have you not set mine honour at the stake,
And baited it with all the unmuzzled thoughts
That tyrannous heart can think? To one of your receiv-
ing

Enough

Enough is fhewn ; a cyprus, not a bofom,
Hides my poor heart : So let me hear you fpeak.

Vio. I pity you.

Oli. That's a degree to love.

Vio. No, not a grife; for 'tis a vulgar proof,
That very oft we pity enemies.

Oli. Why, then, methinks, 'tis time to fmile again :
O world, how apt the poor are to be proud !
If one fhould be a prey, how much the better
To fall before the lion, than the wolf ?   [*Clock ftrikes.*
The clock upbraids me with the wafte of time.—
Be not afraid, good youth, I will not have you :
And yet, when wit and youth is come to harveft,
Your wife is like to reap a proper man :
There lies your way, due weft.

Vio.   Then weftward-hoe :
Grace, and good difpofition 'tend your ladyfhip !
You'll nothing, madam, to my lord by me ?

Oli. Stay :
I pr'ythee, tell me, what thou think'ft of me.

Vio. That you do think, you are not what you are.

Oli. If I think fo, I think the fame of you.

Vio Then think you right ; I am not what I am.

Oli. I would, you were as I would have you be !

Vio. Would it be better, madam, than I am,
I wifh it might ; for now I am your fool.

Oli. O, what a deal of fcorn looks beautiful
In the contempt and anger of his lip !
A murd'rous guilt fhows not itfelf more foon
Than love that would feem hid : love's night is noon.
Cefario, by the rofes of the fpring,
By maidhood, honour, truth, and every thing,
I love thee fo, that, maugre all thy pride,
Nor wit, nor reafon, can my paffion hide.

7   Do

Do not extort thy reasons from this clause,
For, that I woo, thou therefore hast no cause ;
But, rather, reason thus with reason fetter :
Love sought is good, but given unsought, is better.

Vio. By innocence I swear, and by my youth,
I have one heart, one bosom, and one truth,
And that no woman has ; nor never none
Shall mistress be of it, save I alone.
And so adieu, good madam; never more
Will I my master's tears to you deplore.

Oli. Yet come again : for thou, perhaps, may'st move
That heart, which now abhors, to like his love. [*Exeunt.*

SCENE II.

A room in Olivia's *house.*

Enter Sir Toby Belch, Sir Andrew Ague-cheek,
and Fabian.

Sir And. No, faith, I'll not stay a jot longer.

Sir To. Thy reason, dear venom, give thy reason.

Fab. You must needs yield your reason, sir Andrew.

Sir And. Marry, I saw your niece do more favours to the count's serving man, than ever she bestowed upon me; I saw't i'the orchard.

Sir To. Did she see thee the while, old boy ? tell me that.

Sir And. As plain as I see you now.

Fab. This was a great argument of love in her toward you.

Sir And. 'Slight ' will you make an ass o' me ?

Fab. I will prove it legitimate, sir, upon the oaths of judgement and reason.

Sir To. And they have been grand jury-men, since before Noah was a sailor.

Fab.

Fab. She did fhow favour to the youth in your fight, only to exafperate you, to awake your dormoufe valour, to put fire in your heart, and brimftone in your liver: You fhould then have accofted her; and with fome excellent jefts, fire-new from the mint, you fhould have bang'd the youth into dumbnefs. This was look'd for at your hand, and this was baulk'd: the double gilt of this opportunity you let time wafh off, and you are now failed into the north of my lady's opinion; where you will hang like an icicle on a Dutchman's beard, unlefs you do redeem it by fome laudable attempt, either of valour, or policy.

Sir And. And't be any way, it muft be with valour; for policy I hate: I had as lief be a Brownift, as a politician.

Sir To. Why then, build me thy fortunes upon the bafis of valour. Challenge me the count's youth to fight with him; hurt him in eleven places; my niece fhall take note of it: and affure thyfelf, there is no love-broker in the world can more prevail in man's commendation with woman, than report of valour.

Fab. There is no way but this, fir Andrew.

Sir And. Will either of you bear me a challenge to him?

Sir To. Go, write it in a martial hand; be curft and brief; it is no matter how witty, fo it be eloquent, and full of invention: taunt him with the licence of ink: if thou *thou'ft* him fome thrice, it fhall not be amifs; and as many lies as will lie in thy fheet of paper, although the fheet were big enough for the bed of Ware in England, fet 'em down; go, about it. Let there be gall enough in thy ink; though thou write with a goofe-pen, no matter: About it.

Sir And. Where fhall I find you?

Sir To. We'll call thee at the *cubiculo*: Go.

[Exit Sir Andrew.

Fab.

Fab. This is a dear manakin to you, fir Toby.

Sir To. I have been dear to him, lad; fome two thoufand ftrong, or fo.

Fab. We fhall have a rare letter from him: but you'll
not deliver it.

Sir To. Never truft me then; and by all means ftir on
the youth to an anfwer. I think, oxen and wainropes
cannot hale them together. For Andrew, if he were
open'd, and you find fo much blood in his liver as will
clog the foot of a flea, I'll eat the reft of the anatomy.

Fab. And his oppofite, the youth, bears in his vifage
no great prefage of cruelty.

Enter MARIA.

Sir To. Look, where the youngeft wren of nine comes.

Mar. If you defire the fpleen, and will laugh yourfelves
into ftitches, follow me: yon' gull Malvolio is turned
heathen, a very renegado; for there is no Chriftian, that
means to be fav'd by believing rightly, can ever believe
fuch impoffible paffages of groffnefs. He's in yellow ftockings.

Sir To. And crofs-garter'd?

Mar. Moft villainoufly; like a pedant that keeps a
fchool i'the church.—I have dogg'd him, like his murderer: He does obey every point of the letter that I dropp'd
to betray him. He does fmile his face into more lines,
than are in the new map, with the augmentation of the
Indies. you have not feen fuch a thing as 'tis; I can
hardly forbear hurling things at him. I know, my lady
will ftrike him; if fhe do, he'll fmile, and take't for a
great favour.

Sir To. Come, bring us, bring us where he is. [*Exeunt.*

SCENE

SCENE III.

A Street.

Enter ANTONIO *and* SEBASTIAN.

Seb. I would not, by my will, have troubled you;
But, fince you make your pleafure of your pains,
I will no further chide you.

 Ant. I could not ftay behind you; my defire,
More fharp than filed fteel, did fpur me forth;
And not all love to fee you, (though fo much,
As might have drawn one to a longer voyage,)
But jealoufy what might befall your travel,
Being fkillefs in thefe parts; which to a ftranger,
Unguided, and unfriended, often prove
Rough and unhofpitable: My willing love,
The rather by thefe arguments of fear,
Set forth in your purfuit.

 Seb.   My kind Antonio,
I can no other anfwer make, but, thanks,
And thanks, and ever thanks: Often good turns
Are fhuffled off with fuch uncurrent pay:
But, were my worth, as is my confcience, firm,
You fhould find better dealing. What's to do?
Shall we go fee the reliques of this town?

 Ant. To-morrow, fir; beft, firft, go fee your lodging.

 Seb. I am not weary, and 'tis long to night;
I pray you, let us fatisfy our eyes
With the memorials, and the things of fame,
That do renown this city.

 Ant.   'Would, you'd pardon me;
I do not without danger walk thefe ftreets:

       E   Once,

Once, in a fea-fight, 'gainft the Count his gallies,
I did fome fervice ; of fuch note, indeed,
That, were I ta'en here, it would fcarce be anfwer'd.
   Seb. Belike, you flew great number of his people.
   Ant. The offence is not of fuch a bloody nature ;
Albeit the quality of the time, and quarrel,
Might well have given us bloody argument.
It might have fince been anfwer'd in repaying
What we took from them ; which, for traffick's fake,
Moft of our city did : only myfelf ftood out :
For which, if I be lapfed in this place,
I fhall pay dear.
   Seb.   Do not then walk too open.
   Ant. It doth not fit me. Hold, fir, here's my purfe :
In the fouth fuburbs, at the Elephant,
Is beft to lodge : I will befpeak our diet,
Whiles you beguile the time, and feed your knowledge
With viewing of the town ; there fhall you have me.
   Seb. Why I your purfe ?
   Ant. Haply, your eye fhall light upon fome toy
You have defire to purchafe ; and your ftore,
I think, is not for idle markets, fir.
   Seb. I'll be your purfe-bearer, and leave you for
An hour.
   Ant.   To the Elephant.—
   Seb.   I do remember. [*Exeunt.*

SCENE

SCENE IV.

Olivia's *Garden.*

Enter OLIVIA, *and* MARIA.

Oli. I have fent after him : He fays, he'll come;
How fhall I feaft him ; what beftow on him ?
For youth is bought more oft, than begg'd, or borrow'd.
I fpeak too loud.——
Where is Malvolio ?—he is fad, and civil,
And fuits well for a fervant with my fortunes ;—
Where is Malvolio ?

    Mar.   He's coming, madam ;
But in ftrange manner. He is fure poffefs'd.

    Oli. Why, what's the matter ? does he rave ?

    Mar.   No, madam,
He does nothing but fmile : your ladyfhip
Were beft have guard about you, if he come ;
For, fure, the man is tainted in his wits.

    Oli. Go call him hither.—I'm as mad as he,
If fad and merry madnefs equal be.——

Enter MALVOLIO.

How now, Malvolio ?

    Mal. Sweet lady, ho, ho.   [*Smiles fantaftically.*

    Oli. Smil'ft thou ?
I fent for thee upon a fad occafion.

    Mal. Sad, lady ? I could be fad : This does make fome
obftruction in the blood, this crofs-gartering ; But what
of that ? if it pleafe the eye of one, it is with me as the
very true fonnet is : *Pleafe one, and pleafe all.*

Oli. Why, how doſt thou, man? what is the matter with thee?

Mal. Not black in my mind, though yellow in my legs: It did come to his hands, and commands ſhall be executed. I think, we do know the ſweet Roman hand.

Oli. Wilt thou go to bed, Malvolio?

Mal. To bed? ay, ſweet-heart; and I'll come to thee.

Oli. God comfort thee! Why doſt thou ſmile ſo, and kiſs thy hand ſo oft?

Mar. How do you, Malvolio?

Mal. At your requeſt? Yes; Nightingales anſwer daws.

Mar. Why appear you with this ridiculous boldneſs before my lady?

Mal. *Be not afraid of greatneſs:*—'Twas well writ.

Oli. What meaneſt thou by that, Malvolio?

Mal. *Some are born great,—*

Oli. Ha?

Mal. *Some atchieve greatneſs,——*

Oli. What ſay'ſt thou?

Mal. *And ſome have greatneſs thruſt upon them.*

Oli. Heaven reſtore thee!

Mal. *Remember, who commended thy yellow ſtockings;—*

Oli. Thy yellow ſtockings?

Mal. *And wiſh'd to ſee thee croſs-garter'd.*

Oli. Croſs-garter'd?

Mal. *Go to: thou art made, if thou deſireſt to be ſo;—*

Oli. Am I made?

Mal. *If not, let me ſee thee a ſervant ſtill.*

Oli. Why, this is very midſummer madneſs.

Enter Servant.

Scr. Madam, the young gentleman of the count Orſino's

Thornton, del.   Grangano.

Twelfth Night.

Act 3.^d Sc. 4.th

Oli. Why, this is very midsummer's Madness.

Published by Vernon and Hood, Poultry June 1 1799

no's is return'd; I could hardly entreat him back: he attends your ladyfhip's pleafure.

Oli. I'll come to him. [*Exit* Servant.] Good Maria, let this fellow be look'd to. Where's my coufin Toby? Let fome of my people have a fpecial care of him; I would not have him mifcarry for the half of my dowry.

[*Exeunt* OLIVIA *and* MARIA.

Mal. Oh, ho! do you come near me now? no worfe man than fir Toby to look to me? This concurs directly with the letter: fhe fends him on purpofe, that I may appear ftubborn to him; for fhe incites me to that in the letter. *Caft thy humble flough,* fays fhe;—*be oppofite with a kinfman, furly with fervants,—let thy tongue tang with arguments of ftate,—put thyfelf into the trick of fingularity;*—— and, confequently, fets down the manner how; as, a fad face, a reverend carriage, a flow tongue, in the habit of fome fir of note, and fo forth. I have limed her; but it is Jove's doing, and Jove make me thankful! And, when fhe went away now, *Let this fellow be look'd to:* Fellow! not Malvolio, nor after my degree, but fellow. Why, every thing adheres together; that no dram of a fcruple, no fcruple of a fcruple, no obftacle, no incredulous or unfafe circumftance,—What can be faid? Nothing, that can be, can come between me and the full profpect of my hopes. Well, Jove, not I, is the doer of this, and he is to be thanked.

Re-enter MARIA, *with* SIR TOBY BELCH, *and* FABIAN.

Sir To. Which way is he, in the name of fanctity? If all the devils in hell be drawn in little, and Legion himfelf poffeffed him, yet I'll fpeak to him.

Fab. Here he is, here he is:—How is't with you, fir? how is't with you, man?

Mal.

Mal. Go off; I difcard you; let me enjoy my private; go off.

Mar. Lo, how hollow the fiend fpeaks within him! did not I tell you?—Sir Toby, my lady prays you to have a care of him.

Mal. Ah, ha! does fhe fo?

Sir To. Go to, go to; peace, peace, we muft deal gently with him; let me alone. How do you, Malvolio? how is't with you? What, man! defy the devil: confider, he's an enemy to mankind.

Mal. Do you know what you fay?

Mar. La you, an you fpeak ill of the devil, how he takes it at heart! Pray God, he be not bewitch'd!

Fab. Carry his water to the wife woman.

Mar. Marry, and it fhall be done to-morrow morning, if I live. My lady would not lofe him for more than I'll fay.

Mal. How now, miftrefs?

Mar. O lord!

Sir To. Pr'ythee, hold thy peace; this is not the way: Do you not fee, you move him? let me alone with him.

Fab. No way but gentlenefs; gently, gently: the fiend is rough, and will not be roughly ufed.

Sir To. Why, how now, my bawcock? how doft thou, chuck?

Mal. Sir?

Sir To. Ay, Biddy, come with me. What, man! 'tis not for gravity to play at cherry-pit with Satan: Hang him, foul collier!

Mar. Get him to fay his prayers; good fir Toby, get him to pray.

Mal. My prayers, minx?

Mar. No, I warrant you, he will not hear of godlinefs.

Mal. Go, hang yourfelves all! you are idle fhallow
things;

things : I am not of your element ; you ſhall know more
hereafter.　　　　　　　　　　　　　　　[*Exit.*

Sir To. Is't poſſible ?

Fab. If this were play'd upon a ſtage now, I could condemn it as an improbable fiction.

Sir To. His very genius hath taken the infection of the
device, man.

Mar. Nay, purſue him now; leſt the device take air,
and taint.

Fab. Why, we ſhall make him mad, indeed.

Mar. The houſe will be the quieter.

Sir To. Come, we'll have him in a dark room, and
bound.　My niece is already in the belief that he is mad ;
we may carry it thus, for our pleaſure, and his penance,
till our very paſtime, tired out of breath, prompt us to
have mercy on him : at which time, we will bring the
device to the bar, and crown thee for a finder of madmen.
But ſee, but ſee.

Enter Sir Andrew Ague-cheek.

Fab. More matter for a May morning.

Sir And. Here's the challenge, read it; I warrant, there's
vinegar and pepper in't.

Fab. Is't ſo ſawcy?

Sir And. Ay, is it, I warrant him : do but read.

Sir To. Give me. [*reads.*] *Youth, whatſoever thou art,
thou art but a ſcurvy fellow.*

Fab. Good, and valiant.

Sir To. *Wonder not, nor admire not in thy mind, why I do
call thee ſo, for I will ſhow thee no reaſon for't.*

Fab. A good note : that keeps you from the blow of
the law.

Sir To. *Thou comeſt to the lady Olivia, and in my ſight* ſ

ufes thee kindly : but thou lieft in thy throat, that is not the mat-
ter I challenge thee for.

Fab. Very brief, and exceeding good fenfe-lefs.

Sir To. *I will way-lay thee going home; where if it be thy*
chance to kill me,——

Fab. Good.

Sir To. *Thou kill'ft me like a rogue and a villain.*

Fab. Still you keep o'the windy fide of the law: Good.

Sir To. *Fare thee well; And God have mercy upon one of*
our fouls! He may have mercy upon mine; but my hope is bet-
ter, and fo look to thyfelf. Thy friend, as thou ufeft him, and
thy fworn enemy, ANDREW AGUE-CHEEK.

Sir To. If this letter move him not, his legs cannot;
I'll give't him.

Mar. You may have very fit occafion for't; he is now
in fome commerce with my lady, and will by and by
depart.

Sir To. Go, fir Andrew; fcout me for him at the corner
of the orchard, like a bum-bailiff: fo foon as ever thou
feeft him, draw; and, as thou draw'ft, fwear horrible: for
it comes to pafs oft, that a terrible oath, with a fwagger-
ing accent fharply twang'd off, gives manhood more approbation than ever proof itfelf would have earn'd him.
Away.

Sir And. Nay, let me alone for fwearing.   [*Exit.*

Sir To. Now will not I deliver his letter: for the behaviour of the young gentleman gives him out to be of
good capacity and breeding; his employment between his
lord and my niece confirms no lefs; therefore this letter,
being fo excellently ignorant, will breed no terror in the
youth, he will find it comes from a clodpole. But, fir, I
will deliver his challenge by word of mouth; fet upon
Ague-cheek a notable report of valour; and drive the
gentleman, (as, I know, his youth will aptly receive it,)

3   into

into a moſt hideous opinion of his rage, ſkill, fury, and impetuoſity. This will ſo fright them both, that they will kill one another by the look, like cockatrices.

Enter OLIVIA *and* VIOLA.

Fab. Here he comes with your niece: give them way, till he take leave, and preſently after him.

Sir To. I will meditate the while upon ſome horrid meſ-ſage for a challenge.

　　　　　[*Exeunt* SIR TOBY, FABIAN, *and* MARIA.

Oli. I have ſaid too much unto a heart of ſtone,
And laid mine honour too unchary out:
There's ſomething in me, that reproves my fault;
But ſuch a headſtrong potent fault it is,
That it but mocks reproof.

Vio. With the ſame 'haviour that your paſſion bears,
Go on my maſter's griefs.

Oli. Here, wear this jewel for me, 'tis my picture;
Refuſe it not, it hath no tongue to vex you:
And, I beſeech you, come again to-morrow.
What ſhall you aſk of me, that I'll deny;
That honour, ſav'd, may upon aſking give?

Vio. Nothing but this, your true love for my maſter.

Oli. How with mine honour may I give him that
Which I have given to you?

Vio.　　　　　　　　I will acquit you.

Oli. Well, come again to-morrow: Fare thee well;
A fiend, like thee, might bear my ſoul to hell.　[*Exit.*

Re-enter SIR TOBY BELCH, *and* FABIAN.

Sir To. Gentleman, God ſave thee.
Vio. And you, ſr.

　　　　　　　　　　　　　　　　　　Sir

Sir To. That defence thou haft, betake thee to't: of what nature the wrongs are thou haft done him, I know not; but thy intercepter, full of defpight, bloody as the hunter, attends thee at the orchard end: difmount thy tuck, be yare in thy preparation, for thy affailant is quick, fkilful, and deadly.

Vio. You miftake, fir; I am fure, no man hath any quarrel to me; my remembrance is very free and clear from any image of offence done to any man.

Sir To. You'll find it otherwife, I affure you: therefore, if you hold your life at any price, betake you to your guard; for your oppofite hath in him what youth, ftrength, fkill, and wrath, can furnifh man withal.

Vio. I pray you, fir, what is he?

Sir To. He is knight, dubb'd with unhack'd rapier, and on carpet confideration; but he is a devil in private brawl: fouls and bodies hath he divorced three; and his incenfement at this moment is fo implacable, that fatisfaction can be none but by pangs of death and fepulchre: hob, nob, is his word; give't, or take't.

Vio. I will return again into the houfe, and defire fome conduct of the lady. I am no fighter. I have heard of fome kind of men, that put quarrels purpofely on others, to tafte their valour: belike this is a man of that quirk.

Sir To. Sir, no; his indignation derives itfelf out of a very competent injury; therefore, get you on, and give him his defire. Back you fhall not to the houfe, unlefs you undertake that with me, which with as much fafety you might anfwer him: therefore, on, or ftrip your fword ftark naked; for meddle you muft, that's certain, or forfwear to wear iron about you.

Vio. This is as uncivil, as ftrange. I befeech you, do me this courteous office, as to know of the knight what
my

my offence to him is; it is fomething of my negligence, nothing of my purpofe.

Sir To. I will do fo. Signior Fabian, ftay you by this gentleman till my return.   [*Exit* SIR TOBY.

Vio. Pray you, fir, do you know of this matter?

Fab. I know, the knight is incenfed againft you, even to a mortal arbitrement; but nothing of the circumftance more.

Vio. I befeech you, what manner of man is he?

Fab. Nothing of that wonderful promife, to read him by his form, as you are like to find him in the proof of his valour. He is, indeed, fir, the moft fkilful, bloody, and fatal oppofite that you could poffibly have found in any part of Illyria: Will you walk towards him? I will make your peace with him, if I can.

Vio. I fhall be much bound to you for't: I am one, that had rather go with fir prieft, than fir knight: I care not who knows fo much of my mettle.   [*Exeunt.*

Re-enter SIR TOBY, *with* SIR ANDREW.

Sir To. Why, man, he's a very devil; I have not feen fuch a virago. I had a pafs with him, rapier, fcabbard, and all, and he gives me the ftuck-in, with fuch a mortal motion, that it is inevitable; and on the anfwer, he pays you as furely as your feet hit the ground they ftep on: They fay, he has been fencer to the Sophy.

Sir And. Pox on't, I'll not meddle with him.

Sir To. Ay, but he will not now be pacified: Fabian can fcarce hold him yonder.

Sir And. Plague on't; an I thought he had been valiant, and fo cunning in fence, I'd have feen him damn'd ere I'd have challeng'd him. Let him let the matter flip, and I'll give him my horfe, grey Capilet.

Sir To.

Sir To. I'll make the motion: Stand here, make a good
fhow on't; this fhall end without the perdition of fouls:
Marry, I'll ride your horfe as well as I ride you.

                                          [*Afide.*

Re-enter FABIAN *and* VIOLA.

I have his horfe [*To* FAB.] to take up the quarrel; I have
perfuaded him, the youth's a devil.

    Fab. He is as horribly conceited of him; and pants,
and looks pale, as if a bear were at his heels.

    Sir To. There's no remedy, fir; he will fight with you
for his oath fake: marry, he hath better bethought him
of his quarrel, and he finds that now fcarce to be worth
talking of: therefore draw, for the fupportance of his
vow; he protefts, he will not hurt you.

    Vio. Pray God defend me! A little thing would make
me tell them how much I lack of a man.   [*Afide.*

    Fab. Give ground, if you fee him furious.

    Sir To. Come, fir Andrew, there's no remedy; the gen-
tleman will, for his honour's fake, have one bout with
you: he cannot by the duello avoid it: but he has promis'd me, as he is a gentleman and a foldier, he will not
hurt you. Come on; to't.

    Sir And. Pray God, he keep his oath!   [*draws.*

Enter ANTONIO.

    Vio. I do affure you, 'tis againft my will.   [*draws.*

    Ant. Put up your fword;—If this young gentleman
Have done offence, I take the fault on me;
If you offend him, I for him defy you.   [*drawing.*

    Sir To. You, fir? why, what are you?

                                             Ant.

Ant. One, fir, that for his love dares yet do more
Than you have heard him brag to you he will.

Sir To. Nay, if you be an undertaker, I am for you.
                            [*draws.*

Enter two Officers.

Fab. O good fir Toby, hold; here come the officers.

Sir To. I'll be with you anon.   [*To* ANTONIO.

Vio. Pray, fir, put up your fword, if you pleafe.
                      [*To* SIR ANDREW.

Sir And. Marry, will I, fir;—and, for that I promis'd
you, I'll be as good as my word: He will bear you eafily,
and reins well.

1 *Off.* This is the man; do thy office.

2 *Off.* Antonio, I arreft thee at the fuit
Of count Orfino.

   Ant.   You do miftake me, fir.

1 *Off.* No, fir, no jot; I know your favour well,
Though now you have no fea-cap on your head.—
Take him away; he knows, I know him well.

   Ant. I muft obey.—This comes with feeking you;
But there's no remedy; I fhall anfwer it.
What will you do? Now my neceffity
Makes me to afk you for my purfe: It grieves me
Much more, for what I cannot do for you,
Than what befalls myfelf.   You ftand amaz'd;
But be of comfort.

2 *Off.* Come, fir, away.

   Ant. I muft entreat of you fome of that money.

   Vio. What money, fir?
For the fair kindnefs you have fhow'd me here,
And, part, being prompted by your prefent trouble,
Out of my lean and low ability

I'll lend you fomething : my having is not much;
I'll make divifion of my prefent with you :
Hold, there is half my coffer.

Ant.   Will you deny me now?
Is't poffible, that my deferts to you
Can lack perfuafion? Do not tempt my mifery,
Left that it make me fo unfound a man,
As to upbraid you with thofe kindneffes
That I have done for you.

Vio.   I know of none;
Nor know I you by voice, or any feature :
I hate ingratitude more in a man,
Than lying, vainnefs, babbling, drunkennefs,
Or any taint of vice, whofe ftrong corruption
Inhabits our frail blood.

Ant.   O heavens themfelves!

2 *Off.* Come, fir, I pray you, go.

Ant. Let me fpeak a little. This youth that you fee here,
I fnatch'd one half out of the jaws of death;
Reliev'd him with fuch fanctity of love,——
And to his image, which, methought, did promife
Moft venerable worth, did I devotion.

1 *Off.* What's that to us? The time goes by; away.

Ant. But, O, how vile an idol proves this god!—
Thou haft, Sebaftian, done good feature fhame.—
In nature there's no blemifh, but the mind;
None can be call'd deform'd, but the unkind :
Virtue is beauty; but the beauteous-evil
Are empty trunks, o'erflourifh'd by the devil.

1 *Off.* The man grows mad; away with him.
Come, come, fir.

Ant. Lead me on.   [*Exeunt* Officers, *with* ANTONIO.

Vio. Methinks, his words do from fuch paffion fly,
That he believes himfelf; fo do not I.

5   Prove

Prove true, imagination, O, prove true,
That I, dear brother, be now ta'en for you!

Sir To. Come hither, knight; come hither, Fabian;
we'll whisper o'er a couplet or two of moft fage faws.

Vio. He nam'd Sebaftian; I my brother know
Yet living in my glafs; even fuch, and fo,
In favour was my brother; and he went
Still in this fafhion, colour, ornament,
For him I imitate: O, if it prove,
Tempefts are kind, and falt waves frefh in love!   [*Exit.*

Sir To. A very difhoneft paltry boy, and more a coward
than a hare: his difhonefty appears, in leaving his friend
here in neceffity, and denying him; and for his coward-
fhip, afk Fabian.

Fab. A coward, a moft devout coward, religious in it.

Sir And. 'Slid, I'll after him again, and beat him.

Sir To. Do, cuff him foundly, but never draw thy
fword.

Sir And. An I do not,—   [*Exit.*

Fab. Come, let's fee the event.

Sir To. I dare lay any money, 'twill be nothing yet.
                                                  [*Exeunt.*

ACT

ACT IV.   SCENE I.

The Street before Olivia's *House.*

Enter SEBASTIAN *and* Clown.

Clo. Will you make me believe, that I am not fent for
you?

Seb. Go to, go to, thou art a foolifh fellow;
Let me be clear of thee.

Clo. Well held out, i'faith! No, I do not know you;
nor I am not fent to you by my lady, to bid you come
fpeak with her; nor your name is not mafter Cefario; nor
this is not my nofe neither.—Nothing, that is fo, is fo.

Seb. I pr'ythee, vent thy folly fomewhere elfe;
Thou know'ft not me.

Clo. Vent my folly! He has heard that word of fome
great man, and now applies it to a fool. Vent my folly!
I am afraid this great lubber the world will prove a cock-
ney.—I pr'ythee now, ungird thy ftrangenefs, and tell me
what I fhall vent to my lady; Shall I vent to her, that
thou art coming?

Seb. I pr'ythee, foolifh Greek, depart from me;
There's money for thee; if you tarry longer,
I fhall give worfe payment.

Clo. By my troth, thou haft an open hand:—Thefe
wife men, that give fools money, get themfelves a good
report after fourteen years' purchafe.

Enter

Enter SIR TOBY, SIR ANDREW, *and* FABIAN.

Sir And. Now, fir, have I met you again? there's for
you. [*Striking* SEBASTIAN.

Seb. Why, there's for thee, and there, and there:
Are all the people mad? [*Beating* SIR ANDREW.

Sir To. Hold, fir, or I'll throw your dagger o'er the
houfe.

Clo. This will I tell my lady ftraight: I would not be
in fome of your coats for two-pence. [*Exit* Clown.

Sir To. Come on, fir; hold. [*Holding* SEBASTIAN.

Sir And. Nay, let him alone, I'll go another way to
work with him; I'll have an action of battery againft
him, if there be any law in Illyria: though I ftruck him
firft, yet it's no matter for that.

Seb. Let go thy hand.

Sir To. Come, fir, I will not let you go. Come, my
young foldier, put up your iron: you are well flefh'd;
come on.

Seb. I will be free from thee. What wouldft thou now?
If thou dar'ft tempt me further, draw thy fword. [*draws.*

Sir To. What, what? Nay, then I muft have an ounce
or two of this malapert blood from you. [*draws.*

Enter OLIVIA.

Oli. Hold, Toby; on thy life, I charge thee, hold.

Sir To. Madam?

Oli. Will it be ever thus? Ungracious wretch,
Fit for the mountains, and the barbarous caves,
Where manners ne'er were preach'd! out of my fight!

F Be

Be not offended, dear Cefario :——
Rudefby, be gone !—I pr'ythee, gentle friend,

    [*Exeunt* SIR TOBY, SIR ANDREW, *and* FABIAN.

Let thy fair wifdom, not thy paffion, fway
In this uncivil and unjuft extent
Againft thy peace. Go with me to my houfe ;
And hear thou there how many fruitlefs pranks
This ruffian hath botch'd up, that thou thereby
May'ft fmile at this : thou fhalt not choofe but go ;
Do not deny : Befhrew his foul for me,
He ftarted one poor heart of mine in thee.

  Seb. What relifh is in this ? how runs the ftream ?
Or I am mad, or elfe this is a dream :—
Let fancy ftill my fenfe in Lethe fteep ;
If it be thus to dream, ftill let me fleep !

    Oli. Nay, come, I pr'ythee : 'Would, thou'dft be rul'd
      by me !

    Seb. Madam, I will.

    Oli.   O, fay fo, and fo be !   [*Exeunt.*

SCENE II.

A room in Olivia's *houfe.*

Enter MARIA *and* Clown.

  Mar. Nay, I pr'ythee, put on this gown, and this
beard ; make him believe, thou art fir Topas the curate ;
do it quickly : I'll call fir Toby the whilft.

    [*Exit* MARIA.

  Clo. Well, I'll put it on, and I will diffemble myfelf
in't ; and I would I were the firft that ever diffembled in
fuch a gown. I am not tall enough to become the function

tion well; nor lean enough to be thought a good student: but to be said, an honest man, and a good housekeeper, goes as fairly, as to say, a careful man, and a great scholar. The competitors enter.

Enter SIR TOBY BELCH, *and* MARIA.

Sir To. Jove bless thee, master parson.

Clo. Bonos dies, sir Toby: for as the old hermit of Prague, that never saw pen and ink, very wittily said to a niece of king Gorboduc, *That, that is, is:* so I, being master parson, am master parson; For what is that, but that; and is, but is?

Sir To. To him, sir Topas.

Clo. What, hoa, I say,—Peace in this prison!

Sir To. The knave counterfeits well; a good knave.

Mal. [*in an inner chamber.*] Who calls there?

Clo. Sir Topas, the curate, who comes to visit Malvolio the lunatick.

Mal. Sir Topas, sir Topas, good sir Topas, go to my lady.

Clo. Out, hyperbolical fiend! how vexest thou this man? talkest thou nothing but of ladies?

Sir To. Well said, master parson.

Mal. Sir Topas, never was man thus wrong'd: good sir Topas, do not think I am mad; they have laid me here in hideous darkness.

Clo. Fye, thou dishonest Sathan! I call thee by the most modest terms; for I am one of those gentle ones, that will use the devil himself with courtesy; Say'st thou, that house is dark?

Mal. As hell, sir Topas.

Clo. Why, it hath bay windows transparent as barricadoes, and the clear stones towards the south-north are as

lustrous

luſtrous as ebony; and yet complaineſt thou of obſtruction?

Mal. I am not mad, ſir Topas; I ſay to you, this houſe
is dark.

Clo. Madman, thou erreſt: I ſay, there is no darkneſs,
but ignorance; in which thou art more puzzled, than the
Egyptians in their fog.

Mal. I ſay, this houſe is as dark as ignorance, though
ignorance were as dark as hell; and I ſay, there was never
man thus abuſed: I am no more mad than you are; make
the trial of it in any conſtant queſtion.

Clo. What is the opinion of Pythagoras, concerning
wild-fowl?

' *Mal.* That the ſoul of our grandam might haply inhabit
a bird.

Clo. What think'ſt thou of his opinion?

Mal. I think nobly of the ſoul, and no way approve his
opinion.

Clo. Fare thee well: Remain thou ſtill in darkneſs:
thou ſhalt hold the opinion of Pythagoras, ere I will allow
of thy wits; and fear to kill a woodcock, leſt thou diſ-
poſſeſs the ſoul of thy grandam. Fare thee well.

Mal. Sir Topas, ſir Topas,—

Sir To. My moſt exquiſite ſir Topas!

Clo. Nay, I am for all waters.

Mar. Thou might'ſt have done this without thy beard,
and gown; he ſees thee not.

Sir To. To him in thine own voice, and bring me word
how thou find'ſt him: I would, we were well rid of this
knavery. If he may be conveniently deliver'd, I would
he were; for I am now ſo far in offence with my niece,
that I cannot purſue with any ſafety this ſport to the
upſhot. Come by and by to my chamber.

[*Exeunt* SIR TOBY *and* MARIA.

Clo.

Clo. *Hey Robin, jolly Robin,*
    Tell me how thy lády does.   [*Singing.*

Mal. Fool,—

Clo. *My lady is unkind, perdy.*

Mal. Fool,—

Clo. *Alas, why is she so?*

Mal. Fool, I fay ;—

Clo. *She loves another*—Who calls, ha?

Mal. Good fool, as ever thou wilt deferve well at my hand, help me to a candle, and pen, ink, and paper ; as I am a gentleman, I will live to be thankful to thee for't.

Clo. Mafter Malvolio!

Mal. Ay, good fool.

Clo. Alas, fir, how fell you befides your five wits?

Mal. Fool, there was never man fo notorioufly abufed : I am as well in my wits, fool, as thou àrt.

Clo. But as well? then you are mad, indeed, if you be no better in your wits than a fool.

Mal. They have here property'd me ; keep me in dark-nefs, fend minifters to me, affes, and do all they can to face me out of my wits.

Clo. Advife you what you fay ; the minifter is here.—Malvolio, Malvolio, thy wits the heavens reftore! en-deavour thyfelf to fleep, and leave thy vain bibble babble.

Mal. Sir Topas,——

Clo. Maintain no words with him, good fellow.—Who, I, fir? not I, fir. God b'w'you, good fir Topas.—Marry, amen.—I will, fir, I will.

Mal. Fool, fool, fool, I fay,—

Clo. Alas, fir, be patient. What fay you, fir? I am fhent for fpeaking to you.

Mal. Good fool, help me to fome light, and fome pa-per; I tell thee, I am as well in my wits, as any man in Illyria.

Clo. Well-a-day,—that you were, fir!

Mal. By this hand, I am: Good fool, fome ink, paper, and light, and convey what I will fet down to my lady; it fhall advantage thee more than ever the bearing of letter did.

Clo. I will help you to't. But tell me true, are you not mad indeed? or do you but counterfeit?

Mal. Believe me, I am not; I tell thee true.

Clo. Nay, I'll ne'er believe a madman, till I fee his brains. I will fetch you light, and paper, and ink.

Mal. Fool, I'll requite it in the higheft degree: I pr'ythee, be gone.

Clo.   *I am gone, fir,*
            And anon, fir,
        I'll be with you again,
            In a trice,
            Like to the old vice,
        Your need to fuftain;
        Who with dagger of lath,
        In his rage and his wrath,
            Cries, ah, ha! to the devil:
        Like a mad lad,
        Pare thy nails, dad,
            Adieu, goodman drivel.   [Exit.

SCENE III.

Olivia's *Garden.*

Enter SEBASTIAN.

Seb. This is the air; that is the glorious fun;
This pearl fhe gave me, I do feel't, and fee't;

                                                And

And though 'tis wonder that enwraps me thus,
Yet 'tis not madneſs.　Where's Antonio then?
I could not find him at the Elephant:
Yet there he was; and there I found this credit,
That he did range the town to ſeek me out.
His counſel now might do me golden ſervice:
For though my ſoul diſputes well with my ſenſe,
That this may be ſome error, but no madneſs,
Yet doth this accident and flood of fortune
So far exceed all inſtance, all diſcourſe,
That I am ready to diſtruſt mine eyes,
And wrangle with my reaſon, that perſuades me
To any other truſt, but that I am mad,
Or elſe the lady's mad; yet, if 'twere ſo,
She could not ſway her houſe, command her followers,
Take, and give back, affairs, and their diſpatch,
With ſuch a ſmooth, diſcreet, and ſtable bearing,
As, I perceive, ſhe does: there's ſomething in't,
That is deceivable.　But here comes the lady.

Enter OLIVIA, *and a* Prieſt.

Oli. Blame not this haſte of mine: If you mean well,
Now go with me, and with this holy man,
Into the chantry by: there, before him,
And underneath that conſecrated roof,
Plight me the full aſſurance of your faith;
That my moſt jealous and too doubtful ſoul
May live at peace: He ſhall conceal it,
Whiles you are willing it ſhall come to note;
What time we will our celebration keep
According to my birth.—What do you ſay?

F 4

Seb.

Seb. I'll follow this good man, and go with you ;
And, having fworn truth, ever will be true.

　　Oli. Then lead the way, good father ;——And heavens
　　　　fo fhine,
That they may fairly note this act of mine!　　　　[*Exeunt.*

ACT

ACT V.   SCENE I.

The Street before Olivia's *House.*

Enter Clown, *and* FABIAN.

Fab. Now, as thou loveft me, let me fee his letter.

Clo. Good mafter Fabian, grant me another requeft.

Fab. Any thing.

Clo. Do not defire to fee this letter.

Fab. That is, to give a dog, and, in recompence, defire my dog again.

Enter DUKE, VIOLA, *and Attendants.*

Duke. Belong you to the lady Olivia, friends?

Clo. Ay, fir; we are fome of her trappings.

Duke. I know thee well; How doft thou, my good fellow?

Clo. Truly, fir, the better for my foes, and the worfe
for my friends.

Duke. Juft the contrary; the better for thy friends.

Clo. No, fir, the worfe.

Duke. How can that be?

Clo. Marry, fir, they praife me, and make an afs of me;
now my foes tell me plainly, I am an afs: fo that by my
foes, fir, I profit in the knowledge of myfelf; and by my
friends I am abufed: fo that, conclufions to be as kiffes,
if your four negatives make your two affirmatives, why,
then the worfe for my friends, and the better for my foes.

Duke. Why, this is excellent.

Clo.

Clo. By my troth, fir, no; though it pleafe you to be one of my friends.

Duke. Thou fhalt not be the worfe for me; there's gold.

Clo. But that it would be double-dealing, fir, I would you could make it another.

Duke. O, you give me ill counfel.

Clo. Put your grace in your pocket, fir, for this once, and let your flefh and blood obey it.

Duke. Well, I will be fo much a finner to be a double dealer; there's another.

Clo. *Primo, fecundo, tertio,* is a good play; and the old faying is, the third pays for all: the *triplex,* fir, is a good tripping meafure; or the bells of St. Bennet, fir, may put you in mind; One, two, three.

Duke. You can fool no more money out of me at this throw: if you will let your lady know, I am here to fpeak with her, and bring her along with you, it may awake my bounty further.

Clo. Marry, fir, lullaby to your bounty, till I come again. I go, fir; but I would not have you to think, that my defire of having is the fin of covetoufnefs: but, as you fay, fir, let your bounty take a nap, I will awake it anon. [*Exit* Clown.

Enter ANTONIO, *and* Officers.

Vio Here comes the man, fir, that did refcue me.

Duke. That face of his I do remember well;
Yet, when I faw it laft, it was befmear'd
As black as Vulcan, in the fmoke of war:
A bawbling veffel was he captain of,
For fhallow draught, and bulk, unprizable;
With which fuch fcathful grapple did he make
With the moft noble bottom of our fleet,

That

That very envy, and the tongue of loſs,
Cry'd fame and honour on him.—What's the matter?

    1 *Off.* Orſino, this is that Antonio,
That took the Phœnix, and her fraught, from Candy;
And this is he, that did the Tiger board,
When your young nephew Titus loſt his leg:
Here in the ſtreets, deſperate of ſhame, and ſtate,
In private brabble did we apprehend him.

    Vio. He did me kindneſs, ſir; drew on my ſide;
But, in concluſion, put ſtrange ſpeech upon me,
I know not what 'twas, but diſtraction.

    Duke. Notable pirate! thou ſalt-water chief!
What fooliſh boldneſs brought thee to their mercies,
Whom thou, in terms ſo bloody, and ſo dear,
Haſt made thine enemies?

    Ant.   Orſino, noble ſir,
Be pleas'd that I ſhake off theſe names you give me;
Antonio never yet was thief, or pirate,
Though, I confeſs, on baſe and ground enough,
Orſino's enemy.   A witchcraft drew me hither:
That moſt ingrateful boy there, by your ſide,
From the rude ſea's enrag'd and foamy mouth
Did I redeem; a wreck paſt hope he was:
His life I gave him, and did thereto add
My love, without retention, or reſtraint,
All his in dedication: for his ſake,
Did I expoſe myſelf, pure for his love,
Into the danger of this adverſe town;
Drew to defend him, when he was beſet:
Where being apprehended, his falſe cunning,
(Not meaning to partake with me in danger,)
Taught him to face me out of his acquaintance,
And grew a twenty-years-removed thing,
While one would wink; deny'd me mine own purſe,

                                        Which

Which I had recommended to his ufe
Not half an hour bet... —.

 Vio.   How can this be?

 Duke. When came he to this town?

 Ant. To-day, my lord; and for three months before,
(No interim, not a minute's vacancy,)
Both day and night did we keep company.

   Enter OLIVIA *and Attendants.*

 Duke. Here comes the countefs; now heaven walks on
   earth.——
But for thee, fellow, fellow, thy words are madnefs:
Three months this youth hath tended upon me;
But more of that anon.——Take him afide.

 Oli. What would my lord, but that he may not have,
Wherein Olivia may feem ferviceable?—
Cefario, you do not keep promife with me.

 Vio. Madam?

 Duke. Gracious Olivia,—

 Oli. What do you fay, Cefario?——Good my lord,——

 Vio. My lord would fpeak, my duty hufhes me.

 Oli. If it be aught to the old tune, my lord,
It is as fat and fulfome to mine ear,
As howling after mufick.

 Duke.   Still fo cruel?

 Oli. Still fo conftant, lord.

 Duke. What! to perverfenefs? you uncivil lady,
To whofe ingrate and unaufpicious altars
My foul the faithfull'ft offerings hath breath'd out,
That e'er devotion tender'd! What fhall I do?

 Oli. Even what it pleafe my lord, that fhall become him.

 Duke. Why fhould I not, had I the heart to do it,
Like to the Egyptian thief, at point of death,

            Kill

Kill what I love; a favage jealoufy,
That fometime favours nobly ?—But hear me this:
Since you to non-regardance caft my faith,
And that I partly know the inftrument
That fcrews me from my true place in your favour,
Live you, the marble-breafted tyrant, ftill;
But this, your minion, whom, I know, you love,
And whom, by heaven I fwear, I tender dearly,
Him will I tear out of that cruel eye,
Where he fits crowned in his mafter's fpite.—
Come boy, with me; my thoughts are ripe in mifchief:
I 'll facrifice the lamb that I do love,
To fpite a raven's heart within a dove.   [*Going.*

 Vio. And I, moft jocund, apt, and willingly,
To do you reft, a thoufand deaths would die. [*Following.*

 Oli. Where goes Cefario?
 Vio.   After him I love,
More than I love thefe eyes, more than my life,
More, by all mores, than e'er I fhall love wife:
If I do feign, you witneffes above,
Punifh my life, for tainting of my love!

 Oli. Ah me, detefted! how am I beguil'd!
 Vio. Who does beguile you? who does do you wrong?
 Oli. Haft thou forgot thyfelf? Is it fo long?—
Call forth the holy father.   [*Exit an Attendant.*
 Duke.   Come, away.   [*To* VIOLA.
 Oli. Whither, my lord?—Cefario, hufband, ftay.
 Duke. Hufband?
 Oli.   Ay, hufband; Can he that deny?
 Duke. Her hufband, firrah?
 Vio.   No, my lord, not I.
 Oli. Alas, it is the bafenefs of thy fear,
That makes thee ftrangle thy propriety:
Fear not, Cefario, take thy fortunes up;

                                        Be

Be that thou know'ft thou art, and then thou art
As great as that thou fear'ft—O, welcome, father!

Re-enter Attendant, and Prieft.

Father, I charge thee, by thy reverence,
Here to unfold (though lately we intended
To keep in darknefs, what occafion now
Reveals before 'tis ripe,) what thou doft know,
Hath newly paft between this youth and me.
   Prieft. A contract of eternal bond of love,
Confirm'd by mutual joinder of your hands,
Attefted by the holy clofe of lips,
Strengthen'd by interchangement of your rings;
And all the ceremony of this compáct
Seal'd in my function, by my teftimony :
Since when, my watch hath told me, toward my grave,
I have travell'd but two hours.
   Duke. O, thou diffembling cub ! what wilt thou be,
When time hath fow'd a grizzle on thy cafe ?
Or will not elfe thy craft fo quickly grow,
That thine own trip fhall be thine overthrow ?
Farewell, and take her; but direct thy feet,
Where thou and I henceforth may never meet.
   Vio. My lord, I do proteft,—
   Oli.   O, do not fwear ;
Hold little faith, though thou haft too much fear.

Enter SIR ANDREW AGUE-CHEEK, *with his head broke.*

   Sir And. For the love of God, a furgeon ; fend one prefently to Sir Toby.
   Oli. What's the matter ?
   Sir And. He has broke my head acrofs, and has given
fir

fir Toby a bloody coxcomb too: for the love of God, your help: I had rather than forty pound, I were at home.

Oli. Who has done this, fir Andrew?

Sir And. The count's gentleman, one Cefario: we took him for a coward, but he's the very devil incardinate.

Duke. My gentleman, Cefario?

Sir And. Od's lifelings, here he is:—You broke my head for nothing; and that that I did, I was fet on to do't by fir Toby.

Vio. Why do you fpeak to me? I never hurt you: You drew your fword upon me, without caufe; But I befpake you fair, and hurt you not.

Sir And. If a bloody coxcomb be a hurt, you have hurt me; I think, you fet nothing by a bloody coxcomb.

Enter Sir TOBY BELCH, *drunk, led by the* Clown.

Here comes fir Toby halting, you fhall hear more: but if he had not been in drink, he would have tickled you othergates than he did.

Duke. How now, gentleman? how is't with you?

Sir To. That's all one; he has hurt me, and there's the end on't—Sot, did'ft fee Dick furgeon, fot?

Clo. O he's drunk, fir Toby, an hour agone; his eyes were fet at eight i'the morning.

Sir To. Then he's a rogue. After a paffy-meafure, or a pavin, I hate a drunken rogue.

Oli. Away with him: Who hath made this havock with them?

Sir And. I'll help you, fir Toby, becaufe we'll be dreff-ed together.

Sir To. Will you help an afs-head, and a coxcomb, and a knave? a thin-faced knave, a gull?

· *Oli.* Get him to bed, and let his hurt be look'd to.

    [*Exeunt* Clown, Sir Toby, *and* Sir Andrew.

Enter Sebastian.

Seb. I am forry, madam, I have hurt your kinfman;
But, had it been the brother of my blood,
I muft have done no lefs, with wit, and fafety.
You throw a ftrange regard upon me, and
By that I do perceive it hath offended you;   ᵥ
Pardon me, fweet one, even for the vows
We made each other but fo late ago.

   Duke. One face, one voice, one habit, and two perfons;
A natural perfpective, that is, and is not.

   Seb. Antonio, O my dear Antonio!
How have the hours rack'd and tortur'd me,
Since I have loft thee?

   Ant. Sebaftian are you?

   Seb.   Fear'ft thou that, Antonio?

   Ant. How have you made divifion of yourfelf?—
An apple, cleft in two, is not more twin
Than thefe two creatures. Which is Sebaftian?

   Oli. Moft wonderful!

   Seb. Do I ftand there? I never had a brother:
Nor can there be that deity in my nature,
Of here and every where. I had a fifter,
Whom the blind waves and furges have devour'd:—
Of charity, what kin are you to me?   [*To* Viola.
What countryman? what name? what parentage?

   Vio. Of Meffaline: Sebaftian was my father;
Such a Sebaftian was my brother too,
So went he fuited to his watery tomb:
If fpirits can affume both form and fuit
You come to fright us.

Seb.   A fpirit I am, indeed;
But am in that dimenfion grofsly clad,
Which from the womb I did participate.
Were you a woman, as the reft goes even,
I fhould my tears let fall upon your cheek,
And fay—Thrice welcome, drowned Viola!
  Vio. My father had a mole upon his brow.
  Seb. And fo had mine.
  Vio. And died that day when Viola from her birth
Had number'd thirteen years.
  Seb. O, that record is lively in my foul!
He finifhed, indeed, his mortal act,
That day that made my fifter thirteen years.
  Vio. If nothing lets to make us happy both,
But this my mafculine ufurp'd attire,
Do not embrace me, till each circumftance
Of place, time, fortune, do cohere, and jump,
That I am Viola: which to confirm,
I'll bring you to a captain in this town,
Where lie my maiden weeds; by whofe gentle help
I was preferv'd, to ferve this noble count:
All the occurrence of my fortune fince
Hath been between this lady, and this lord.
  Seb. So comes it, lady, you have been miftook:
                              [*To* OLIVIA.

But nature to her bias drew in that.
You would have been contracted to a maid;
Nor are you therein, by my life, deceiv'd,
You are betroth'd both to a maid and man.
  Duke. Be not amaz'd; right noble is his blood.—
If this be fo, as yet the glafs feems true,
I fhall have fhare in this moft happy wreck:
Boy, thou haft faid to me a thoufand times, [*To* VIOLA.
Thou never fhould'ft love woman like to me.

           •   G   Vi·

Vio. And all thofe fayings will I over-fwear;
And all thofe fwearings keep as true in foul,
As doth that orbed continent the fire
That fevers day from night.

Duke.   Give me thy hand;
And let me fee thee in thy woman's weeds.

Vio. The captain, that did bring me firft on fhore,
Hath my maid's garments: he, upon fome action,
Is now in durance; at Malvolio's fuit,
A gentleman, and follower of my lady's.

Oli. He fhall enlarge him:—Fetch Malvolio hither:—
And yet, alas, now I remember me,
They fay, poor gentleman, he's much diftract.

Re-enter Clown, *with a letter.*

A moft extracting frenzy of mine own
From my remembrance clearly banifh'd his.—
How does he, firrah?

Clo. Truly, madam, he holds Belzebub at the ftave's
end, as well as a man in his cafe may do: he has here
writ a letter to you, I fhould have given it you to-day
morning; but as a madman's epiftles are no gofpels, fo it
fkills not much, when they are delivered.

Oli. Open it, and read it.

Clo. Look then to be well edified, when the fool deli-
vers the madman.—*By the Lord, madam,*—

Oli. How now! art thou mad?

Clo. No, madam, I do but read madnefs: an your ladyfhip will have it as it ought to be, you muft allow *vox.*

Oli. Pr'ythee, read i'thy right wits.

Clo. So I do, madonna; but to read his right wits, is
to read thus: therefore perpend, my princefs, and give
ear.

                                        Oli.

Oli. Read it you, firrah. [*To* FABIAN.

Fab. [reads.] *By the Lord, madam, you wrong me, and the world fhall know it : though you have put me into darknefs, and given your drunken coufin rule over me, yet have I the benefit of my fenfes as well as your ladyfhip. I have your own letter that induced me to the femblance I put on ; with the which I doubt not but to do myfelf much right, or you much fhame. Think of me as you pleafe. I leave my duty a little unthought of, and fpeak out of my injury. The madly-ufed* MALVOLIO.

Oli. Did he write this ?

Clo. Ay, madam.

Duke. This favours not much of diftraction.

Oli. See him deliver'd, Fabian ; bring him hither.

[*Exit* FABIAN.

My lord, fo pleafe you, thefe things further thought on,
To think me as well a fifter as a wife,
One day fhall crown the alliance on't, fo pleafe you,
Here at my houfe, and at my proper coft.

Duke. Madam, I am moft apt to embrace your offer.—
Your mafter quits you ; [*To* VIOLA.] and, for your fer-
            vice done him,   •
So much againft the mettle of your fex,
So far beneath your foft and tender breeding,
And fince you call'd me mafter for fo long,
Here is my hand ; you fhall from this time be
Your mafter's miftrefs.

Oli.   A fifter ?—you are fhe.

Re-enter FABIAN, *with* MALVOLIO.

Duke. Is this the madman ?

Oli.   Ay, my lord, this fame :

How now, Malvolio ?

                G 2   *Mal.*

Mal.   Madam, you have done me wrong,
Notorious wrong.

Oli.   Have I, Malvolio? no.

Mal. Lady, you have. Pray you, perufe that letter:
You muft not now deny it is your hand,
Write from it, if you can, in hand, or phrafe;
Or fay, 'tis not your feal, nor your invention:
You can fay none of this: Well, grant it then,
And tell me, in the modefty of honour,
Why you have given me fuch clear lights of favour;
Bade me come fmiling, and crofs-garter'd to you,
To put on yellow ftockings, and to frown
Upon fir Toby, and the lighter people:
And, acting this in an obedient hope,
Why have you fuffer'd me to be imprifon'd,
Kept in a dark houfe, vifited by the prieft,
And made the moft notorious geck, and gull,
That e'er invention play'd on? tell me why.

Oli. Alas, Malvolio, this is not my writing,
Though, I confefs, much like the character:
But, out of queftion, 'tis Maria's hand.
And now I do bethink me, it was fhe
Firft told me, thou waft mad; then cam'ft in fmiling,
And in fuch forms which here were prefuppos'd
Upon thee in the letter. Pr'ythee, be content:
This practice hath moft fhrewdly pafs'd upon thee;
But, when we know the grounds and authors of it,
Thou fhalt be both the plaintiff and the judge
Of thine own caufe.

Fab.   Good madam, hear me fpeak;
And let no quarrel, nor no brawl to come,
Taint the condition of this prefent hour,
Which I have wonder'd at. In hope it fhall not,
Moft freely I confefs, myfelf, and Toby,

I

Set this device againſt Malvolio here,
Upon ſome ſtubborn and uncourteous parts
We had conceiv'd againſt him : Maria writ
The letter, at ſir Toby's great importance ;
In recompence whereof, he hath married her.
How with a ſportful malice it was follow'd,
May rather pluck on laughter than revenge ;
If that the injuries be juſtly weigh'd,
That have on both ſides paſt.

 Oli. Alas, poor fool ! how have they baffled thee ?

 Clo. Why, *ſome are born great, ſome atcbieve greatneſs, and ſome have greatneſs thrown upon them.* I was one, ſir, in this interlude ; one ſir Topas, ſir ; but that's all one : —*By the Lord, fool, I am not mad ;*—But do you remember ? *Madam, why laugh you at ſuch a barren raſcal ? an you ſmile not, he's gagg'd:* And thus the whirligig of time brings in his revenges.

 Mal. I'll be revenged on the whole pack of you. [*Exit.*

 Oli. He hath been moſt notoriouſly abus'd.

 Duke. Purſue him, and entreat him to a peace :—
He hath not told us of the captain yet ;
When that is known, and golden time convents,
A ſolemn combination ſhall be made
Of our dear ſouls—Mean time, ſweet ſiſter,
We will not part from hence.—Ceſario, come ;
For ſo you ſhall be, while you are a man ;
But, when in other habits you are ſeen,
Orſino's miſtreſs, and his fancy's queen. [*Exeunt.*

SONG.

SONG.

Clo.   *When that I was and a little tiny boy,*
       With hey, ho, the wind and the rain,
    A foolish thing was but a toy,
       For the rain it raineth every day.

    But when I came to man's estate,
       With hey, ho, the wind and the rain,
    'Gainst knave and thief men shut their gate,
       For the rain it raineth every day.

    But when I came, alas! to wive,
       With hey, ho, the wind and the rain,
    By swaggering could I never thrive,
       For the rain it raineth every day.

    But when I came unto my bed,
       With hey, ho, the wind and the rain,
    With toss-pots still had drunken head,
       For the rain it raineth every day.

    A great while ago the world begun,
       With hey, ho, the wind and the rain,
    But that's all one, our play is done,
       And we'll strive to please you every day.   [Exit.

Singleton del   J.J. Van den Berghe sculp 1800.

Measure for Measure

Act 5 Scene 2.

Pub. Apr 20 1800 by Vernor & Hood Poultry

Harding's Edition.

MEASURE FOR MEASURE,

A

COMEDY.

BY

WILLIAM SHAKSPEARE.

ACCURATELY PRINTED

FROM THE TEXT OF

Mr. STEEVENS's LAST EDITION.

Ornamented with Plates.

London:

PUBLISHED BY E. HARDING, NO. 98, PALL-MALL;
J. WRIGHT, PICCADILLY; G. SAEL, STRAND;
AND VERNOR AND HOOD, POULTRY.

1799.

OBSERVATIONS.

THE ſtory is taken from *Cinthio's Novels*, Decad. 8, Novel 5. POPE.

We are ſent to Cinthio for the plot of *Meaſure for Meaſure,* and Shakſpeare's judgment hath been attacked for ſome deviations from him in the conduct of it, when probably all he knew of the matter was from Madam *Iſabella,* in *The Heptameron* of *Whetſtone,* Lond. 4to, 1582.—She *reports,* in the fourth dayes Exerciſe, the rare *Hiſtorie of Promos and Caſſandra.* A marginal note informs us, that *Whetſtone* was the author of the *Comedie* on that ſubject; which likewiſe had probably fallen into the hands of Shakſpeare. FARMER.

There is perhaps not one of Shakſpeare's plays more darkened than this by the peculiarities of its author, and the unſkilfulneſs of its editors, by diſtortions of phraſe, or negligence of tranſcription. JOHNSON.

Dr. Johnſon's remark is ſo juſt reſpecting the corruptions of this play, that I ſhall not attempt much reformation in its metre, which is too often rough, redundant, and irregular.

Shakſpeare took the fable of this play from the *Promos and Caſſandra* of George Whetſtone, publiſhed in 1578.

A hint, like a ſeed, is more or leſs prolific, according to the qualities of the ſoil on which it is thrown. This ſtory, which in the hands of Whetſtone produced little more than barren inſipidity, under the culture of Shakſpeare became fertile of entertainment. The curious reader will find that the old play of *Promos and Caſſandra* exhibits an almoſt complete embryo of *Meaſure for Meaſure;* yet the hints on which it is formed are ſo ſlight, that is is nearly as impoſſible to detect them, as it is to point out in the acorn the future ramifications of the oak.

Whetſtone opens his play thus :

Act I. Scene i.

" Promos, Mayor, Shirife, Sworde bearer : one with a bunche of
keyes : Phallax, *Promos Man.*

" You officers which now in *Julio* ſtaye,
" Know you your leadge, the King of *Hungarie,*

" Sent

" Sent me to *Promos*, to joyne with you in fway :
" That ftyll we may to *Juftice* have an eye.
" And now to fhow my rule and power at lardge,
" Attentivelie his letters patents heare :
" *Phallax*, reade out my Soveraines chardge.
Phal. " A you commaunde I wyll : give heedeful eare.

    Phallax *readeth the Kinges Letters Pattents, which*
    muft be fayre written in parchment, with fome
    great counterfeat zeale.

Pro. " Loe, here you fee what is our Soveraignes wyl,
" Loe, heare his wifh, that right, not might, beare fwaye :
" Loe, heare his care, to weede from good the yll,
" To fcoorge the wights, good lawes that difobay.
" Such zeale he beares, unto the common weale,
" (How fo he byds, the ignoraunt to fave)
" As he commaundes, the lewde doo rigor feele, &c. &c. &c.

——— ——— ——— ———

Prov. " Both fwoorde and keies, unto my princes ufe,
" I do receyve, and gladlie take my chardge.
" It refteth now, for to reforme abufe,
" We poynt a tyme of councell more at lardge,
" To treate of which, a whyle we wyll depart.
Al. fpeak. " To worke your wyll, we yeelde a willing hart.

                                        Exeunt."

See the piece itfelf among *Six old plays on which Shakfpeare founded*, &c. publifhed by S. Leacroft, Charing-crofs. STEEVENS.

Meafure for Meafure was, I believe, written in 1603. MALONE.

PERSONS REPRESENTED.

VINCENTIO, *duke of* Vienna.

ANGELO, *lord deputy in the duke's absence.*

ESCALUS, *an ancient lord, joined with* Angelo *in the deputation.*

CLAUDIO, *a young gentleman.*

LUCIO, *a fantastick.*

Two other like gentlemen.

VARRIUS, *a gentleman, servant to the duke.*

Provost.

THOMAS,
PETER, } *two friars.*

A justice.

ELBOW, *a simple constable.*

FROTH, *a foolish gentleman.*

Clown, servant to Mrs. Over-done.

ABHORSON, *an executioner.*

BARNARDINE, *a dissolute prisoner.*

ISABELLA, *sister to* Claudio.

MARIANA, *betrothed to* Angelo.

JULIET, *beloved by* Claudio.

FRANCISCA, *a nun.*

Mistress OVER-DONE, *a bawd.*

Lords, Gentlemen, Guards, Officers, and other Attendants.

SCENE, Vienna.

MEASURE FOR MEASURE.

ACT I. SCENE I.

An Apartment in the DUKE'S *palace.*

Enter Duke, ESCALUS, Lords, *and Attendants.*

Duke.

ESCALUS,—
    Escal. My lord.
   Duke. Of government the properties to unfold,
Would feem in me to affect fpeech and difcourfe;
Since I am put to know, that your own fcience,
Exceeds, in that, the lifts of all advice
My ftrength can give you: Then no more remains,
But that to your fufficiency, as your worth is able,
And let them work. The nature of our people,
Our city's inftitutions, and the terms
For common juftice, you are as pregnant in,
As art and practice hath enriched any
That we remember: There is our commiffion,
From which we would not have you warp.—Call hither,
I fay, bid come before us Angelo.— [*Exit an Attendant.*
What figure of us think you he will bear?
For you muft know, we have with fpecial foul
Elected him our abfence to fupply;
Lent him our terror, dreft him with our love;

And given his deputation all the organs
Of our own power : What think you of it ?
   Eſcal. If any in Vienna be of worth
To undergo ſuch ample grace and honour,
It is lord Angelo.

Enter ANGELO.

   Duke.   Look, where he comes.
   Ang. Always obedient to your grace's will,
I come to know your pleaſure.
   Duke.   Angelo,
There is a kind of charaæter in thy life,
That, to the obſerver, doth thy hiſtory
Fully unfold : Thyſelf and thy belongings
Are not thine own ſo proper, as to waſte
Thyſelf upon thy virtues, them on thee.
Heaven doth with us, as we with torches do ;
Not light them for themſelves : for if our virtues
Did not go forth of us, 'twere all alike
As if we had them not.   Spirits are not finely touch'd,
But to fine iſſues : nor nature never lends
The ſmalleſt ſcruple of her excellence,
But, like a thrifty goddeſs, ſhe determines
Herſelf the glory of a creditor,
Both thanks and uſe.   But I do bend my ſpeech
To one that can my part in him advértiſe ;
Hold therefore, Angelo ;
In our remove, be thou at full ourſelf ;
Mortality and mercy in Vienna
Live in thy tongue and heart : Old Eſcalus,
Though firſt in queſtion, is thy ſecondary :
Take thy commiſſion.
   Ang.   Now, good my lord,

Le

Let there be fome more teft made of my metal,
Before fo noble and fo great a figure
Be ftamp'd upon it.

　　Duke.　　　　　No more evafion :
We have with a leaven'd and prepared choice
Proceeded to you ; therefore take your honours.
Our hafte from hence is of fo quick condition,
That it prefers itfelf, and leaves unqueftion'd
Matters of needful value.　We fhall write to you,
As time and our concernings fhall impórtune,
How it goes with us ; and do look to know
What doth befal you here.　So, fare you well :
To the hopeful execution do I leave you
Of your commiffions.

　　Ang.　　　　　　Yet, give leave, my lord,
That we may bring you fomething on the way.

　　Duke. My hafte may not admit it ;
Nor need you, on mine honour, have to do
With any fcruple : your fcope is as mine own ;
So to enforce, or qualify the laws,
As to your foul feems good.　Give me your hand ;
I'll privily away : I love the people,
But do not like to ftage me to their eyes :
Though it do well, I do not relifh well
Their loud applaufe, and *aves* vehement ;
Nor do I think the man of fafe difcretion,
That does affect it.　Once more, fare you well.

　　Ang. The heavens give fafety to your purpofes !
　　Efcal. Lead forth, and bring you back in happinefs !
　　Duke. I thank you : Fare you well.　　　　　[*Exit.*
　　Efcal. I fhall defire you, fir, to give me leave
To have free fpeech with you ; and it concerns me
To look into the bottom of my place :

　　　　　　　　　B 2　　　　　　　　　A power

A power I have; but of what ftrength and nature
I am not yet inftructed.

Ang. 'Tis fo with me :—Let us withdraw together,
And we may foon our fatisfaction have
Touching that point.

Efcal.   I'll wait upon your honour. [*Exeunt.*

SCENE II.

A Street.

Enter LUCIO, *and two* Gentlemen.

Lucio. If the duke, with the other dukes, come not to
compofition with the king of Hungary, why, then all the
dukes fall upon the king.

1 *Gent.* Heaven grant us its peace, but not the king of
Hungary's!

2 *Gent.* Amen.

Lucio. Thou concludeft like the fanctimonious pirate,
that went to fea with the ten commandments, but fcraped
one out of the table.

2 *Gent.* Thou fhalt not fteal ?

Lucio. Ay, that he razed.

1 *Gent.* Why, 'twas a commandment to command the
captain and all the reft from their functions; they put
forth to fteal : There's not a foldier of us all, that, in the
thankfgiving before meat, doth relifh the petition well that
prays for peace.

2 *Gent.* I never heard any foldier diflike it.

Lucio. I believe thee; for, I think, thou never waft
where grace was faid.

2 *Gent.* No ? a dozen times at leaft.

1 *Gent.* What ? in metre ?

                                        Lucio.

Lucio. In any proportion, or in any language.

1 *Gent.* I think, or in any religion.

Lucio. Ay! why not? Grace is grace, despite of all controversy: As for example; Thou thyself art a wicked villain, despite of all grace.

1 *Gent.* Well, there went but a pair of sheers between us.

Lucio. I grant; as there may between the lists and the velvet: Thou art the list.

1 *Gent.* And thou the velvet: thou art good velvet; thou art a three-pil'd piece, I warrant thee: I had as lief be a list of an English kersey, as be pil'd, as thou art pil'd, for a French velvet. Do I speak feelingly now?

Lucio. I think thou dost; and, indeed, with most painful feeling of thy speech: I will, out of thine own confession, learn to begin thy health; but, whilst I live, forget to drink after thee.

1 *Gent.* I think, I have done myself wrong; have I not?

2 *Gent.* Yes, that thou hast; whether thou art tainted, or free.

Lucio. Behold, behold, where madam Mitigation comes! I have purchased as many diseases under her roof, as come to—

2 *Gent.* To what, I pray?

1 *Gent.* Judge.

2 *Gent.* To three thousand dollars a year.

1 *Gent.* Ay, and more.

Lucio. A French crown more.

1 *Gent.* Thou art always figuring diseases in me: but thou art full of error; I am sound.

Lucio. Nay, not as one would say, healthy; but so found, as things that are hollow: thy bones are hollow; impiety has made a feast of thee.

Ente

Enter Bawd.

1 *Gent.* How now? Which of your hips has the moft profound fciatica?

Bawd. Well, well; there's one yonder arrefted, and carry'd to prifon, was worth five thoufand of you all.

1 *Gent.* Who's that, I pray thee?

Bawd. Marry, fir, that's Claudio, fignior Claudio.

1 *Gent.* Claudio to prifcn! 'tis not fo.

Bawd. Nay, but I know, 'tis fo: I faw him arrefted; faw him carried away; and, which is more, within thefe three days his head's to be chopped off.

Lucio. But, after all this fooling, I would not have it fo: Art thou fure of this?

Bawd. I am too fure of it: and it is for getting madam Julietta with child.

Lucio. Believe me, this may be: he promifed to meet me two hours fince; and he was ever precife in promife-keeping.

2 *Gent.* Befides, you know, it draws fomething near to the fpeech we had to fuch a purpofe.

1 *Gent.* But moft of all, agreeing with the proclamation.

Lucio. Away; let's go learn the truth of it.

             [*Exeunt* Lucio, *and* Gentlemen.

Bawd. Thus, what with the war, what with the fweat, what with the gallows, and what with poverty, I am cuftom-fhrunk. How now? what's the news with you?

Enter Clown.

Clo. Yonder man is carried to prifon.

Bawd. Well; what has he done?

Clo. A woman.

Bawd. But what's his offence?

Clo. Groping for trouts in a peculiar river.

Bawd. What, is there a maid with child by him?

Clo. No; but there's a woman with maid by him: You have not heard of the proclamation, have you?

Bawd. What proclamation, man?

Clo. All houſes in the ſuburbs of Vienna muſt be pluck'd down.

Bawd. And what ſhall become of thoſe in the city?

Clo. They ſhall ſtand for ſeed: they had gone down too, but that a wiſe burgher put in for them.

Bawd. But ſhall all our houſes of reſort in the ſuburbs be pull'd down?

Clo. To the ground, miſtreſs.

Bawd. Why, here's a change, indeed, in the common-wealth! What ſhall become of me?

Clo. Come; fear not you: good counſellors lack no clients: though you change your place, you need not change your trade; I'll be your tapſter ſtill. Courage; there will be pity taken on you: you that have worn your eyes almoſt out in the ſervice, you will be conſidered.

Bawd. What's to do here, Thomas Tapſter? Let's withdraw.

Clo. Here comes ſignior Claudio, led by the provoſt to priſon: and there's madam Juliet.   [*Exeunt.*

SCENE III.

The fame.

Enter Provoſt, CLAUDIO, JULIET, *and* Officers; LUCIO, *and two* Gentlemen.

Claud. Fellow, why doſt thou ſhow me thus to the world?
Bear me to priſon, where I am committed.

Prov. I do it not in evil diſpoſition,
But from lord Angelo by ſpecial charge.

Claud. Thus can the demi-god, Authority,
Make us pay down for our offence by weight.—
The words of heaven;—on whom it will, it will;
On whom it will not, ſo; yet ſtill 'tis juſt.

Lucio. Why, how now, Claudio? whence comes this
reſtraint?

Claud. From too much liberty, my Lucio, liberty:
As ſurfeit is the father of much faſt,
So every ſcope by the immoderate uſe
Turns to reſtraint: Our natures do purſue,
(Like rats that ravin down their proper bane,)
A thirſty evil; and when we drink, we die.

Lucio. If I could ſpeak ſo wiſely under an arreſt, I
would ſend for certain of my creditors: And yet, to ſay
the truth, I had as lief have the foppery of freedom, as
the morality of impriſonment.—What's thy offence,
Claudio?

Claud. What, but to ſpeak of would offend again.

Lucio. What is it? murder?

Claud. No.

Lucio. Lechery?

Claud. Call it ſo.

Prov.

Prov. Away, fir; you muſt go.

Claud. One word, good friend:—Lucio, a word with
　　you.　　　　　　　　　　　　　　[*Takes him aſide.*

Lucio. A hundred, if they'll do you any good.—
Is lechery ſo look'd after?

Claud. Thus ſtands it with me:—Upon a true contráct,
I got poſſeſſion of Julietta's bed;
You know the lady; ſhe is faſt my wife,
Save that we do the denunciation lack
Of outward order: this we came not to,
Only for propagation of a dower
Remaining in the coffer of her friends;
From whom we thought it meet to hide our love,
Till time had made them for us. But it chances,
The ſtealth of our moſt mutual entertainment,
With charaćter too groſs, is writ on Juliet.

Lucio. With child, perhaps?

Claud. Unhappily, even ſo.
And the new deputy now for the duke,—
Whether it be the fault and glimpſe of newneſs;
Or whether that the body public be　　·
A horſe whereon the governor doth ride,
Who, newly in the ſeat, that it may know
He can command, lets it ſtraight feel the ſpur:
Whether the tyranny be in his place,
Or in his eminence that fills it up,
I ſtagger in:—But this new governor
Awakes me all the enrolled penalties,
Which have, like unſcour'd armour, hung by the wall
So long, that nineteen zodiacks have gone round,
And none of them been worn; and, for a name,
Now puts the drowſy and neglećted ać
Freſhly on me:—'tis, ſurely, for a name.

Lucio. I warrant, it is: and thy head ſtands ſo tickle on
　　　　　　　　　　　　　　　　　　thy

thy fhoulders, that a milk-maid, if fhe be in love, may
figh it off.   Send after the duke, and appeal to him.

Claud. I have done fo, but he's not to be found.
I pr'ythee, Lucio, do me this kind fervice :
This day my fifter fhould the cloifter enter,
And there receive her approbation :
Acquaint her with the danger of my ftate ;
Implore her, in my voice, that fhe make friends
To the ftrict deputy; bid herfelf affay him ;
I have great hope in that : for in her youth
There is a prone and fpeechlefs dialect,
Such as moves men ; befide, fhe hath profperous art
When fhe will play with reafon and difcourfe,
And well fhe can perfuade.

Lucio. I pray, fhe may : as well for the encouragement
of the like, which elfe would ftand under grievous impo-
fition ; as for the enjoying of thy life, who I would be
forry fhould be thus foolifhly loft at a game of tick-tack.
I'll to her.

Claud. I thank you, good friend Lucio.

Lucio. Within two hours,——

Claud. Come, officer, away.   [*Exeunt.*

SCENE   IV.

A Monaftery.

Enter Duke, *and Friar* THOMAS.

Duke. No; holy father; throw away that thought;
Believe not that the dribbling dart of love
Can pierce a cómplete bofom : why I defire thee
To give me fecret harbour, hath a purpofe

                                    More

More grave and wrinkled than the aims and ends
Of burning youth.
    Fri.   May your grace fpeak of it?
    Duke. My holy fir, none better knows than you
How I have ever lov'd the life remov'd;
And held in idle price to haunt affemblies,
Where youth, and coft, and witlefs bravery keeps.
I have deliver'd to lord Angelo
(A man of ftricture, and firm abftinence,)
My abfolute power and place here in Vienna,
And he fuppofes me travell'd to Poland;
For fo I have ftrew'd it in the common ear,
And fo it is receiv'd: Now, pious fir,
You will demand of me, why I do this?
    Fri. Gladly, my lord.
    Duke. We have ftrict ftatutes, and moft biting laws,
(The needful bits and curbs for head-ftrong fteeds,)
Which for thefe fourteen years we have let fleep;
Even like an o'er-grown lion in a cave,
That goes not out to prey: Now, as fond fathers
Having bound up the threat'ning twigs of birch,
Only to ftick it in their children's fight,
For terror, not to ufe; in time the rod
Becomes more mock'd, than fear'd: fo our decrees,
Dead to infliction, to themfelves are dead;
And liberty plucks juftice by the nofe;
The baby beats the nurfe, and quite athwart
Goes all decorum.
    Fri.   It refted in your grace
To unloofe this tied-up juftice, when you pleas'd:
And it in you more dreadful would have feem'd,
Than in lord Angelo.
    Duke.   I do fear, too dreadful:
Sith 'twas my fault to give the people fcope,

                        'Twould

'Twould be my tyranny to ftrike, and gall them,
For what I bid them do: For we bid this be done,
When evil deeds have their permiffive pafs,
And not the punifhment.   Therefore, indeed, my father,
I have on Angelo impos'd the office;
Who may, in the ambufh of my name, ftrike home,
And yet my nature never in the fight,
To do it flander: And to behold his fway,
I will, as 'twere a brother of your order,
Vifit both prince and people: therefore, I pr'ythee,
Supply me with the habit, and inftruct me
How I may formally in perfon bear me
Like a true friar.   More reafons for this action,
At our more leifure fhall I render you;
Only, this one:—Lord Angelo is precife;
Stands at a guard with envy; fcarce confeffes
That his blood flows, or that his appetite
Is more to bread than ftone: Hence fhall we fee,
If power change purpofe, what our feemers be.   [*Exeunt.*

SCENE V.

A Nunnery.

Enter ISABELLA *and* FRANCISCA.

Ifab. And have you nuns no further privileges?
Fran. Are not thefe large enough?
Ifab. Yes, truly: I fpeak not as defiring more;
But rather wifhing a more ftrict reftraint
Upon the fifter-hood, the votarifts of faint Clare.
Lucio. Ho! Peace be in this place!   [*Within.*]
Ifab.   Who's that which calls?
Fran. It is a man's voice: Gentle Ifabella,
                              Turn

Turn you the key, and know his bufinefs of him ;
You may, I may not ; you are yet unfworn :
When you have vow'd, you muft not fpeak with men,
But in the prefence of the priorefs :
Then, if you fpeak, you muft not fhow your face ;
Or, if you fhow your face, you muft not fpeak.
He calls again ; I pray you, anfwer him.

                       [Exit FRANCISCA.

   Ifab. Peace and profperity ! Who is't that calls?

Enter LUCIO.

   Lucio. Hail, virgin, if you be ; as thofe cheek-rofes
Proclaim you are no lefs ! Can you fo ftead me,
As bring me to the fight of Ifabella,
A novice of this place, and the fair fifter
To her unhappy brother Claudio ?
   Ifab. Why her unhappy brother ? let me afk ;
The rather, for I now muft make you know
I am that Ifabella, and his fifter.
   Lucio. Gentle and fair, your brother kindly greets you :
Not to be weary with you, he's in prifon.
   Ifab. Woe me ! For what ?
   Lucio. For that, which, if myfelf might be his judge,
He fhould receive his punifhment in thanks :
He hath got his friend with child.
   Ifab. Sir, make me not your ftory.
   Lucio.   It is true.
I would not—though 'tis my familiar fin
With maids to feem the lapwing, and to jeft,
Tongue far from heart,—play with all virgins fo :
I hold you as a thing enfky'd, and fainted ;
By your renouncement, an immortal fpirit ;

                            And

And to be talk'd with in fincerity,
As with a faint.

  Ifab. You do blafpheme the good, in mocking me.

  Lucio. Do not believe it. Fewnefs and truth, 'tis thus:
Your brother and his lover have embrac'd :
As thofe that feed grow full ; as bloffoming time,
That from the feednefs the bare fallow brings
To teeming foifon ; even fo·her plenteous womb
Expreffeth bis full tilth and hufbandry.   •

  Ifab. Some one with child by him ?—My coufin Juliet ? ·

  Lucio. Is fhe your coufin ? ·

  Ifab. Adoptedly ; as fchool-maids change their names,
By vain though apt affection.

  Lucio.   She it is.

  Ifab. O, let him marry her !

  Lucio.   This is the point.
The duke is very ftrangely gone from hence ;
Bore many gentlemen, myfelf being one,
In hand, and hope of action : but we do learn
By thofe that know the very nerves of ftate,
His givings out were of an infinite diftance
From his true meant defign.   Upon his place,   .
And with full line of his authority,
Governs lord Angelo; a man, whofe blood
Is very fnow-broth ; one who never feels
The wanton ftings and motions of the fenfe ;
But doth rebate and blunt his natural edge
With profits of the mind, ftudy and faft.
He (to give fear to ufe and liberty,
Which have, for long, run by the hideous law,
As mice by lions,) hath pick'd out an act,
Under whofe heavy fenfe your brother's life
Falls into forfeit : he arrefts him on it ;
And follows clofe the rigour of the ftatute,

                            To

To make him an example : all hope is gone,
Unlefs you have the grace by your fair prayer
To foften Angelo : and that's my pith
Of bufinefs, 'twixt you and your poor brother.
   Ifab. Doth he fo feek his life ?
   Lucio.   Has cenfur'd him
Already ; and, as I hear, the provoft hath
A warrant for his execution.
   Ifab. Alas! what poor ability's in me
To do him good ?
   Lucio.   Affay the power you have.
   Ifab. My power! alas! I doubt,—
   Lucio.   Our doubts are traitors,
And make us lofe the good we oft might win,
By fearing to attempt : Go to lord Angelo,
And let him learn to know, when maidens fue,
Men give like gods ; but when they weep and kneel,
All their petitions are as freely theirs
As they themfelves would owe them.
   Ifab. I'll fee what I can do.
   Lucio.   But, fpeedily.
   Ifab. I will about it ftraight ;
No longer ftaying but to give the mother
Notice of my affair. I humbly thank you :
Commend me to my brother : foon at night
I'll fend him certain word of my fuccefs.
   Lucio. I take my leave of you.
   Ifab.   Good fir, adieu.
                               [*Exeunt.*

                               ACT

ACT II.   SCENE I.

A Hall in Angelo's *Houſe.*

Enter ANGELO, ESCALUS, *a* Juſtice, Provoſt, Officers, *and other Attendants.*

Ang. We muſt not make a ſcare-crow of the law,
Setting it up to fear the birds of prey,
And let it keep one ſhape, till cuſtom make it
Their perch, and not their terror.
   Eſcal.   Ay, but yet
Let us be keen, and rather cut a little,
Than fall, and bruiſe to death : Alas! this gentleman,
Whom I would ſave, had a moſt noble father.
Let but your honour know,
(Whom I believe to be moſt ſtrait in virtue,)
That, in the working of your own affections,
Had time coher'd with place, or place with wiſhing,
Or that the reſolute acting of your blood
Could have attain'd the effect of your own purpoſe,
Whether you had not ſometime in your life
Err'd in this point which now you cenſure him,
And pull'd the law upon you.
   Ang. 'Tis one thing to be tempted, Eſcalus,
Another thing to fall.   I not deny,
The jury, paſſing on the priſoner's life,
May, in the ſworn twelve, have a thief or two
Guiltier than him they try : What's open made to juſtice,
That juſtice ſeizes.   What know the laws,
That thieves do paſs on thieves ? 'Tis very pregnant,
The jewel that we find, we ſtoop and take it,
                                 Becauſe

Becaufe we fee it; but what we do not fee,
We tread upon, and never think of it.
You may not fo extenuate his offence,
For I have had fuch faults; but rather tell me,
When I, that cenfure him, do fo offend,
Let mine own judgement pattern out my death,
And nothing come in partial. Sir, he muft die.

Efcal. Be it as your wifdom will.

Ang.　　　　　　　　Where is the provoft?

Prov. Here, if it like your honour.

Ang.　　　　　　　　See that Claudio
Be executed by nine to-morrow morning:
Bring him his confeffor, let him be prepar'd;
For that's the utmoft of his pilgrimage.　[*Exit* Provoft.

Efcal. Well, heaven forgive him! and forgive us all!
Some rife by fin, and fome by virtue fall:
Some run from brakes of vice, and anfwer none;
And fome condemned for a fault alone.

Enter ELBOW, FROTH, Clown, Officers, &c.

Elb. Come, bring them away: if thefe be good people
in a common-weal, that do nothing but ufe their abufes in
common houfes, I know no law: bring them away.

Ang. How now, fir! What's your name? and what's
the matter?

Elb. If it pleafe your honour, I am the poor duke's
conftable, and my name is Elbow; I do lean upon juftice,
fir, and do bring in here before your good honour two
notorious benefactors.

Ang. Benefactors? Well; what benefactors are they?
are they not malefactors?

Elb. If it pleafe your honour, I know not well what
they are: but precife villains they are, that I am fure of;

C　　　　　　　　　　　　and

and void of all profanation in the world, that good chriftians ought to have.

Efcal. This comes off well; here's a wife officer.

Ang. Go to: What quality are they of? Elbow is your
name? Why doft thou not fpeak, Elbow?

Clo. He cannot, fir; he's out at elbow.

Ang. What are you, fir?

Elb. He, fir? a tapfter, fir; parcel-bawd; one that
ferves a bad woman; whofe houfe, fir, was, as they fay,
pluck'd down in the fuburbs; and now fhe profeffes a
hot-houfe, which, I think, is a very ill houfe too.

Efcal. How know you that?

Elb. My wife, fir, whom I deteft before heaven and
your honour,—

Efcal. How! thy wife?

Elb. Ay, fir; whom, I thank heaven, is an honeft woman;—

Efcal. Doft thou deteft her therefore?

Elb. I fay, fir, I will deteft myfelf alfo, as well as fhe,
that this houfe, if it be not a bawd's houfe, it is pity of
her life, for it is a naughty houfe.

Efcal. How doft thou know that, conftable?

Elb. Marry, fir, by my wife; who, if fhe had been a
woman cardinally given, might have been accufed in fornication, adultery, and all uncleanlinefs there.

Efcal. By the woman's means?

Elb. Ay, fir, by miftrefs Over-done's means: but as
fhe fpit in his face, fo fhe defy'd him.

Clo. Sir, if it pleafe your honour, this is not fo.

Elb. Prove it before thefe varlets here, thou honourable
man, prove it.

Efcal. Do you hear how he mifplaces?   [*To* Angelo.

Clo. Sir, fhe came in great with child; and longing
(faving your honour's reverence,) for ftew'd prunes; fir,

5   we

we had but two in the houfe, which at that very diftant time ftood, as it were, in a fruit-difh, a difh of fome three-pence; your honours have feen fuch difhes; they are not China difhes, but very good difhes.

Efcal. Go to, go to; no matter for the difh, fir.

Clo. No, indeed, fir, not of a pin; you are therein in the right: but, to the point: As I fay, this miftrefs Elbow, being, as I fay, with child, and being great belly'd, and longing, as I faid, for prunes; and having but two in the difh, as I faid, mafter Froth here, this very man, having eaten the reft, as I faid, and, as I fay, paying for them very honeftly!—for, as you know, mafter Froth, I could not give you three-pence again.

Froth. No, indeed.

Clo. Very well: you being then, if you be remember'd, cracking the ftones of the forefaid prunes—

Froth. Ay, fo I did, indeed.

Clo. Why, very well: I telling you then, if you be remember'd, that fuch a one, and fuch a one, were paft cure of the thing you wot of, unlefs they kept very good diet, as I told you—

Froth. All this is true.

Clo. Why, very well then.

Efcal. Come, you are a tedious fool: to the purpofe.— What was done to Elbow's wife, that he hath caufe to complain of? Come me to what was done to her.

Clo. Sir, your honour cannot come to that yet.

Efcal. No, fir, nor I mean it not.

Clo. Sir, but you fhall come to it, by your honour's leave: And, I befeech you, look into mafter Froth here, fir; a man of fourfcore pound a year; whofe father died at Hallowmas:—Was't not at Hallowmas, mafter Froth?

Froth. All-hollond eve.

Clo.

Clo. Why, very well; I hope here be truths: He, fir, fitting, as I fay, in a lower ch ir, fir;—'twas in the *Bunch of Grapes*, where, indeed, you have a delight to fit: Have you not?

Froth. I have fo; becaufe it is an open room, and good for winter.

Clo. Why, very well then;—I hope here be truths.

Ang. This will laft out a night in Ruffia,
When nights are longeft there: I'll take my leave,
And leave you to the hearing of the caufe;
Hoping, you'll find good caufe to whip them all.

Efcal. I think no lefs: Good morrow to your lordfhip.
                    [*Exit* ANGELO.
Now, fir, come on: What was done to Elbow's wife, once more?

Clo. Once, fir? there was nothing done to her once.

Elb. I befeech you, fir, afk him what this man did to my wife.

Clo. I befeech your honour, afk me.

Efcal. Well, fir; What did this gentleman to her?

Clo. I befeech you, fir, look in this gentleman's face:
—Good mafter Froth, look upon his honour; 'tis for a good purpofe: Doth your honour mark his face?

Efcal. Ay, fir, very well.

Clo. Nay, I befeech you, mark it well.

Efcal. Well, I do fo.

Clo. Doth your honour fee any harm in his face?

Efcal. Why, no.

Clo. I'll be fuppofed upon a book, his face is the worft thing about him: Good then; if his face be the worft thing about him, how could mafter Froth do the conftable's wife any harm? I would know that of your honour.

Efcal. He's in the right: Conftable, what fay you to it?
                                        Elb.

Elb. Firſt, an it like you, the houſe is a reſpected houſe; next, this is a reſpected fellow; and his miſtreſs is a re-ſpected woman.

Clo. By this hand, ſir, his wife is a more reſpected per-ſon than any of us all.

Elb. Varlet, thou lieſt; thou lieſt, wicked varlet: the time is yet to come, that ſhe was ever reſpected with man, woman, or child.

Clo. Sir, ſhe was reſpected with him before he married with her.

Eſcal. Which is the wiſer here? Juſtice, or Iniquity?—Is this true?

Elb. O thou caitiff! O thou varlet! O thou wicked Hannibal! I reſpected with her, before I was married to her? If ever I was reſpected with her, or ſhe with me, let not your worſhip think me the poor duke's officer:—Prove this, thou wicked Hannibal, or I'll have mine action of battery on thee.

Eſcal. If he took you a box o' the ear, you might have your action of ſlander too.

Elb. Marry, I thank your good worſhip for it: What is't your worſhip's pleaſure I ſhall do with this wicked caitiff?

Eſcal. Truly, officer, becauſe he hath ſome offences in him, that thou wouldſt diſcover if thou couldſt, let him continue in his courſes, till thou know'ſt what they are.

Elb. Marry, I thank your worſhip for it:—Thou ſeeſt, thou wicked varlet now, what's come upon thee; thou art to continue now, thou varlet; thou art to continue.

Eſcal. Where were you born, friend?   [*To* FROTH.

Froth. Here in Vienna, ſir.

Eſcal. Are you of fourſcore pounds a year?

Froth. Yes, and't pleaſe you, ſir.

Eſcal. So.—What trade are you of, ſir? [*To the* Clown.

Clo.

Clo. A tapfter ; a poor widow's tapfter.

Efcal. Your miftrefs's name ?

Clo. Miftrefs Over-done.

Efcal. Hath fhe had any more than one hufband ?

Clo. Nine, fir; Over-done by the laft.

Efcal. Nine !—Come hither to me, mafter Froth. Mafter Froth, I would not have you acquainted with tapfters;
they will draw you, mafter Froth, and you will hang
them : Get you gone, and let me hear no more of you.

Froth. I thank your worfhip: For mine own part, I
never come into any room in a taphoufe, but I am drawn
in.

Efcal. Well ; no more of it, mafter Froth : farewell.
[*Exit* FROTH.]—Come you hither to me, mafter tapfter ;
what's your name, mafter tapfter ?

Clo. Pompey.

Efcal. What elfe ?

Clo. Bum, fir.

Efcal. 'Troth, and your bum is the greateft thing about
you ; fo that, in the beaftlieft fenfe, you are Pompey the
great. Pompey, you are partly a bawd, Pompey, howfoever you colour it in being a tapfter. Are you not ?
come, tell me true; it fhall be the better for you.

Clo. Truly, fir, I am a poor fellow, that would live.

Efcal. How would you live, Pompey ? by being a bawd ?
What do you think of the trade Pompey ? is it a lawful
trade ?

Clo. If the law would allow it, fir.

Efcal. But the law will not allow it, Pompey ; nor it
fhall not be allowed in Vienna.

Clo. Does your worfhip mean to geld and fpay all the
youth in the city ?

Efcal. No, Pompey.

Clo. Truly, fir, in my poor opinion, they will to't then :

If

If your worſhip will take order for the drabs and the knaves, you need not to fear the bawds.

Eſcal. There are pretty orders beginning, I can tell you : it is but heading and hanging.

Clo. If you head and hang all that offend that way but for ten year together, you'll be glad to give out a com-miſſion for more heads. If this law hold in Vienna ten year, I'll rent the faireſt houſe in it, after three pence a bay. If you live to ſee this come to paſs, ſay, Pompey told you ſo.

Eſcal. Thank you, good Pompey: and, in requital of your prophecy, hark you,—I adviſe you, let me not find you before me again upon any complaint whatſoever, no, not for dwelling where you do; if I do, Pompey, I ſhall beat you to your tent, and prove a ſhrewd Cæſar to you; in plain dealing, Pompey, I ſhall have you whipt : ſo for this time, Pompey, fare you well.

Clo. I thank your worſhip for your good counſel; but I ſhall follow it, as the fleſh and fortune ſhall better de-termine.

Whip me ? No, no ; let carman whip his jade ;
The valiant heart's not whipt out of his trade.   [*Exit.*

Eſcal. Come hither to me, maſter Elbow; come hither, maſter conſtable. How long have you been in this place of conſtable ?

Elb. Seven year and a half, ſir.

Eſcal. I thought, by your readineſs in the office, you had continued in it ſome time : You ſay, ſeven years to-gether ?

Elb. And a half, ſir.

Eſcal. Alas! it hath been great pains to you! They do you wrong to put you ſo oft upon't : Are there not men in your ward ſufficient to ſerve it ?

Elb. Faith, ſir, few of any wit in ſuch matters : as they

are chofen, they are glad to choofe me for them; I do it
for fome piece of money, and go through with all.

Efcal. Look you, bring me in the names of fome fix or
feven, the moft fufficient of your parifh.

Elb. To your worfhip's houfe, fir ?

Efcal. To my houfe : Fare you well.   [*Exit* ELBOW.
What's o'clock, think you ?

Juft. Eleven, fir.

Efcal. I pray you home to dinner with me.

Juft. I humbly thank you.

Efcal. It grieves me for the death of Claudio ;
But there's no remedy.

Juft. Lord Angelo is fevere.

Efcal.   It is but needful :
Mercy is not itfelf, that oft looks fo ;
Pardon is ftill the nurfe of fecond woe :
But yet,—Poor Claudio !—There's no remedy.
Come, fir.   [*Exeunt.*

SCENE II.

Another Room in the fame.

Enter Provoft, *and a* Servant.

Serv. He's hearing of a caufe ; he will come ftraight.
I'll tell him of you.

Prov. Pray you, do.   [*Exit* Servant.]   I'll know
His pleafure ; may be, he will relent : Alas,
He hath but as offended in a dream !
All fects, all ages fmack of this vice ; and he
To die for it !—

                                     Enter

Singleton del   Hopwood sc

Measure for Measure

Act 2. Scene 2.

Pub May 1 1800 by Vernor & Hood Poultry

Enter ANGELO.

Ang. Now, what's the matter, provoſt?

Prov. Is it your will Claudio ſhall die to-morrow?

Ang. Did I not tell thee, yea? hadſt thou not order?
Why doſt thou aſk again?

Prov. Leſt I might be too raſh:
Under your good correction, I have ſeen,
When, after execution, judgement hath
Repented o'er his doom.

Ang. Go to; let that be mine:
Do you your office, or give up your place,
And you ſhall well be ſpar'd.

Prov. I crave your honour's pardon.—
What ſhall be done, ſir, with the groaning Juliet?
She's very near her hour.

Ang. Diſpoſe of her
To ſome more fitter place; and that with ſpeed.

Re-enter Servant.

Serv. Here is the ſiſter of the man condemn'd,
Deſires acceſs to you.

Ang. Hath he a ſiſter?

Prov. Ay, my good lord; a very virtuous maid,
And to be ſhortly of a ſiſterhood,
If not already.

Ang. Well, let her be admitted. [*Exit* Servant.
See you, the fornicatreſs be remov'd;
Let her have needful, but not laviſh, means;
There ſhall be order for it.

Enter

Enter LUCIO *and* ISABELLA.

Prov. Save your honour!   [*Offering to retire.*

Ang. Stay a little while.—[*To* ISAB.]   You are wel-
     come: What's your will?

Isab. I am a woeful suitor to your honour,
Please but your honour hear me.

     Ang.   Well; what's your suit?

Isab. There is a vice, that most I do abhor,
And most desire should meet the blow of justice;
For which I would not plead, but that I must;
For which I must not plead, but that I am
At war, 'twixt will, and will not.

     Ang.   Well; the matter?

Isab. I have a brother is condemn'd to die:
I do beseech you, let it be his fault,
And not my brother.

     Prov.   Heaven give thee moving graces!

     Ang. Condemn the fault, and not the actor of it!
Why, every fault's condemn'd, ere it be done:
Mine were the very cypher of a function,
To find the faults, whose fine stands in record,
And let go by the actor.

     Isab.   O just, but severe law!
I had a brother then.—Heaven keep your honour!

                         [*Retiring.*

     Lucio. [*To* ISAB.] Give not o'er so: to him again, in-
     treat him;
Kneel down before him, hang upon his gown;
You are too cold: if you should need a pin,
You could not with more tame a tongue desire it:
To him, I say.

     Isab. Must he needs die?

                         Ang.

Ang.   Maiden, no remedy.

Iſab. Yes; I do think that you might pardon him,
And neither heaven, nor man, grieve at the mercy.

Ang. I will not do't.

Iſab.   But can you, if you would?

Ang. Look, what I will not, that I cannot do.

Iſab. But might you do't, and do the world no wrong,
If ſo your heart were touch'd with that remorſe
As mine is to him?

Ang.   He's ſentenc'd; 'tis too late.

Lucio. You are too cold.   [*To* ISABELLA.

Iſab. Too late? why, no; I, that do ſpeak a word,
May call it back again: Well believe this,
No ceremony that to great ones 'longs,
Not the king's crown, nor the deputed ſword,
The marſhal's truncheon, nor the judge's robe,
Become them with one half ſo good a grace,
As mercy does. If he had been as you,
And you as he, you would have ſlipt like him;
But he, like you, would not have been ſo ſtern.

Ang. Pray you, begone.

Iſab. I would to heaven I had your potency,
And you were Iſabel! ſhould it then be thus?
No; I would tell what 'twere to be a judge,
And what a priſoner.

Lucio. Ay, touch him: there's the vein.   [*Aſide.*

Ang. Your brother is a forfeit of the law,
And you but waſte your words.

Iſab.   Alas! alas!
Why, all the ſouls that were, were forfeit once;
And He that might the vantage beſt have took,
Found out the remedy: How would you be,
If he, which is the top of judgement, ſhould
But judge you as you are? O, think on that;

                        And

And mercy then will breathe within your lips,
Like man new made.

 Ang.   Be you content, fair maid;
It is the law, not I, condemns your brother:
Were he my kinfman, brother, or my fon,
It fhould be thus with him;—he muft die to-morrow.

 Ifab. To-morrow? O, that's fudden! Spare him, fpare
   him;
He's not prepar'd for death! Even for our kitchens
We kill the fowl of feafon; fhall we ferve heaven
With lefs refpect than we do minifter
To our grofs felves? Good, good my lord, bethink you:
Who is it that hath died for this offence?
There's many have committed it.

 Lucio.   Ay, well faid.

 Ang. The law hath not been dead, though it hath flept:
Thofe many had not dar'd to do that evil,
If the firft man that did the edict infringe,
Had anfwer'd for his deed: now, 'tis awake;
Takes note of what is done; and, like a prophet,
Looks in a glafs, that fhows what future evils,
(Either now, or by remiffnefs new-conceiv'd,
And fo in progrefs to be hatch'd and born,)
Are now to have no fucceffive degrees,
But, where they live, to end.

 Ifab.   Yet fhow fome pity.

 Ang. I fhow it moft of all, when I fhow juftice;
For then I pity thofe I do not know,
Which a difmifs'd offence would after gall;
And do him right, that, anfwering one foul wrong,
Lives not to act another. Be fatisfied;
Your brother dies to-morrow; be content.

 Ifab. So you muft be the firft, that gives this fentence;
And he, that fuffers: O, it is excellent

         To

To have a giant's ſtrength; but it is tyrannous,
To uſe it like a giant.

 Lucio.   That's well ſaid.

 Iſab. Could great men thunder
As Jove himſelf does, Jove would ne'er be quiet,
For every pelting, petty officer,
Would uſe his heaven for thunder; nothing but thunder.—
Merciful heaven!
Thou rather, with thy ſharp and ſulphurous bolt,
Split'ſt the unwedgeable and gnarled oak,
Than the ſoft myrtle ;—O, but man, proud man!
Dreſt in a little brief authority;
Moſt ignorant of what he's moſt aſſur'd,
His glaſſy eſſence,—like an angry ape,
Plays ſuch fantaſtick tricks before high heaven,
As make the angels weep; who, with our ſpleens,
Would all themſelves laugh mortal.

 Lucio. O, to him, to him, wench; he will relent;
He's coming; I perceiv't.

 Prov.   Pray heaven ſhe win him!

 Iſab. We cannot weigh our brother with ourſelf:
Great men may jeſt with ſaints: 'tis wit in them;
But, in the leſs, foul profanation.

 Lucio. Thou'rt in the right, girl; more o' that.

 Iſab. That in the captain's but a cholerick word,
Which in the ſoldier is flat blaſphemy.

 Lucio. Art advis'd o' that? more on't.

 Ang. Why do you put theſe ſayings upon me?

 Iſab. Becauſe authority, though it err like others,
Hath yet a kind of medicine in itſelf,
That ſkins the vice o' the top: Go to your boſom;
Knock there; and aſk your heart, what it doth know
That's like my brother's fault: if it confeſs
A natural guiltineſs, ſuch as is his,

               Let

Let it not found a thought upon your tongue
Againſt my brother's life.

Ang.   She ſpeaks, and 'tis
Such ſenſe, that my ſenſe breeds with it.——Fare you well.

Iſab. Gentle my lord, turn back.

Ang. I will bethink me :—Come again to-morrow.

Iſab. Hark, how I'll bribe you : Good my lord, turn
      back.

Ang. How! bribe me?

Iſab. Ay, with ſuch gifts that heaven ſhall ſhare with
      you.

Lucio. You had marr'd all elſe.

Iſab. Not with fond ſhekels of the teſted gold,
Or ſtones, whoſe rates are either rich, or poor,
As fancy values them : but with true prayers,
That ſhall be up at heaven, and enter there,
Ere ſun-riſe ; prayers from preſerved ſouls,
From faſting maids, whoſe minds are dedicate
To nothing temporal.

Ang.   Well : come to me
To-morrow.

Lucio.   Go to ; it is well ; away.   [*Aſide to* ISABEL.

Iſab. Heaven keep your honour ſafe !

Ang.   Amen : for I
Am that way going to temptation,   [*Aſide.*
Where prayers croſs.

Iſab.   At what hour to-morrow
Shall I attend your lordſhip ?

Ang.   At any time 'fore noon.

Iſab. Save your honour !

         [*Exeunt* LUCIO, ISABELLA, *and* Provoſt.

Ang.   From thee ; even from thy virtue !—
What's this ? what's this ? Is this her fault, or mine ?
The tempter, or the tempted, who ſins moſt ? Ha !

                        Not

Not fhe; nor doth fhe tempt: but it is I,
That lying by the violet, in the fun,
Do, as the carrion does, not as the flower,
Corrupt with virtuous feafon. Can it be,
That modefty may more betray our fenfe
Than woman's lightnefs? Having wafte ground enough,
Shall we defire to raze the fanctuary,
And pitch our evils there? O, fie, fie, fie!
What doft thou? or what art thou, Angelo?
Doft thou defire her foully, for thofe things
That make her good? O, let her brother live:
Thieves for their robbery have authority,
When judges fteal themfelves. What? do I love her,
That I defire to hear her fpeak again,
And feaft upon her eyes? What is't I dream on?
O cunning enemy, that, to catch a faint,
With faints doft bait thy hook! Moft dangerous
Is that temptation, that doth goad us on
To fin in loving virtue: never could the ftrumpet,
With all her double vigour, art, and nature,
Once ftir my temper; but this virtuous maid
Subdues me quite;—Ever, till now,
When men were fond, I fmil'd, and wonder'd how.

[*Exit.*

SCENE III.

A Room in a Prifon.

Enter Duke, *habited like a Friar, and* Provoft.

Duke. Hail to you, provoft! fo, I think you are.
Prov. I am the provoft: What's your will, good friar?
Duke. Bound by my charity, and my blefs'd order,

I come

I come to vifit the afflicted fpirits
Here in the prifon: do me the common right
To let me fee them; and to make me know
The nature of their crimes, that I may minifter
To them accordingly.

   Prov. I would do more than that, if more were needful.

         Enter JULIET.

Look, here comes one; a gentlewoman of mine,
Who falling in the flames of her own youth,
Hath blifter'd her report: She is with child;
And he that got it, fentenc'd: a young man
More fit to do another fuch offence,
Than die for this.
   Duke.   When muft he die?
   Prov. As I do think, to-morrow.—
I have provided for you; ftay a while,   [*To* JULIET.
And you fhall be conducted.
   Duke. Repent you, fair one, of the fin you carry?
   Juliet. I do; and bear the fhame moft patiently.
   Duke. I'll teach you how you fhall arraign your con-
        fcience,
And try your penitence, if it be found,
Or hollowly put on.
   Juliet.   I'll gladly learn.
   Duke. Love you the man that wrong'd you?
   Juliet. Yes, as I love the woman that wrong'd him.
   Duke. So then, it feems, your moft offenceful act
Was mutually committed?
   Juliet.   Mutually.
   Duke. Then was your fin of heavier kind than his.
   Juliet. I do confefs it, and repent it, father.
   Duke. 'Tis meet fo, daughter: But left you do repent,

                          As

As that the fin hath brought you to this fhame,—
Which forrow is always toward ourfelves, not heaven;
Showing, we'd not fpare heaven, as we love it,
But as we ftand in fear,—

Juliet. I do repent me, as it is an evil;
And take the fhame with joy.

Duke.   There reft.
Your partner, as I hear, muft die to-morrow,
And I am going with inftruction to him.—
Grace go with you! *Benedicite!*   [*Exit.*

Juliet. Muft die to-morrow! O, injurious love,
That refpites me a life, whofe very comfort
Is ftill a dying horror!

Prov.   'Tis pity of him.   [*Exeunt.*

SCENE IV.

A Room in Angelo's *Houfe.*

Enter ANGELO.

Ang. When I would pray and think, I think and pray
To feveral fubjects: heaven hath my empty words;
Whilft my invention, hearing not my tongue,
Anchors on Ifabel: Heaven in my mouth,
As if I did but only chew his name;
And in my heart, the ftrong and fwelling evil
Of my conception: The ftate, whereon I ftudied,
Is like a good thing, being often read,
Grown fear'd and tedious; yea, my gravity,
Wherein (let no man hear me) I take pride,
Could I, with boot, change for an idle plume,
Which the air beats for vain. O place! O form!
How often doft thou with thy cafe, thy habit,

D   Wrench

Wrench awe from fools, and tie the wifer fouls
To thy falfe feeming? Blood, thou ftill art blood :
Let's write good angel on the devil's horn,
'Tis not the devil's creft.

Enter Servant.

How now, who's there?

  Serv.   One Ifabel, a fifter,
Defires accefs to you.

  Ang.   Teach her the way.   [*Exit* Se
O heavens!
Why does my blood thus mufter to my heart;
Making both it unable for itfelf,
And difpoffeffing all my other parts
Of neceffary fitnefs?
So play the foolifh throngs with one that fwoons;
Come all to help him, and fo ftop the air
By which he fhould revive : and even fo
The general, fubject to a well-wifh'd king,
Quit their own part, and in obfequious fondnefs
Crowd to his prefence, where their untaught love
Muft needs appear offence.

Enter ISABELLA.

How now, fair maid?

  Ifab.   I am come to know your pleafur

  Ang. That you might know it, would much bet
      pleafe me,
Than to demand what 'tis. Your brother cannot live

  Ifab. Even fo?—Heaven keep your honour! [*Retiri*

  Ang. Yet may he live a while; and, it may be,
As long as you, or I: Yet he muft die.

Isab. Under your fentence?

Ang. Yea.

Isab. When, I befeech you? that in his reprieve,
Longer, or fhorter, he may be fo fitted,
That his foul ficken not.

Ang. Ha! Fie, thefe filthy vices! It were as good
To pardon him, that hath from nature ftolen
A man already made, as to remit
Their faucy fweetnefs, that do coin heaven's image,
In ftamps that are forbid: 'tis all as eafy
Falfely to take away a life true made,
As to put mettle in reftrained means,
To make a falfe one.

Isab. 'Tis fet down fo in heaven, but not in earth.

Ang. Say you fo? then I fhall poze you quickly.
Which had you rather, That the moft juft law
Now took your brother's life; or, to redeem him,
Give up your body to fuch fweet uncleannefs,
As fhe that he hath ftain'd?

Isab.   Sir, believe this,
I had rather give my body than my foul.

Ang. I talk not of your foul; Our compell'd fins
Stand more for number than accompt.

Isab.   How fay you?

Ang. Nay, I'll not warrant that; for I can fpeak
Againft the thing I fay. Anfwer to this;—
I, now the voice of the recorded law,
Pronounce a fentence on your brother's life:
Might there not be a charity in fin,
To fave this brother's life?

Isab.   Pleafe you to do't,
I'll take it as a peril to my foul,
It is no fin at all, but charity.

Ang.

Ang. Pleas'd you to do't, at peril of your foul,
Were equal poize of fin and charity.

Ifab. That I do beg his life, if it be fin,
Heaven, let me bear it! you granting of my fuit,
If that be fin, I'll make it my morn prayer
To have it added to the faults of mine,
And nothing of your, anfwer.

Ang.   Nay, but hear me:
Your fenfe purfues not mine: either you are ignoran
Or feem fo, craftily; and that's not good.

Ifab. Let me be ignorant, and in nothing good,
But gracioufly to know I am no better.

Ang. Thus wifdom wifhes to appear moft bright,
When it doth tax itfelf: as thefe black mafks
Proclaim an enfhield beauty ten times louder
Than beauty could difplayed.—But mark me;
To be received plain, I'll fpeak more grofs:
Your brother is to die.

Ifab. So.

Ang. And his offence is fo, as it appears
Accountant to the law upon that pain.

Ifab. True.

Ang. Admit no other way to fave his life,
(As I fubfcribe not that, nor any other,
But in the lofs of queftion,) that you, his fifter,
Finding yourfelf defir'd of fuch a perfon,
Whofe credit with the judge, or own great place,
Could fetch your brother from the manacles
Of the all-binding law; and that there were
No earthly mean to fave him, but that either
You muft lay down the treafures of your body
To this fuppofed, or elfe let him fuffer;
What would you do?

Isab. As much for my poor brother, as myself:
That is, Were I under the terms of death,
The impreſſion of keen whips I'd wear as rubies,
And ſtrip myſelf to death, as to a bed
That longing I have been ſick for, ere I'd yield
My body up to ſhame.

   Ang.   Then muſt your brother die.

   Isab. And 'twere the cheaper way:
Better it were, a brother died at once,
Than that a ſiſter, by redeeming him,
Should die for ever.

   Ang. Were not you then as cruel as the ſentence
That you have ſlander'd ſo?

   Isab. Ignomy in ranſom, and free pardon,
Are of two houſes: lawful mercy is
Nothing akin to foul redemption.

   Ang. You ſeem'd of late to make the law a tyrant;
And rather prov'd the ſliding of your brother
A merriment than a vice.

   Isab. O, pardon me, my lord; it oft falls out,
To have what we'd have, we ſpeak not what we mean:
I ſomething do excuſe the thing I hate,
For his advantage that I dearly love.

   Ang. We are all frail.

   Isab.   Elſe let my brother die,
If not a feodary, but only he,
Owe, and ſucceed by weakneſs.

   Ang.   Nay, women are frail too.

   Isab. Ay, as the glaſſes where they view themſelves;
Which are as eaſy broke as they make forms.
Women!—Help heaven! men their creation mar
In profiting by them. Nay, call us ten times frail;
For we are ſoft as our complexions are,
And credulous to falſe prints.

                         Ang.

Ang.   I think it well :
And from this teftimony of your own fex,
(Since, I fuppofe, we are made to be no ftronger
Than faults may fhake our frames,) let me be bold ;—
I do arreft your words ; Be that you are,
That is, a woman ; if you be more, you're none ;
If you be one, (as you are well exprefs'd
By all external warrants,) fhow it now,
By putting on the deftin'd livery.

    Ifab. I have no tongue but one : gentle my lord,
Let me intreat you fpeak the former language.

    Ang. Plainly conceive, I love you.

    Ifab. My brother did love Juliet ; and you tell me,
That he fhall die for it.

    Ang. He fhall not, Ifabel, if you give me love.

    Ifab. I know, your virtue hath a licence in't,
Which feems a little fouler than it is,
To pluck on others.

    Ang.   Believe me, on mine honour,
My words exprefs my purpofe.

    Ifab. Ha ! little honour to be much believ'd,
And moft pernicious purpofe !—Seeming, feeming !—
I will proclaim thee, Angelo ; look for't :
Sign me a prefent pardon for my brother,
Or, with an out-ftretch'd throat, I'll tell the world
Aloud, what man thou art.

    Ang.   Who will believe thee, Ifabel?
My unfoil'd name, the aufterenefs of my life,
My vouch againft you, and my place i'the ftate,
Will fo your accufation over-weigh,
That you fhall ftifle in your own report,
And fmell of calumny. I have begun ;
And now I give my fenfual race the rein :
Fit thy confent to my fharp appetite ;

                                 Lay

Lay by all nicety, and prolixious blushes,
That banish what they sue for ; redeem thy brother
By yielding up thy body to my will ;
Or else he must not only die the death,
But thy unkindness shall his death draw out
To lingering sufferance : answer me to-morrow,
Or, by the affection that now guides me most,
I'll prove a tyrant to him : As for you,
Say what you can, my false o'erweighs your true. [*Exit.*

    Isab. To whom should I complain ? Did I tell this,
Who would believe me ? O perilous mouths,
That bear in them one and the self-same tongue,
Either of condemnation or approof !
Bidding the law make court'sy to their will ;
Hooking both right and wrong to the appetite,
To follow, as it draws ! I'll to my brother :
Though he hath fallen by prompture of the blood,
Yet hath he in him such a mind of honour,
That had he twenty heads to tender down
On twenty bloody blocks, he'd yield them up,
Before his sister should her body stoop
To such abhorr'd pollution.
Then Isabel, live chaste, and, brother, die :
More than our brother is our chastity.
I'll tell him yet of Angelo's request,
And fit his mind to death, for his soul's rest. [*Exit.*

ACT III.   SCENE I.

A Room in the Prison.

Enter Duke, Claudio, *and* Provost.

Duke. So, then you hope of pardon from lord Angelo?

Claud. The miserable have no other medicine,
But only hope:
I have hope to live, and am prepar'd to die.

Duke. Be absolute for death; either death, or life,
Shall thereby be the sweeter.   Reason thus with life,—
If I do lose thee, I do lose a thing
That none but fools would keep: a breath thou art,
(Servile to all the skiey influences,)
That dost this habitation, where thou keep'st,
Hourly afflict: merely, thou art death's fool;
For him thou labour'st by thy flight to shun,
And yet run'st toward him still: Thou art not noble;
For all the accommodations that thou bear'st,
Are nurs'd by baseness: Thou art by no means valiant;
For thou dost fear the soft and tender fork
Of a poor worm: Thy best of rest is sleep,
And that thou oft provok'st; yet grossly fear'st
Thy death, which is no more.   Thou art not thyself;
For thou exist'st on many a thousand grains
That issue out of dust: Happy thou art not:
For what thou hast not, still thou striv'st to get;
And what thou hast, forget'st: Thou art not certain;
For thy complexion shifts to strange effects,
After the moon: If thou art rich, thou art poor;
For, like an ass, whose back with ingots bows,

Tho

Singleton del.

Measure for Measure.

Act 3. Scene 1.

Pub.d May 1, 1800. by Vernor & Hood Poultry

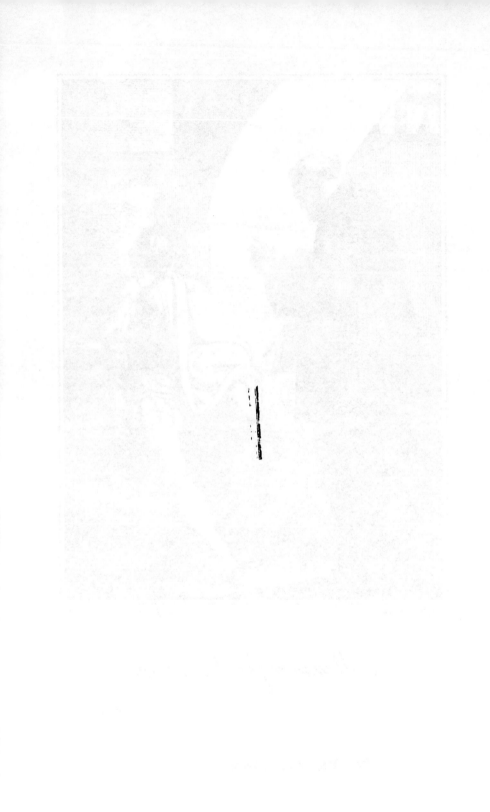

Thou bear'ft thy heavy riches but a journey,
And death unloads thee : Friend haft thou none;
For thine own bowels, which do call thee fire,
The mere effufion of thy proper loins,
Do curfe the gout, ferpigo, and the rheum,
For ending thee no fooner: Thou haft nor youth, nor age;
But, as it were, an after-dinner's fleep,
Dreaming on both : for all thy bleffed youth
Becomes as aged, and doth beg the alms
Of palfied eld; and when thou art old, and rich,
Thou haft neither heat, affection, limb, nor beauty,
To make thy riches pleafant.   What's yet in this,
That bears the name of life? Yet in this life
Lie hid more thoufand deaths : yet death we fear,
That makes thefe odds all even.

   Claud.   I humbly thank you.
To fue to live, I find, I feek to die ;
And, feeking death, find life: Let it come on.

Enter ISABELLA.

  Ifab. What, ho! Peace here ; grace and good company!
  Prov. Who's there ? come in, the wifh deferves a wel-
     come.
  Duke. Dear fir, ere long I'll vifit you again.
  Claud. Moft holy fir, I thank you.
  Ifab. My bufinefs is a word or two with Claudio.
  Prov. And very welcome.   Look, fignior, here's your
     fifter.
  Duke. Provoft, a word with you.
  Prov.   As many as you pleafe.
  Duke. Bring them to fpeak, where I may be conceal'd,
Yet hear them.   [*Exeunt* Duke *and* Provoft.
  Claud.   Now, fifter, what's the comfort ?

                                Ifab.

Isab. Why, as all comforts are; most good in deed:
Lord Angelo, having affairs to heaven,
Intends you for his swift embassador,
Where you shall be an everlasting leiger:
Therefore your best appointment make with speed;
To-morrow you set on.
 Claud.   Is there no remedy?
 Isab. None, but such remedy, as, to save a head,
To cleave a heart in twain.
 Claud.   But is there any?
 Isab. Yes, brother, you may live;
There is a devilish mercy in the judge,
If you'll implore it, that will free your life,
But fetter you till death.
 Claud.   Perpetual durance?
 Isab. Ay, just, perpetual durance; a restraint,
Though all the world's vastidity you had,
To a determin'd scope.
 Claud.   But in what nature?
 Isab. In such a one as (you consenting to't)
Would bark your honour from that trunk you bear,
And leave you naked.
 Claud.   Let me know the point.
 Isab. O, I do fear thee, Claudio; and I quake,
Lest thou a feverous life should'st entertain,
And six or seven winters more respect
Than a perpetual honour. Dar'st thou die?
The sense of death is most in apprehension;
And the poor beetle, that we tread upon,
In corporal sufferance finds a pang as great
As when a giant dies.
 Claud.   Why give you me this shame?
Think you I can a resolution fetch
From flowery tenderness? If I must die, .

I will

I will encounter darkneſs as a bride,
And hug it in mine arms.

   Iſab. There ſpake my brother; there my father's grave
Did utter forth a voice! Yes, thou muſt die :
Thou art too noble to conſerve a life
In baſe appliances. This outward-ſainted deputy,—
Whoſe ſettled viſage and deliberate word
Nips youth i'the head, and follies doth enmew,
As falcon doth the fowl,—is yet a devil;
His filth within being caſt, he would appear
A pond as deep as hell.

   Claud.   The princely Angelo?

   Iſab. O, 'tis the cunning livery of hell,
The damned'ſt body to inveſt and cover
In princely guards! Doſt thou think, Claudio,
If I would yield him my virginity,
Thou might'ſt be freed?

   Claud.   O, heavens! it cannot be.

   Iſab. Yes, he would give it thee, from this rank offence,
So to offend him ſtill : This night's the time
That I ſhould do what I abhor to name,
Or elſe thou dieſt to-morrow.

   Claud.   Thou ſhalt not do't.

   Iſab. O, were it but my life,
I'd throw it down for your deliverance
As frankly as a pin.

   Claud.   Thanks, dear Iſabel.

   Iſab. Be ready, Claudio, for your death to-morrow.

   Claud. Yes.—Has he affections in him,
That thus can make him bite the law by the noſe,
When he would force it? Sure it is no ſin;
Or of the deadly ſeven it is the leaſt.

   Iſab. Which is the leaſt?

   Claud. If it were damnable, he, being ſo wiſe,

                              Why·

Why, would he for the momentary trick
Be perdurably fin'd ?—O Ifabel !
  Ifab. What fays my brother?
  Claud.   Death is a fearful thing.
  Ifab. And fhamed life a hateful.
  Claud. Ay, but to die, and go we know not where ;
To lie in cold obftruction, and to rot ;
This fenfible warm motion to become
A kneaded clod ; and the delighted fpirit
To bathe in fiery floods, or to refide
In thrilling regions of thick-ribbed ice ;
To be imprifon'd in the viewlefs winds,
And blown with reftlefs violence round about
The pendant world ; or to be worfe than worft
Of thofe, that lawlefs and incertain thoughts
Imagine howling !—'tis too horrible !
The wearieft and moft loathed worldly life,
That age, ach, penury, and imprifonment
Can lay on nature, is a paradife
To what we fear of death.
  Ifab. Alas ! alas !
  Claud.   Sweet fifter, let me live :
What fin you do to fave a brother's life,
Nature difpenfes with the deed fo far,
That it becomes a virtue.
  Ifab.   O, you beaft !
O, faithlefs coward ! O, difhoneft wretch !
Wilt thou be made a man out of my vice ?
Is't not a kind of inceft, to take life
From thine own fifter's fhame ? What fhould I think ?
Heaven fhield, my mother play'd my father fair !
For fuch a warped flip of wildernefs
Ne'er iffu'd from his blood. Take my defiance :
Die ; perifh ! might but my bending down

5   Reprieve

Reprieve thee from thy fate, it fhould proceed :
I'll pray a thoufand prayers for thy death,
No word to fave thee.

Claud. Nay, hear me, Ifabel.

Ifab.   O, fie, fie, fie!
Thy fin's not accidental, but a trade :
Mercy to thee would prove itfelf a bawd :
'Tis beft that thou dieft quickly.   [*Going.*

Claud.   O hear me, Ifabella.

Re-enter Duke.

Duke. Vouchfafe a word, young fifter, but one word.

Ifab. What is your will?

Duke. Might you difpenfe with your leifure, I would by and by have fome fpeech with you : the fatisfaction I would require, is likewife your own benefit.

Ifab. I have no fuperfluous leifure; my ftay muft be ftolen out of other affairs; but I will attend you a while.

Duke. [*To* CLAUDIO, *afide.*] Son, I have overheard what hath paft between you and your fifter. Angelo had never the purpofe to corrupt her; only he hath made an affay of her virtue, to practife his judgement with the difpofition of natures: fhe, having the truth of honour in her, hath made him that gracious denial which he is moft glad to receive: I am confeffor to Angelo, and I know this to be true; therefore prepare yourfelf to death : Do not fatisfy your refolution with hopes that are fallible : to-morrow you muft die; go to your knees, and make ready.

Claud. Let me afk my fifter pardon. I am fo out of love with life, that I will fue to be rid of it.

Duke. Hold you there : Farewell.   [*Exit* CLAUDIO.
                                          Re-enter

Re-enter Provoſt.

Provoſt, a word with you.

Prov. What's your will, father?

Duke. That now you are come, you will be gone: Leave me a while with the maid; my mind promiſes with my habit, no loſs ſhall touch her by my company.

Prov. In good time.   [*Exit* Provoſt.

Duke. The hand that hath made you fair, hath made you good: the goodneſs, that is cheap in beauty, makes beauty brief in goodneſs; but grace, being the ſoul of your complexion, ſhould keep the body of it ever fair. The aſſault, that Angelo hath made to you, fortune hath convey'd to my underſtanding; and, but that frailty hath examples for his falling, I ſhould wonder at Angelo. How would you do to content this ſubſtitute, and to ſave your brother?

Iſab. I am now going to reſolve him: I had rather my brother die by the law, than my ſon ſhould be unlawfully born. But O, how much is the good duke deceived in Angelo! If ever he return, and I can ſpeak to him, I will open my lips in vain, or diſcover his government.

Duke. That ſhall not be much amiſs: Yet, as the matter now ſtands, he will avoid your accuſation; he made trial of you only.—Therefore faſten your ear on my adviſings; to the love I have in doing good, a remedy preſents itſelf. I do make myſelf believe, that you may moſt uprighteouſly do a poor wronged lady a merited benefit; redeem your brother from the angry law; do no ſtain to your own gracious perſon; and much pleaſe the abſent duke, if, peradventure, he ſhall ever return to have hearing of this buſineſs.

Iſab. Let me hear you ſpeak further; I have ſpirit to
do

do any thing that appears not foul in the truth of my
spirit.

Duke. Virtue is bold, and goodness never fearful.
Have you not heard speak of Mariana the sister of Frederick, the great soldier, who miscarried at sea?

Isab. I have heard of the lady, and good words went
with her name.

Duke. Her should this Angelo have married; was af-
fianced to her by oath, and the nuptial appointed: between which time of the contract, and limit of the solem-
nity, her brother Frederick was wrecked at sea, having in
that perish'd vessel the dowry of his sister. But mark,
how heavily this befel to the poor gentlewoman: there
she lost a noble and renowned brother, in his love toward
her ever most kind and natural; with him the portion and
sinew of her fortune, her marriage-dowry; with both,
her combinate husband, this well-seeming Angelo!

Isab. Can this be so? Did Angelo so leave her?

Duke. Left her in her tears, and dry'd not one of them
with his comfort; swallowed his vows whole, pretending, in
her, discoveries of dishonour: in few, bestowed her on
her own lamentation, which she yet wears for his sake;
and he, a marble to her tears, is washed with them, but
relents not.

Isab. What a merit were it in death, to take this poor
maid from the world! What corruption in this life, that
it will let this man live!—But how out of this can she
avail?

Duke. It is a rupture that you may easily heal: and the
cure of it not only saves your brother, but keeps you
from dishonour in doing it.

Isab. Show me how, good father.

Duke. This fore-named maid hath yet in her the continuance

tinuance of her firſt affection; his unjuſt unkindneſs, that
in all reaſon ſhould have quenched her love, hath, like an
impediment in the current, made it more violent and un-
ruly. Go you to Angelo; anſwer his requiring with a
plauſible obedience; agree with his demands to the point:
only refer yourſelf to this advantage,—firſt, that your ſtay
with him may not be long; that the time may have all
ſhadow and ſilence in it; and the place anſwer to conve-
nience: this being granted in courſe, now follows all.
We ſhall adviſe this wronged maid to ſtead up your appointment, go in your place; if the encounter acknowledge itſelf hereafter, it may compel him to her recompence: and here, by this, is your brother ſaved, your
honour untainted, the poor Mariana advantaged, and the
corrupt deputy ſcaled. The maid will I frame, and make
fit for his attempt. If you think well to carry this as you
may, the doubleneſs of the benefit defends the deceit from
reproof. What think you of it?

Iſab. The image of it gives me content already; and, I
truſt, it will grow to a moſt proſperous perfection.

Duke. It lies much in your holding up: Haſte you
ſpeedily to Angelo; if for this night he entreat you to
his bed, give him promiſe of ſatisfaction. I will preſently to St. Luke's! there, at the moated grange reſides this
dejected Mariana: At that place call upon me; and diſpatch with Angelo, that it may be quickly.

Iſab. I thank you for this comfort: Fare you well, good
father.   [*Exeunt ſeverally.*

SCENE

SCENE II.

The Street before the Prison.

Enter Duke *as a Friar;* to him ELBOW, Clown, *and*
Officers.

Elb. Nay, if there be no remedy for it, but that you
will needs buy and fell men and women like beafts, we
fhall have all the world drink brown and white baftard.

Duke. O, heavens! what ftuff is here?

Clo. 'Twas never merry world, fince, of two ufuries,
the merrieft was put down, and the worfer allow'd by
order of law a furr'd gown to keep him warm; and furr'd
with fox and lamb-fkins too, to fignify, that craft, being
richer than innocency, ftands for the facing.

Elb. Come your way, fir:—Blefs you, good father friar.

Duke. And you, good brother father: What offence
hath this man made you, fir?

Elb. Marry, fir, he hath offended the law; and, fir, we
take him to be a thief too, fir; for we have found upon
him, fir, a ftrange pick-lock, which we have fent to the
deputy.

Duke. Fie, firrah; a bawd, a wicked bawd!
The evil that thou caufeft to be done,
That is thy means to live: Do thou but think
What 'tis to cram a maw, or clothe a back,
From fuch a filthy vice: fay to thyfelf,—
From their abominable and beaftly touches
I drink, I eat, array myfelf, and live.
Canft thou believe thy living is a life,
So ftinkingly depending? Go, mend, go, mend.

Clo. Indeed, it does ftink in fome fort, fir; but yet, fir,
I would prove——

E　　　　　　　　Duk

Duke. Nay, if the devil have given thee proofs for fin,
Thou wilt prove his. Take him to prifon, officer;
Correction and inſtruction muſt both work,
Ere this rude beaſt will profit.

Elb. He muſt before the deputy, ſir; he has given him
warning: the deputy cannot abide a whore-maſter: if he
be a whore-monger, and comes before him, he were as
good go a mile on his errand.

Duke. That we were all, as ſome would ſeem to be,
Free from our faults, as faults from ſeeming, free!

Enter LUCIO.

Elb. His neck will come to your waiſt, a cord, ſir.

Clo. I ſpy comfort; I cry, bail: Here's a gentleman,
and a friend of mine.

Lucio. How now, noble Pompey? What, at the heels
of Cæſar? Art thou led in triumph? What, is there none
of Pygmalion's images, newly made woman, to be had
now, for putting the hand in the pocket and extracting
it clutch'd? What reply? Ha? What ſay'ſt thou to this
tune, matter, and method? Is't not drown'd i' the laſt
rain? Ha? What ſay'ſt thou, trot? Is the world as it
was, man? Which is the way? Is it ſad, and few words?
Or how? The trick of it?

Duke. Still thus, and thus! ſtill worſe!

Lucio. How doth my dear morſel, thy miſtreſs? Pro-
cures ſhe ſtill? Ha?

Clo. Troth, ſir, ſhe hath eaten up all her beef, and ſhe
is herſelf in the tub.

Lucio. Why, 'tis good; it is the right of it; it muſt be
ſo: Ever your freſh whore, and your powder'd bawd:
An unſhunn'd conſequence; it muſt be ſo: Art going to
priſon, Pompey?

Clo.

Clo. Yes, faith, fir.

Lucio. Why 'tis not amifs, Pompey: Farewell: Go; fay, I fent thee thither. For debt, Pompey? Or how?

Elb. For being a bawd, for being a bawd.

Lucio. Well, then imprifon him: If imprifonment be the due of a bawd, why, 'tis his right: Bawd is he, doubt-lefs, and of antiquity too; bawd-born. Farewell, good Pompey: Commend me to the prifon, Pompey: You will turn good hufband now, Pompey; you will keep the houfe.

Clo. I hope, fir, your good worfhip will be my bail.

Lucio. No, indeed, will I not, Pompey; it is not the wear. I will pray, Pompey, to increafe your bondage: if you take it not patiently, why, your mettle is the more: Adieu, trufty Pompey.—Blefs you, friar.

Duke. And you.

Lucio. Does Bridget paint ftill, Pompey? Ha?

Elb. Come your ways, fir; come.

Clo. You will not bail me then, fir?

Lucio. Then, Pompey? nor now.—What news abroad, friar? What news?

Elb. Come your ways, fir; come.

Lucio. Go,—to kennel, Pompey, go:

[*Exeunt* ELBOW, Clown, *and* Officers.

What news, friar, of the duke?

Duke. I know none: Can you tell me of any?

Lucio. Some fay, he is with the emperor of Ruffia; other fome, he is in Rome: But where is he, think you?

Duke. I know not where: But wherefoever, I wifh him well.

Lucio. It was a mad fantaftical trick of him, to fteal from the ftate, and ufurp the beggary he was never born to. Lord Angelo dukes it well in his abfence; he puts tranfgreffion to't.

E 2

Duke.

Duke. He does well in't.

Lucio. A little more lenity to lechery would do no harm in him: fomething too crabbed that way, friar.

Duke. It is too general a vice, and feverity muft cure it.

Lucio. Yes, in good footh, the vice is of a great kindred; it is well ally'd: but it is impoffible to extirp it quite, friar, till eating and drinking be put down. They fay, this Angelo was not made by man and woman, after the downright way of creation: Is it true, think you?

Duke. How fhould he be made then?

Lucio. Some report, a fea-maid fpawn'd him:—Some, that he was begot between two ftock-fifhes:—But it is certain, that when he makes water, his urine is congeal'd ice; that I know to be true: and he is a motion ungenerative, that's infallible.

Duke. You are pleafant, fir; and fpeak apace.

Lucio. Why, what a ruthlefs thing is this in him, for the rebellion of a cod-piece, to take away the life of a man? Would the duke, that is abfent, have done this? Ere he would have hang'd a man for the getting a hundred baftards, he would have paid for the nurfing a thoufand: He had fome feeling of the fport; he knew the fervice, and that inftructed him to mercy.

Duke. I never heard the abfent duke much detected for women; he was not inclined that way.

Lucio. O, fir, you are deceived.

Duke. 'Tis not poffible.

Lucio. Who? not the duke? yes, your beggar of fifty; —and his ufe was, to put a ducat in her clack-difh: the duke had crotchets in him: He would be drunk too; that let me inform you.

Duke. You do him wrong, furely.

Lucio. Sir, I was an inward of his: A fhy fellow was

the

the duke: and, I believe, I know the caufe of his with-drawing.

Duke. What, I pr'ythee, might be the caufe?

Lucio. No,—pardon;—'tis a fecret muſt be lock'd within the teeth and the lips: but this I can let you under-ſtand,—The greater file of the fubject held the duke to be wife.

Duke. Wife? why, no queſtion but he was.

Lucio. A very fuperficial, ignorant, unweighing fellow.

Duke. Either this is envy in you, folly, or miſtaking; the very ſtream of his life, and the bufineſs he hath helm-ed, muſt, upon a warranted need, give him a better pro-clamation. Let him be but teſtimonied in his own bring-ings forth, and he ſhall appear to the envious, a ſcholar, a ſtateſman, and a ſoldier: Therefore, you ſpeak unſkil-fully; or, if your knowledge be more, it is much darken'd in your malice.

Lucio. Sir, I know him, and I love him.

Duke. Love talks with better knowledge, and know-ledge with dearer love.

Lucio. Come, fir, I know what I know.

Duke. I can hardly believe that, ſince you know not what you ſpeak. But, if ever the duke return, (as our prayers are he may,) let me defire you to make your an-ſwer before him: If it be honeſt you have ſpoke, you have courage to maintain it: I am bound to call upon you; and, I pray you, your name?

Lucio. Sir, my name is Lucio; well known to the duke.

Duke. He ſhall know you better, fir, if I may live to report you.

Lucio. I fear you not.

Duke. O, you hope the duke will return no more; or you imagine me too unhurtful an oppoſite. But, indeed, I can do you little harm: you'll forſwear this again.

Lucio.

Lucio. I'll be hang'd firſt: thou art deceived in me, friar. But no more of this: Canſt thou tell, if Claudio die to-morrow, or no?

Duke. Why ſhould he die, ſir?

Lucio. Why? for filling a bottle with a tun-diſh. I would, the duke, we talk of, were return'd again: this ungenitur'd agent will unpeople the province with continency; ſparrows muſt not build in his houſe-eaves, becauſe they are lecherous. The duke yet would have dark deeds darkly anſwer'd; he would never bring them to light: would he were return'd! Marry, this Claudio is condemn'd for untruſſing. Farewell, good friar; I pr'ythee, pray for me. The duke, I ſay to thee again, would eat mutton on Fridays. He's now paſt it; yet, and I ſay to thee, he would mouth with a beggar, though ſhe ſmelt brown bread and garlick: ſay, that I ſaid ſo. Farewell.

[*Exit.*

Duke. No might nor greatneſs in mortality
Can cenſure 'ſcape; back-wounding calumny
The whiteſt virtue ſtrikes: What king ſo ſtrong,
Can tie the gall up in the ſlanderous tongue?
But who comes here?

Enter ESCALUS, Provoſt, Bawd, *and* Officers.

Eſcal. Go, away with her to priſon.

Bawd. Good my lord, be good to me; your honour is accounted a merciful man: good my lord.

Eſcal. Double and treble admonition, and ſtill forfeit in the ſame kind? This would make mercy ſwear, and play the tyrant.

Prov. A bawd of eleven years continuance, may it pleaſe your honour.

Bawd. My lord, this is one Lucio's information againſt

me;

me: miftrefs Kate Keep-down was with child by him in
the duke's time, he promifed her marriage; his child
is a year and a quarter old, come Philip and Jacob:
I have kept it myfelf; and fee how he goes about to
abufe me.

Efcal. That fellow is a fellow of much licence:—let
him be called before us.—Away with her to prifon: Go
to; no more words. [*Exeunt* Bawd *and* Officers.] Provoft, my brother Angelo will not be alter'd, Claudio muft
die to-morrow: let him be furnifhed with divines, and
have all charitable preparation: if my brother wrought
by my pity, it fhould not be fo with him.

Prov. So pleafe you, this friar hath been with him, and
advifed him for the entertainment of death.

Efcal. Good even, good father.

Duke. Blifs and goodnefs on you!

Efcal. Of whence are you?

Duke. Not of this country, though my chance is now
To ufe it for my time: I am a brother
Of gracious order, late come from the fee,
In fpecial bufinefs from his holinefs.

Efcal. What news abroad i' the world?

Duke. None, but that there is fo great a fever on goodnefs, that the diffolution of it muft cure it: novelty
is only in requeft; and it is as dangerous to be aged in
any kind of courfe, as it is virtuous to be conftant in any
undertaking. There is fcarce truth enough alive, to
make focieties fecure; but fecurity enough, to make fel-
lowfhips accurs'd: much upon this riddle runs the wifdom
of the world. This news is old enough, yet it is every
day's news. I pray you, fir, of what difpofition was the
duke?

Efcal. One, that, above all other ftrifes, contended efpecially to know himfelf.

Duke.

Duke. What pleasure was he given to ?

Escal. Rather rejoicing to see another merry, than merry at any thing which profess'd to make him rejoice : a gentleman of all temperance. But leave we him to his events, with a prayer they may prove prosperous ; and let me desire to know how you find Claudio prepared. I am made to understand, that you have lent him visitation.

Duke. He professes to have received no sinister measure from his judge, but most willingly humbles himself to the determination of justice : yet had he framed to himself, by the instruction of his frailty, many deceiving promises of life ; which I, by my good leisure, have discredited to him, and now is he resolved to die.

Escal. You have paid the heavens your function, and the prisoner the very debt of your calling. I have labour'd for the poor gentleman, to the extremest shore of my modesty ; but my brother justice have I found so severe, that he hath forced me to tell him, he is indeed—justice.

Duke. If his own life answer the straitness of his proceeding, it shall become him well ; wherein if he chance to fail, he hath sentenced himself.

Escal. I am going to visit the prisoner : Fare you well.

Duke. Peace be with you !

[*Exeunt* ESCALUS *and* Provost.

He, who the sword of heaven will bear,
Should be as holy as severe :
Pattern in himself to know,
Grace to stand, and virtue go ;
More nor less to others paying,
Than by self-offences weighing.
Shame to him, whose cruel striking
Kills for faults of his own liking !

Twice

Twice treble ſhame on Angelo,
To weed my vice, and let his grow!
O, what may man within him hide,
Though angel on the outward ſide!
How may likeneſs, made in crimes,
Making practice on the times,
Draw with idle ſpiders' ſtrings
Moſt pond'rous and ſubſtantial things!
Craft againſt vice I muſt apply:
With Angelo to-night ſhall lie
His old betrothed, but deſpis'd;
So diſguiſe ſhall, by the diſguis'd,
Pay with falſhood falſe exacting,
And perform an old contracting.   [*Exit.*

AC

ACT IV.   SCENE I.

A Room in Mariana's *House.*

MARIANA *discovered sitting; a Boy singing.*

SONG.

Take, oh take those lips away,
That so sweetly were forsworn;
And those eyes, the break of day,
Lights that do mislead the morn:
But my kisses bring again,
                        bring again,
Seals of love, but seal'd in vain,
                        seal'd in vain.

Mari. Break off thy song, and haste thee quick aw
Here comes a man of comfort, whose advice
Hath often still'd my brawling discontent.— [*Exit*

Enter Duke.

I cry you mercy, sir; and well could wish
You had not found me here so musical:
Let me excuse me, and believe me so,—
My mirth it much displeas'd, but pleas'd my woe.
   Duke. 'Tis good: though musick oft hath such a ch
To make bad, good, and good provoke to harm.
I pray you, tell me, hath any body inquired for me
to-day? much upon this time have I promis'd he
meet.

Mari. You have not been inquired after: I have fat here all day.

Enter ISABELLA.

Duke. I do conftantly believe you:—The time is come, even now. I fhall crave your forbearance a little; may be, I will call upon you anon, for fome advantage to yourfelf.

Mari. I am always bound to you.   [*Exit.*

Duke. Very well met, and welcome.
What is the news from this good deputy?

Ifab. He hath a garden circummur'd with brick,
Whofe weftern fide is with a vineyard back'd;
And to that vineyard is a planched gate,
That makes his opening with this bigger key:
This other doth command a little door,
Which from the vineyard to the garden leads;
There have I made my promife to call on him,
Upon the heavy middle of the night.

    Duke. But fhall you on your knowledge find this way?

    Ifab. I have ta'en a due and wary note upon't;
With whifpering and moft guilty diligence,
In action all of precept, he did fhow me
The way twice o'er.

    Duke.   Are there no other tokens
Between you 'greed, concerning her obfervance?

    Ifab. No, none, but only a repair i' the dark;
And that I have poffefs'd him, my moft ftay
Can be but brief: for I have made him know,
I have a fervant comes with me along,
That ftays upon me; whofe perfuafion is,
I come about my brother.

    Duke.   'Tis well borne up.

                        I have

I have not yet made known to Mariana
A word of this:—What, ho! within! come forth!

Re-enter MARIANA.

I pray you, be acquainted with this maid;
She comes to do you good.
 Ifab.   I do defire the like.
 Duke. Do you perfuade yourfelf that I refpect you?
 Mari. Good friar, I know you do; and have found it.
 Duke. Take then this your companion by the hand,
Who hath a ftory ready for your ear:
I fhall attend your leifure; but make hafte;
The vaporous night approaches.
 Mari.   Will't pleafe you walk afide?
      [*Exeunt* MARIANA *and* ISABELLA.
 Duke. O place and greatnefs, millions of falfe eyes
Are ftuck upon thee! volumes of report
Run with thefe falfe and moft contrarious quefts
Upon thy doings! thoufand 'fcapes of wit
Make thee the father of their idle dream,
And rack thee in their fancies!—Welcome! How agreed?

Re-enter MARIANA *and* ISABELLA.

 Ifab. She'll take the enterprize upon her, father,
If you advife it.
 Duke.   It is not my confent,
But my intreaty too.
 Ifab.   Little have you to fay,
When you depart from him, but, foft and low,
Remember now my brother.
 Mari.   Fear me not.
 Duke. Nor, gentle daughter, fear you not at all:

He

He is your hufband on a pre-contráct :
To bring you thus together, 'tis no fin ;
Sith that the juftice of your.title to him
Doth flourifh the deceit. Come, let us go ;
Our corn's to reap, for yet our tithe's to fow. [*Exeunt.*

SCENE II.

A Room in the Prifon.

Enter Provoft *and* Clown.

Prov. Come hither, firrah : Can you cut off a man's head ?

Clo. If the man be a bachelor, fir, I can : but if he be a married man, he is his wife's head, and I can never cut off a woman's head.

Prov. Come, fir, leave me your fnatches, and yield me a direct anfwer. To-morrow morning are to die Claudio and Barnardine : Here is in our prifon a common executioner, who in his office lacks a helper : if you will take it on you to affift him, it fhall redeem you from your gyves; if not, you fhall have your full time of imprifonment, and your deliverance with an unpitied whipping ; for you have been a notorious bawd.

Clo. Sir, I have been an unlawful bawd, time out of mind ; but yet I will be content to be a lawful hangman. I would be glad to receive fome inftruction from my fellow partner.

Prov. What ho, Abhorfon ! Where's Abhorfon, there?

Enter ABHORSON.

Abhor. Do you call, fir ?

Prov.

Prov. Sirrah, here's a fellow will help you to-m
in your execution : If you think it meet, compound
him by the year, and let him abide here with you ; if
ufe him for the prefent, and difmifs him: He ca
plead his eftimation with you ; he hath been a bawd.

Abhor. A bawd, fir? Fie upon him, he will dif
our myftery.

Prov. Go to, fir; you weigh equally; a feather
turn the fcale.   [E

Clo. Pray, fir, by your good favour, (for, furely, fir,
good favour you have, but that you have a hanging look,)
do you call, fir, your occupation a myftery?

Abhor. Ay, fir; a myftery.

Clo. Painting, fir, I have heard fay, is a myftery; and
your whores, fir, being members of my occupation, ufing
painting, do prove my occupation a myftery: but what
myftery there fhould be in hanging, if I fhould be hang'd,
I cannot imagine.

Abhor. Sir, it is a myftery.

Clo. Proof.

Abhor. Every true man's apparel fits your thief: If it
be too little for your thief, your true man thinks it big
enough; if it be too big for your thief, your thief thinks
it little enough: fo every true man's apparel fits your
thief.

Re-enter Provoft.

Prov. Are you agreed?

Clo. Sir, I will ferve him; for I do find, your hangman
is a more penitent trade than your bawd; he doth oftner
afk forgivenefs.

Prov. You, firrah, provide your block and your axe,
o-morrow four o'clock.

Abhor.

Abhor. Come on, bawd; I will inftruct thee in my trade; follow.

Clo. I do defire to learn, fir; and, I hope, if you have occafion to ufe me for your own turn, you fhall find me yare: for, truly fir, for your kindnefs, I owe you a good turn.

Prov. Call hither Barnardine and Claudio:

[*Exeunt* Clown *and* ABHORSON.

One has my pity; not a jot the other,
Being a murderer, though he were my brother.

Enter CLAUDIO.

Look, here's the warrant, Claudio, for thy death:
'Tis now dead midnight, and by eight to-morrow
Thou muft be made immortal. Where's Barnardine?

Claud. As faft lock'd up in fleep, as guiltlefs labour
When it lies ftarkly in the traveller's bones:
He will not wake.

Prov.   Who can do good on him?
Well, go, prepare yourfelf. But hark, what noife?

[*Knocking within.*

Heaven give your fpirits comfort! [*Exit* CLAUDIO.] By
     and by:—
I hope it is fome pardon, or reprieve,
For the moft gentle Claudio.—Welcome, father.

Enter Duke.

Duke. The beft and wholefomeft fpirits of the night
Envelop you, good Provoft! Who call'd here of late?

Prov. None, fince the curfew rung.

Duke.   Not Ifabel?

Prov. No.

3   Duke.

Duke.   They will then, ere't be long.

Prov. What comfort is for Claudio?

Duke.   There's some in hope.

Prov. It is a bitter deputy.

Duke. Not so, not so; his life is parallel'd
Even with the stroke and line of his great justice;
He doth with holy abstinence subdue
That in himself, which he spurs on his power
To qualify in others: were he meal'd
With that which he corrects, then were he tyrannous;
But this being so, he's just.—Now are they come.—

          [*Knocking within.*—Provost *goes out.*

This is a gentle provost: Seldom, when
The steeled gaoler is the friend of men.—
How now? What noise? That spirit's possess'd with
          haste,
That wounds the unsisting postern with these strokes.

          Provost *returns, speaking to one at the door.*

Prov. There he must stay, until the officer
Arise to let him in; he is call'd up.

Duke. Have you no countermand for Claudio yet,
But he must die to-morrow?

Prov.   None, sir, none.

Duke. As near the dawning, Provost, as it is,
You shall hear more ere morning.

Prov.   Happily,
You something know; yet, I believe, there comes
No countermand; no such example have we:
Besides, upon the very siege of justice,
Lord Angelo hath to the publick ear
Profess'd the contrary.

                              Ente

Enter a Meſſenger.

Duke. This is his lordſhip's man.

Prov. And here comes Claudio's pardon.

Meſſ. My lord hath ſent you this note ; and by me this further charge, that you ſwerve not from the ſmalleſt ar-ticle of it, neither in time, matter, or other circumſtance. Good morrow ; for, as I take it, it is almoſt day.

Prov. I ſhall obey him.   [*Exit* Meſſenger.

Duke. This is his pardon; purchas'd by ſuch ſin, [*Aſide.*
For which the pardoner himſelf is in :
Hence hath offence his quick celerity,
When it is borne in high authority :
When vice makes mercy, mercy's ſo extended,
That for the fault's love, is the offender friended.—
Now, ſir, what news ?

Prov. I told you : Lord Angelo, be-like, thinking me remiſs in mine office, awakens me with this unwonted putting on : methinks, ſtrangely ; for he hath not uſed it before.

Duke. Pray you, let's hear.

Prov. [Reads.] *Whatſoever you may bear to the contrary, let Claudio be executed by four of the clock ; and, in the after-noon, Barnardine : for my better ſatisfaction, let me have Claudio's head ſent me by five. Let this be duly perform'd; with a thought, that more depends on it than we muſt yet de-liver. Thus fail not to do your office, as you will anſwer it at your peril.*
What ſay you to this, ſir ?

Duke. What is that Barnardine, who is to be executed in the afternoon?

Prov. A Bohemian born ; but here nurſed up and bred : one that is a priſoner nine years old.

F   *Duke.*

Duke. How came it, that the abfent duke had not either deliver'd him to his liberty, or executed him? I have heard, it was ever his manner to do fo.

Prov. His friends ftill wrought reprieves for him : And, indeed, his fact, till now in the government of lord Angelo, came not to an undoubtful proof.

Duke. Is it now apparent?

Prov. Moft manifeft, and not denied by himfelf.

Duke. Hath he borne himfelf penitently in prifon? How feems he to be touch'd?

Prov. A man that apprehends death no more dreadfully, but as a drunken fleep; carelefs, recklefs, and fearlefs of what's paft, prefent, or to come; infenfible of mortality, and defperately mortal.

Duke. He wants advice.

Prov. He will hear none: he hath evermore had the liberty of the prifon; give him leave to efcape hence, he would not: drunk many times a day, if not many days entirely drunk. We have very often awaked him, as if to carry him to execution, and fhow'd him a feeming warrant for it: it hath not moved him at all.

Duke. More of him anon. There is written in your brow, Provoft, honefty and conftancy: if I read it not truly, my ancient fkill beguiles me; but in the boldnefs of my cunning, I will lay myfelf in hazard. Claudio, whom here you have a warrant to execute, is no greater forfeit to the law than Angelo who hath fentenced him: To make you underftand this in a manifefted effect, I crave but four days refpite; for the which you are to do me both a prefent and a dangerous courtefy.

Prov. Pray, fir, in what?

Duke. In the delaying death.

Prov. Alack! how may I do it? having the hour limited; and an exprefs command, under penalty, to deliver

liver his head in the view of Angelo? I may make my
cafe as Claudio's, to crofs this in the fmalleft.

Duke. By the vow of mine order, I warrant you, if my
inftructions may be your guide. Let this Barnardine be
this morning executed, and his head borne to Angelo.

Prov. Angelo hath feen them both, and will difcover
the favour.

Duke. O, death's a great difguifer: and you may add
to it. Shave the head, and tie the beard; and fay, it
was the defire of the penitent to be fo bared before his
death: You know, the courfe is common. If any thing
fall to you upon this, more than thanks and good fortune,
by the faint whom I profefs, I will plead againft it with
my life.

Prov. Pardon me, good father; it is againft my oath.

Duke. Were you fworn to the duke, or to the deputy?

Prov. To him, and to his fubftitutes.

Duke. You will think you have made no offence, if the
duke avouch the juftice of your dealing?

Prov. But what likelihood is in that?

Duke. Not a refemblance, but a certainty. Yet fince I
fee you fearful, that neither my coat, integrity, nor my
perfuafion, can with eafe attempt you, I will go further
than I meant, to pluck all fears out of you. Look you,
fir, here is the hand and feal of the duke. You know
the character, I doubt not; and the fignet is not ftrange
to you.

Prov. I know them both.

Duke. The contents of this is the return of the duke;
you fhall anon over-read it at your pleafure; where you
fhall find, within thefe two days he will be here. This
is a thing, that Angelo knows not: for he this very day
receives letters of ftrange tenor; perchance, of the duke's
death; perchance, entering into fome monaftery; but,

by

by chance, nothing of what is writ. Look, the unfold-
ing ftar calls up the fhepherd : Put not yourfelf into amazement, how thefe things fhould be : all difficulties are but
eafy when they are known. Call your executioner, and
off with Barnardine's head : I will give him a prefent
fhrift, and advife him for a better place. Yet you are
amazed; but this fhall abfolutely refolve you. Come
away; it is almoft clear dawn. [*Exeunt.*

SCENE II.

Another Room in the fame.

Enter Clown.

Clo. I am as well acquainted here, as I was in our houfe
of profeffion : one would think, it were miftrefs Over-
done's own houfe, for here be many of her old cuftomers.
Firft, here's young mafter Rafh; he's in for a commodity
of brown paper and old ginger, ninefcore and feventeen
pounds; of which he made five marks, ready money:
marry, then, ginger was not much in requeft, for
the old women were all dead. Then is there here one
mafter Caper, at the fuit of mafter Three-pile the mercer,
for fome four fuits of peach-colour'd fatin, which now
peaches him a beggar. Then have we here young Dizy,
and young mafter Deep-vow, and mafter Copper-fpur,
and mafter Starve-lacky the rapier and dagger-man, and
young Drop-heir that kill'd lufty Pudding, and mafter
Forthright the tilter, and brave mafter Shoe-tye the great
traveller, and wild Half-can that ftabb'd Pots, and, I
think, forty more ; all great doers in our trade, and are
now for the Lord's fake.

Enter

Enter ABHORSON.

Abbor. Sirrah, bring Barnardine hither.

Clo. Mafter Barnardine! you muft rife and be hang'd, mafter Barnardine!

Abbor. What, ho, Barnardine!

Barnar. [*Within.*] A pox o' your throats! Who makes that noife there? What are you?

Clo. Your friends, fir; the hangman: You muft be fo good, fir, to rife and be put to death.

Barnar. [*Within.*] Away, you rogue, away; I am fleepy.

Abbor. Tell him, he muft awake, and that quickly too.

Clo. Pray, mafter Barnardine, awake till you are exe-cuted, and fleep afterwards.

Abbor. Go in to him, and fetch him out.

Clo. He is coming, fir, he is coming: I hear his ftraw ruftle.

Enter BARNARDINE.

Abbor. Is the axe upon the block, firrah?

Clo. Very ready, fir.

Barnar. How now, Abhorfon? what's the news with you?

Abbor. Truly, fir, I would defire you to clap into your prayers; for, look you, the warrant's come.

Barnar. You rogue, I have been drinking all night, I am not fitted for't.

Clo. O, the better, fir; for he that drinks all night, and is hang'd betimes in the morning, may fleep the founder all the next day.

Enter Duke.

Abhor. Look you, fir, here comes your ghoftly father;
Do we jeft now, think you?

Duke. Sir, induced by my charity, and hearing how
haftily you are to depart, I am come to advife you, comfort you, and pray with you.

Barnar. Friar, not I; I have been drinking hard all
night, and I will have more time to prepare me, or they
fhall beat out my brains with billets : I will not confent
to die this day, that's certain.

Duke. O, fir, you muft : and therefore, I befeech you,
Look forward on the journey you fhall go.

Barnar. I fwear, I will not die to-day for any man's
perfuafion.

Duke. But hear you,——

Barnar. Not a word; if you have any thing to fay to
me, come to my ward; for thence will not I to-day.

[*Exit.*

Enter Provoft.

Duke. Unfit to live, or die : O, gravel heart!——
After him, fellows; bring him to the block.

[*Exeunt* ABHORSON *and* Clown.

Prov. Now, fir, how do you find the prifoner?

Duke. A creature unprepar'd, unmeet for death;
And, to tranfport him in the mind he is,
Were damnable.

Prov.   Here in the prifon, father,
There died this morning of a cruel fever
One Ragozine, a moft notorious pirate,
A man of Claudio's years; his beard, and head,

Juft

Juſt of his colour: What if we do omit
This reprobate, till he were well inclin'd;
And ſatisfy the deputy with the viſage
Of Ragozine, more like to Claudio?

 Duke. O, 'tis an accident that heaven provides!
Deſpatch it preſently; the hour draws on
Prefix'd by Angelo: See, this be done,
And ſent according to command; whiles I
Perſuade this rude wretch willingly to die.

 Prov. This ſhall be done, good father, preſently.
But Barnardine muſt die this afternoon:
And how ſhall we continue Claudio,
To ſave me from the danger that might come,
If he were known alive?

 Duke. Let this be done;—Puf them in ſecret holds,
Both Barnardine and Claudio: Ere twice
The ſun hath made his journal greeting to
The under generation, you ſhall find
Your ſafety manifeſted.

 Prov. I am your free dependant.

 Duke.   Quick, deſpatch,
And ſend the head to Angelo.   [*Exit* Provoſt.
Now will I write letters to Angelo,—
The provoſt, he ſhall bear them,—whoſe contents
Shall witneſs to him, I am near at home;
And that, by great injunĉtions, I am bound
To enter publickly: him I'll deſire
To meet me at the conſecrated fount,
A league below the city; and from thence,
By cold gradation and weal-balanced form,
We ſhall proceed with Angelo.

Re-enter Provoſt.

Prov. Here is the head; I'll carry it myſelf.

Duke. Convenient is it: Make a ſwift return;
For I would commune with you of ſuch things,
That want no ear but yours.

Prov.   I'll make all ſpeed.   [*Exit.*

Iſab. [*Within.*] Peace, ho, be here!

Duke. The tongue of Iſabel:—She's come to know,
If yet her brother's pardon be come hither:
But I will keep her ignorant of her good,
To make her heavenly comforts of deſpair,
When it is leaſt expected.

Enter ISABELLA.

Iſab. Ho, by your leave.

Duke. Good morning to you, fair and gracious daugh.
ter.

Iſab. The better, given me by ſo holy a man.
Hath yet the deputy ſent my brother's pardon?

Duke. He hath releas'd him, Iſabel, from the world;
His head is off, and ſent to Angelo.

Iſab. Nay, but it is not ſo.

Duke.   It is no other:
Show your wiſdom, daughter, in your cloſe patience.

Iſab. O, I will to him, and pluck out his eyes.

Duke. You ſhall not be admitted to his ſight.

Iſab. Unhappy Claudio! Wretched Iſabel!
Injurious world! Moſt damned Angelo!

Duke. This nor hurts him, nor profits you a jot:
Forbear it therefore; give your cauſe to heaven.
Mark what I ſay; which you ſhall find,

B5

By every fyllable, a faithful verity :
The duke comes home to-morrow ;—nay, dry your eyes ;
One of our convent, and his confeffor,
Gives me this inftance: Already he hath carried
Notice to Efcalus and Angelo ;
Who do prepare to meet him at the gates,
There to give up their power. If you can, pace your wifdom
In that good path that I would wifh it go ;
And you fhall have your bofom on this wretch,
Grace of the duke, revenges to your heart,
And general honour.

     Ifab.   I am directed by you.

     Duke. This letter then to friar Peter give ;
'Tis he that fent me of the duke's return :
Say, by this token, I defire his company
At Mariana's houfe to-night. Her caufe, and yours,
I'll perfect him withal ; and he fhall bring you
Before the duke ; and to the head of Angelo
Accufe him home, and home. For my poor felf,
I am combined by a facred vow,
And fhall be abfent. Wend you with this letter :
Command thefe fretting waters from your eyes
With a light heart ; truft not my holy order,
If I pervert your courfe.—Who's here ?

Enter LUCIO.

     Lucio.   **Good even!**
Friar, where is the Provoft ?

     Duke.   Not within, fir.

     Lucio. O, pretty Ifabella, I am pale at mine heart, to
fee thine eyes fo red : thou muft be patient : I am fain to
dine and fup with water and bran ; I dare not for my
head fill my belly ; one fruitful meal would fet me to't :
                                           But

But they fay the duke will be here to-morrow. By my
troth, Ifabel, I lov'd thy brother: if the old fantaftical
duke of dark corners had been at home, he had lived.

                                     [*Exit* ISABELLA.

   Duke. Sir, the duke is marvellous little beholden to
your reports; but the beft is, he lives not in them.

   Lucio. Friar, thou knoweft not the duke fo well as I
do: he's a better woodman than thou takeft him for.

   Duke. Well, you'll anfwer this one day. Fare ye well.

   Lucio. Nay, tarry; I'll go along with thee; I can tell
thee pretty tales of the duke.

   Duke. You have told me too many of him already, fir,
if they be true; if not true, none were enough.

   Lucio. I was once before him for getting a wench with
child.

   Duke. Did you fuch a thing?

   Lucio. Yes, marry, did I: but was fain to forfwear it;
they would elfe have married me to the rotten medlar.

   Duke. Sir, your company is fairer than honeft: Reft
you well.

   Lucio. By my troth, I'll go with thee to the lane's end:
If bawdy talk offend you, we'll have very little of it: Nay,
friar, I am a kind of burr, I fhall ftick.   [*Exeunt.*

SCENE IV.

A Room in Angelo's *Houfe.*

Enter ANGELO *and* ESCALUS.

   Efcal. Every letter he hath writ hath difvouch'd other.

   Ang. In moft uneven and diftracted manner. His
actions fhow much like to madnefs: pray heaven, his
                                    wifdom

wifdom be not tainted! And why meet him at the gates,
and re-deliver our authorities there?

Efcal. I guefs not.

Ang. And why fhould we proclaim it in an hour before
his entering, that, if any crave redrefs of injuftice, they
fhould exhibit their petitions in the ftreet?

Efcal. He fhows his reafon for that: to have a defpatch
of complaints; and to deliver us from devices hereafter,
which fhall then have no power to ftand againft us.

Ang. Well, I befeech you, let it be proclaim'd:
Betimes i' the morn, I'll call you at your houfe:
Give notice to fuch men of fort and fuit,
As are to meet him.

Efcal.   I fhall, fir: fare you well.   [*Exit.*

Ang. Good night.—
This deed unfhapes me quite, makes me unpregnant,
And dull to all proceedings. A deflower'd maid!
And by an eminent body, that enforc'd
The law againft it!—But that her tender fhame
Will not proclaim againft her maiden lofs,
How might fhe tongue me? Yet reafon dares her?—no:
For my authority bears a credent bulk,
That no particular fcandal once can touch,
But it confounds the breather. He fhould have liv'd,
Save that his riotous youth, with dangerous fenfe,
Might, in the times to come, have ta'en revenge,
By fo receiving a difhonour'd life,
With ranfom of fuch fhame. 'Would yet he had liv'd!
Alack, when once our grace we have forgot,
Nothing goes right; we would, and we would not. [*Exit.*

SCENE

SCENE·V.

Fields without the Town.

Enter Duke *in his own habit, and Friar* PETER.

Duke. Thefe letters at fit time deliver me.

                           [*Giving letters.*

The provoſt knows our purpofe, and our plot.
The matter being afoot, keep your inſtruction,
And hold you ever to our ſpecial drift;
Though fometimes you do blench from this to that,
As caufe doth miniſter. Go, call at Flavius' houfe,
And tell him where I ſtay: give the like notice,
To Valentinus, Rowland, and to Craſſus,
And bid them bring the trumpets to the gate;
But fend me Flavius firſt.

    F. Peter.   It ſhall be fpeeded well.

                              [*Exit* Friar.

Enter VARRIUS.

  · *Duke.* I thank thee, Varrius; thou haſt made good
        haſte:
Come, we will walk: There's other of our friends
Will greet us here anon, my gentle Varrius.   [*Exeunt.*

SCENE VI.

Street near the City Gate.

Enter ISABELLA *and* MARIANA.

Isab. To speak so indirectly, I am loth;
I would say the truth; but to accuse him so,
That is your part: yet I'm advis'd to do it;
He says, to veil full purpose.
 Mari.   Be rul'd by him.
 Isab. Besides, he tells me, that, if peradventure
He speak against me on the adverse side,
I should not think it strange; for 'tis a physick,
That's bitter to sweet end.
 Mari. I would, friar Peter—
 Isab.   O, peace; the friar is come.

Enter Friar PETER.

 F. Peter. Come, I have found you out a stand most fit,
Where you may have such vantage on the duke,
He shall not pass you: Twice have the trumpets sounded;
The generous and gravest citizens
Have hent the gates, and very near upon
The duke is ent'ring; therefore hence, away.   [*Exeunt.*

            ACT

ACT V.   SCENE I.

A publick Place near the City Gate.

MARIANA *(veil'd)*, ISABELLA, *and* PETER, *at a distance.*
Enter at opposite doors, Duke, VARRIUS, Lords; AN-
GELO, ESCALUS, LUCIO, Provost, Officers, *and*
Citizens.

Duke. My very worthy cousin, fairly met :—
Our old and faithful friend, we are glad to see you.
Ang. and Escal. Happy return be to your royal grace!
Duke. Many and hearty thankings to you both.
We have made inquiry of you; and we hear
Such goodness of your justice, that our soul
Cannot but yield you forth to publick thanks,
Fo e-running more requital.
Ang.   You make my bonds still greater.
Duke. O, your desert speaks loud; and I should wrong it,
To lock it in the wards of covert bosom,
When it deserves with characters of brass
A forted residence, 'gainst the tooth of time,
And razure of oblivion : Give me your hand,
And let the subject see, to make them know
That outward courtesies would fain proclaim
Favours that keep within.—Come, Escalus ;
You must walk by us on our other hand ;—
And good supporters are you.

PETER *and* ISABELLA *come forward,*

F. Peter. Now is your time; speak loud, and kneel
  before him.

                                        Isab.

Isab. Juftice, O royal Duke! Vail your regard
Upon a wrong'd, I'd fain have faid, a maid!
O worthy prince, difhonour not your eye
By throwing it on any other objeft,
Till you have heard me in my true complaint,
And given me juftice, juftice, juftice, juftice!

   Duke. Relate your wrongs: In what? By whom? Be
       brief:
Here is lord Angelo fhall give you juftice;
Reveal yourfelf to him.

   Isab.   O, worthy duke,
You bid me feek redemption of the devil:
Hear me yourfelf; for that which I muft fpeak
Muft either punifh me, not being believ'd,
Or wring redrefs from you: hear me, O, hear me, here.

   Ang. My lord, her wits, I fear me, are not firm:
She hath been a fuitor to me for her brother,
Cut off by courfe of juftice.

   Isab.   By courfe of juftice!

   Ang. And fhe will fpeak moft bitterly, and ftrange.

   Isab. Moft ftrange, but yet moft truly, will I fpeak:
That Angelo's forfworn; is it not ftrange?
That Angelo's a murderer; is't not ftrange?
That Angelo is an adulterous thief,
An hypocrite, a virgin-violator;
Is it not ftrange, and ftrange?

   Duke.   Nay, it is ten times ftrange.

   Isab. It is not truer he is Angelo,
Than this is all as true as it is ftrange:
Nay, it is ten times true; for truth is truth
To the end of reckoning.

   Duke.   Away with her:—Poor foul,
She fpeaks this in the infirmity of fenfe.

   Isab. O prince, I cónjure thee, as thou believ'ft

      6   **There**

There is another comfort than this world,
That thou negle&ct; me not, with that opinion
That I am touch'd with madne&s;: make not impo&ffible; ,
That which but &seems; unlike: 'tis not impo&ffible;,
But one, the wicked'&ft; caitiff on the ground,
May &seem; as ­, as grave, as ju&ft;, as ab&solute;,
As Angelo; even &so; may Angelo,
In all his dre&ffings;, chara&cts;, titles, forms,
Be an arch-villain: believe it, royal prince,
If he be le&fs;, he's nothing; but he's more,
Had I more name for badne&fs;.

 Duke.   By mine hone&fty;,
If &she; be mad, (as I believe no other,)
Her madne&fs; hath the odde&ft; frame of &sense;,
Such a dependency of thing on thing,
As e'er I heard in madne&fs;.

 I&sab;.   O, gracious duke,
Harp not on that; nor do not bani&sh; rea&son;
For inequality: but let your rea&son; &serve;
To make the truth appear, where it &seems; hid;
And hide the fal&se;, &seems; true.

 Duke.   Many that are not mad,
Have, &sure;, more lack of rea&son;.—What would you &say;?

 I&sab;. I am the &sister; of one Claudio,
Condemn'd upon the a&ct; of fornication
To lo&se; his head; condemn'd by Angelo:
I, in probation of a &sisterhood;,
Was &sent; to by my brother: One Lucio
As then the me&ffenger;;—

 Lucio.   That's I, an't like your grace:
I came to her from Claudio, and de&sir'd; her
To try her gracious fortune with lord Angelo,
For her poor brother's pardon.

 I&sab;.   That's he, indeed.

           Duke.

Duke. You were not bid to fpeak.

Lucio.   No, my good lord;
Nor wifh'd to hold my peace.

Duke.   I wifh you now then;
Pray you, take note of it: and when you have
A bufinefs for yourfelf, pray heaven, you then
Be perfect.

Lucio.   I warrant your honour.

Duke. The warrant's for yourfelf; take heed to it.

Ifab. This gentleman told fomewhat of my tale.

Lucio. Right.

Duke. It may be right; but you are in the wrong
To fpeak before your time.—Proceed.

Ifab.   I went
To this pernicious caitiff deputy.

Duke. That's fomewhat madly fpoken.

Ifab.   Pardon it;
The phrafe is to the matter.

Duke. Mended again: the matter;—Proceed.

Ifab. In brief,—to fet the needlefs procefs by,
How I perfuaded, how I pray'd, and kneel'd,
How he refell'd me, and how I reply'd;
(For this was of much length,) the vile conclufion
I now begin with grief and fhame to utter:
He would not, but by gift of my chafte body
To his concupifcible intemperate luft,
Releafe my brother; and, after much debatement,
My fifterly remorfe confutes mine honour,
And I did yield to him: But the next morn betimes,
His purpofe furfeiting, he fends a warrant
For my poor brother's head.

Duke.   This is moft likely!

Ifab. O, that it were as like, as it is true!

                         G   *Duke.*

Duke. By heaven, fond wretch, thou know'ft not what
        thou fpeak'ft ;
Or elfe thou art fuborn'd againft his honour,
In hateful practice : Firft, his integrity
Stands without blemifh :—next, it imports no reafon,
That with fuch vehemency he fhould purfue
Faults proper to himfelf : if he had fo offended,
He would have weigh'd thy brother by himfelf,
And not have cut him off : Some one hath fet you on ;
Confefs the truth, and fay by whofe advice
Thou cam'ft here to complain.

     Ifab.   And is this all ?
Then, oh, you bleffed minifters above,
Keep me in patience ; and, with ripen'd time,
Unfold the evil which is here wrapt up
In countenance !—Heaven fhield your grace from woe,
As I, thus wrong'd, hence unbelieved go !

     Duke. I know, yon'd fain be gone :—An officer !
To prifon with her :—Shall we thus permit
A blafting and a fcandalous breath to fall
On him fo near us ? This needs muft be a practice.
—Who knew of your intent and coming hither ?

     Ifab. One that I would were here, friar Lodowick.

     Duke. A ghoftly father, belike :—Who knows that
        Lodowick ?

     Lucio. My lord, I know him ; 'tis a medling friar ;
I do not like the man : had he been lay, my lord,
For certain words he fpake againft your grace
In your retirement, I had fwing'd him foundly.

     Duke. Words againft me ? This' a good friar, belike !
And to fet on this wretched woman here
Againft our fubftitute !—Let this friar be found.

     Lucio. But yefternight, my lord, fhe and that friar

                                       I faw

I faw them at the prifon: a fawcy friar,
A very fcurvy fellow.

    F. Peter.   Bleffed be your royal grace!
I have ftood by, my lord, and I have heard
Your royal ear abus'd: Firft, hath this woman
Moft wrongfully accus'd your fubftitute;
Who is as free from touch or foil with her,
As fhe from one ungot.

    Duke.   We did believe no lefs.
Know you the friar Lodowick, that fhe fpeaks of?

    F. Peter. I know him for a man divine and holy;
Not fcurvy, nor a temporary medler,
As he's reported by this gentleman;
And, on my truft, a man that never yet
Did, as he vouches, mifreport your grace.

    Lucio. My lord, moft villainoufly; believe it.

    F. Peter. Well, he in time may come to clear himfelf;
But at this inftant he is fick, my lord,
Of a ftrange fever: Upon his mere requeft,
(Being come to knowledge that there was complaint
Intended 'gainft lord Angelo,) came I hither,
To fpeak, as from his mouth, what he doth know
Is true, and falfe; and what he with his oath,
And all probation, will make up full clear,
Whenfoever he's convented. Firft, for this woman;
(To juftify this worthy nobleman,
So vulgarly and perfonally accus'd,)
Her fhall you hear difproved to her eyes,
Till fhe herfelf confefs it.

    Duke.   Good friar, let's hear it.
      [ISABELLA *is carried off, guarded; and* MARIANA
          comes forward.
Do you not fmile at this, lord Angelo?—
O heaven! the vanity of wretched fools!—

               Give

Give us fome feats.—Come, coufin Angelo;
In this I'll be impartial; be you judge
Of your own caufe.—Is this the witnefs, friar?
Firft, let her fhow her face; and, after, fpeak.

   Mari. Pardon, my lord; I will not fhow my face,
Until my hufband bid me.

   Duke.   What, are you married?

   Mari. No, my lord.

   Duke.   Are you a maid?

   Mari.   No, my lord.

   Duke. A widow then?

   Mari.   Neither, my lord.

   Duke.   Why, you
Are nothing then:—Neither maid, widow, nor wife?

   Lucio. My lord, fhe may be a punk; for many of them
are neither maid, widow, nor wife.

   Duke. Silence that fellow: I would, he had fome caufe
To prattle for himfelf.

   Lucio. Well, my lord.

   Mari. My lord, I do confefs I ne'er was married;
And, I confefs, befides, I am no maid:
I have known my hufband; yet my hufband knows not,
That ever he knew me.

   Lucio. He was drunk then, my lord; it can be no better.

   Duke. For the benefit of filence, 'would thou wert fo
too.

   Lucio. Well, my lord.

   Duke. This is no witnefs for lord Angelo.

   Mari. Now I come to't, my lord:
She, that accufes him of fornication,
In felf-fame manner doth accufe my hufband;
And charges him, my lord, with fuch a time,

When

When I'll depofe I had him in mine arms,
With all the effect of love.

Ang.   Charges fhe more than me?

Mari. Not that I know.

Duke.   No? you fay, your hufband.

Mari. Why, juft, my lord, and that is Angelo,
Who thinks, he knows, that he ne'er knew my body,
But knows, he thinks, that he knows Ifabel's.

Ang. This is a ftrange abufe:—Let's fee thy face.

Mari. My hufband bids me; now I will unmafk.

                                      [*Unveiling.*

This is that face, thou cruel Angelo,
Which, once thou 'fwor'ft, was worth the looking on:
This is the hand, which, with a vow'd contract,
Was faft belock'd in thine: this is the body
That took away the match from Ifabel,
And did fupply thee at thy garden-houfe,
In her imagin'd perfon.

Duke.   Know you this woman?

Lucio. Carnally, fhe fays.

Duke.   Sirrah, no more.

Lucio. Enough, my lord.

Ang. My lord, I muft confefs, I know this woman;
And, five years fince, there was fome fpeech of marriage
Betwixt myfelf and her: which was broke off,
Partly, for that her promifed proportions
Came fhort of compofition; but, in chief,
For that her reputation was difvalued
     levity: fince which time, of five years,
     ever fpake with her, faw her, nor heard from her,
  pon my faith and honour.

Mari.   Noble prince,
As there comes light from heaven, and words from breath,
As there is fenfe in truth, and truth in virtue,

                    G 3   I am

I am affianc'd this man's wife, as ſtrongly
As words could make up vows: and, my good lord,
But Tueſday night laſt gone, in his garden-houſe,
He knew me as a wife: As this is true,
Let me in ſafety raiſe me from my knees;
Or elſe for ever be confixed here,
A marble monument!

    Ang.   I did but ſmile till now;
Now, good my lord, give me the ſcope of juſtice;
My patience here is touch'd: I do perceive,
Theſe poor informal women are no more
But inſtruments of ſome more mightier member,
That ſets them on: Let me have way, my lord,
To find this practice out.

    Duke.   Ay, with my heart;
And puniſh them unto your height of pleaſure.—
Thou fooliſh friar; and thou pernicious woman,
Compáct with her that's gone! think'ſt thou, thy oaths,
Though they would ſwear down each particular ſaint,
Were teſtimonies againſt his worth and credit,
That's ſeal'd in approbation?—You, lord Eſcalus,
Sit with my couſin; lend him your kind pains
To find out this abuſe, whence 'tis deriv'd.—
There is another friar that ſet them on;
Let him be ſent for.

    F. Peter. Would he were here, my lord; for he, indeed,
Hath ſet the women on to this complaint:
Your provoſt knows the place where he abides,
And he may fetch him.

    Duke. Go, do it inſtantly.—   [*Exit* Provoſt.
And you, my noble and well-warranted couſin,
Whom it concerns to hear this matter forth,
Do with your injuries as ſeems you beſt,
In any chaſtiſement: I for a while

                                 Will

ill leave you; but ſtir not you, till you have well
etermined upon theſe ſlanderers.

Eſcal. My lord, we'll do it thoroughly.—[*Exit* Duke.]
Signior Lucio, did not you ſay, you knew that friar Lodowick to be a diſhoneſt perſon?

Lucio. Cucullus non facit monachum : honeſt in nothing,
but in his clothes; and one that hath ſpoke moſt villainous ſpeeches of the duke.

Eſcal. We ſhall entreat you to abide here till he come,
and enforce them againſt him: we ſhall find this friar a
notable fellow.

Lucio. As any in Vienna, on my word.

Eſcal. Call that ſame Iſabel here once again; [*To an
Attendant.*] I would ſpeak with her: Pray you, my lord,
give me leave to queſtion; you ſhall ſee how I'll handle
her.

Lucio. Not better than he, by her own report.

Eſcal. Say you?

Lucio. Marry, ſir, I think, if you handled her pri-
vately, ſhe would ſooner confeſs; perchance, publickly
ſhe'll be aſhamed.

Re-enter Officers, *with* ISABELLA; *the* Duke, *in the
Friar's habit, and* Provoſt.

Eſcal. I will go darkly to work with her.

Lucio. That's the way; for women are light at midnight.

Eſcal. Come on, miſtreſs; [*To* ISABELLA.] here's a
gentlewoman denies all that you have ſaid.

Lucio My lord, here comes the raſcal I ſpoke of; here
with the provoſt.

Eſcal. In very good time :—ſpeak not you to him, till
we call upon you.

G 4

Lucio.

Lucio. Mum.

Escal. Come, fir: Did you fet this woman on to flander lord Angelo? they have confefs'd you did.

Duke. 'Tis falfe.

Escal. How! know you where you are?

Duke. Refpect to your great place! and let the devil Be fometime honour'd for his burning throne:—— Where is the duke? 'tis he fhould hear me fpeak.

Escal. The duke's in us; and we will hear you fpeak: Look, you fpeak juftly.

Duke.   Boldly, at leaft:—But, O, poor fouls, Come you to feek the lamb here of the fox? Good night to your redrefs. Is the duke gone? Then is your caufe gone too. The duke's unjuft, Thus to retort your manifeft appeal, And put your trial in the villain's mouth, Which here you come to accufe.

Lucio. This is the rafcal; this is he I fpoke of.

Escal. Why, thou unreverend and unhallow'd friar! Is't not enough, thou haft fuborn'd thefe women To accufe this worthy man; but, in foul mouth, And in the witnefs of his proper ear, To call him villain? And then to glance from him to the duke himfelf; To tax him with injuftice?—Take him hence; To the rack with him:—We'll touze you joint by joint, · But we will know this purpofe:—What! unjuft?

Duke. Be not fo hot; the duke Dare no more ftretch this finger of mine, than he Dare rack his own; his fubject am I not, Nor here provincial: My bufinefs in this ftate Made me a looker-on here in Vienna, Where I have feen corruption boil and bubble, Till it o'er-run the ftew: laws, for all faults;

            But

But faults fo countenanc'd, that the ftrong ftatutes
Stand like the forfeits in a barber's fhop,
As much in mock as mark.

Efcal. Slander to the ftate! Away with him to prifon.

Ang. What can you vouch againft him, fignior Lucio?
Is this the man that you did tell us of?

Lucio. 'Tis he, my lord. Come hither, goodman bald-
pate: Do you know me?

Duke. I remember you, fir, by the found of your voice:
I met you at the prifon, in the abfence of the duke.

Lucio. O, did you fo? And do you remember what you
faid of the duke?

Duke. Moft notedly, fir.

Lucio. Do you fo, fir? And was the duke a flefh-mon-
ger, a fool, and a coward, as you then reported him
to be?

Duke. You muft, fir, change perfons with me, ere you
make that my report: you, indeed, fpoke fo of him; and
much more, much worfe.

Lucio. O thou damnable fellow! Did not I pluck thee
by the nofe, for thy fpeeches?

Duke. I proteft, I love the duke, as I love myfelf.

Ang. Hark! how the villain would clofe now, after his
treafonable abufes.

Efcal. Such a fellow is not to be talk'd withal:—Away
with him to prifon:—Where is the provoft?—Away with
him to prifon; lay bolts enough upon him: let him fpeak
no more:—Away with thofe giglots too, and with the
other confederate companion.

               [*The* Provoft *lays hands on the* Duke.

Duke. Stay, fir; ftay a while.

Ang. What! refifts he? Help him, Lucio.

Lucio. Come, fir; come, fir; come, fir; foh, fir: Why,
you bald-pated, lying rafcal! you muft be hooded, muft

                         you?

you ? Show your knave's vifage, with a pox to you ! fhow
your fheep-biting face, and be hang'd an hour! Will't
not off ? [*Pulls off the friar's hood, and difcovers the* Duke.

Duke. Thou art the firft knave, that e'er made a duke.——
Firft, Provoft, let me bail thefe gentle three :——
Sneak not away, fir ; [*To* Lucio.] for the friar and you
Muft have a word anon :—lay hold on him.

Lucio. This may prove worfe than hanging.

Duke. What you have fpoke, I pardon; fit you down.——
                                              [*To* Escalus.
We'll borrow place of him :—Sir, by your leave :
                                              [*To* Angelo.
Haft thou or word, or wit, or impudence,
That yet can do thee office ? If thou haft,
Rely upon it till my tale be heard,
And hold no longer out.

Ang.   O my dread lord,
I fhould be guiltier than my guiltinefs,
To think I can be undifcernable,
When I perceive, your grace, like power divine,
Hath look'd upon my paffes : Then, good prince,
No longer feffion hold upon my fhame,
But let my trial be mine own confeffion ;
Immediate fentence then, and fequent death,
Is all the grace I beg.

Duke.   Come hither, Mariana :—
Say, waft thou e'er contracted to this woman ?

Ang. I was, my lord.

Duke. Go take her hence, and marry her inftantly.—
Do you the office, friar; which confummate,
Return him here again :—Go with him, Provoft.

     [*Exeunt* Angelo, Mariana, Peter, *and* Provoft.

Efcal My lord, I am more amaz'd at his difhonour,
Than at the ftrangenefs of it.

                                              Duke.

Duke.   Come hither, Ifabel;
Your friar is now your prince: As I was then
Advértifing, and holy to your bufinefs,
Not changing heart with habit, I am ftill
Attorney'd at your fervice.

Ifab.   O, give me pardon,
That I, your vaffal, have employ'd and pain'd
Your unknown fovereignty.

Duke.   You are pardon'd, Ifabel:
And now, dear maid, be you as free to us.
Your brother's death, I know, fits at your heart;
And you may marvel, why I obfcur'd myfelf,
Labouring to fave his life; and would not rather
Make rafh remonftrance of my hidden power,
Than let him fo be loft: O, moft kind maid,
It was the fwift celerity of his death,
Which I did think with flower foot came on,
That brain'd my purpofe: But, peace be with him!
That life is better life, paft fearing death,
Than that which lives to fear: make it your comfort,
So happy is your brother.

Re-enter ANGELO, MARIANA, PETER, *and* Provoft.

Ifab.   I do, my lord.
Duke. For this new-married man, approaching here,
Whofe falt imagination yet hath wrong'd
Your well-defended honour, you muft pardon
For Mariana's fake: but as he adjudg'd your brother,
(Being criminal, in double violation
Of facred chaftity, and of promife-breach,
Thereon dependant, for your brother's life,)
The very mercy of the law cries out
Moft audible, even from his proper tongue,

An'

An Angelo for Claudio, death for death.
Haſte ſtill pays haſte, and leiſure anſwers leiſure ;
Like doth quit like, and *Meaſure* ſtill *for Meaſure.*
Then, Angelo, thy fault's thus manifeſted ;
Which though thou would'ſt deny, denies thee vantage :
We do condemn thee to the very block
Where Claudio ſtoop'd to death, and·with like haſte ;—
Away with him.

    Mari.   O, my moſt gracious lord,
I hope you will not mock me with a huſband !

    Duke. It is your huſband mock'd you with a huſband :
Conſenting to the ſafeguard of your honour,
I thought your marriage fit ; elſe imputation,
For that he knew you, might reproach your life,
And choke your good to come : for his poſſeſſions,
Although by confiſcation they are ours,
We do inſtate and widow you withal,
To buy you a better huſband.

    Mari.   O, my dear lord,
I crave no other, nor no better man.

    Duke. Never crave him ; we are definitive.

    Mari. Gentle, my liege,—   [*Kneeling.*

    Duke.   You do but loſe your labour;
Away with him to death.—Now, ſir, [*To* LUCIO.] to you.

    Mari. O, my good lord !—Sweet Iſabel, take my part;
Lend me your knees, and all my life to come
I'll lend you, all my life to do you ſervice.

    Duke. Againſt all ſenſe you do impórtune her :
Should ſhe kneel down, in mercy of this fact,
Her brother's ghoſt his paved bed would break,
And take her hence in horror.

    Mari.   Iſabel,
Sweet Iſabel, do yet but kneel by me ;
Hold up your hands, ſay nothing, I'll ſpeak all.

                     They

They fay, beft men are moulded out of faults ;
And, for the moft, become much more the better
For being a little bad : fo may my hufband.
O, Ifabel ! will you not lend a knee ?
 Duke. He dies for Claudio's death.
 Ifab.   Moft bounteous fir,
              [*Kneeling.*

Look, if it pleafe you, on this man condemn'd,
As if my brother liv'd : I partly think,
A due fincerity govern'd his deeds,
Till he did look on me ; fince it is fo,
Let him not die : My brother had but juftice,
In that he did the thing for which he died :
For Angelo,
His act did not o'ertake his bad intent;
And muft be buried but as an intent
That perifh'd by the way : thoughts are no fubjects ;
Intents but merely thoughts.
 Mari.   Merely, my lord.
 Duke. Your fuit's unprofitable ; ftand up, I fay.—
I have bethought me of another fault :—
Provoft, how came it, Claudio was beheaded
At an unufual hour ?
 Prov.   It was commanded fo.
 Duke. Had you a fpecial warrant for the deed ?
 Prov. No, my good lord ; it was by private meffage.
 Duke. For which I do difcharge you of your office :
Give up your keys.
 Prov.   Pardon me, noble lord :
I thought it was a fault, but knew it not ;
Yet did repent me, after more advice :
For teftimony whereof, one in the prifon,
That fhould by private order elfe have died,
I have referv'd alive.
               , *Duke.*

Duke.   What's he ?

Prov.   His name is Barnardine.

Duke. I would thou had'ft done fo by Claudio.—
Go, fetch him hither; let me look upon him.

                             [*Exit* Provoft.

Efcal. I am forry, one fo learned and fo wife
As you, lord Angelo, have ftill appear'd,
Should flip fo grofsly, both in the heat of blood,
And lack of temper'd judgement afterward.

Ang. I am forry, that fuch forrow I procure :
And fo deep fticks it in my penitent heart,
That I crave death more willingly than mercy ;
'Tis my deferving, and I do entreat it.

Re-enter Provoft, BARNARDINE, CLAUDIO, *and* JULIET.

Duke. Which is that Barnardine ?

Prov.   This, my lord.

Duke. There was a friar told me of this man :—
Sirrah, thou art faid to have a ftubborn foul,
That apprehends no further than this world,
And fquar'ft thy life according. Thou'rt condemn'd;
But, for thofe earthly faults, I quit them all ;
And pray thee, take this mercy to provide
For better times to come :——Friar, advife him ;
I leave him to your hand.—What muffled fellow's that?

Prov. This is another prifoner, that I fav'd,
That fhould have d:ed when Claudio loft his head ;
As like almoft to Claudio, as himfelf.

                           [*Unmuffles* CLAUDIO.

Duke. If he be like your brother, [*To* ISABELLA.] for
        his fake

Is he pardon'd ; And, for your lovely fake,
Give me your hand, and fay you will be mine,

                                He

He is my brother too : But fitter time for that.
By this, lord Angelo perceives he's fafe ;
Methinks, I fee a quick'ning in his eye :—
Well, Angelo, your evil quits you well :
Look that you love your wife ; her worth, worth yours.—
I find an apt remiffion in myfelf :
And yet here's one in place I cannot pardon ;—
You, firrah, [*To* LUCIO.] that knew me for a fool, a
     coward,
One all of luxury, an afs, a madman ;
Wherein have I fo deferved of you,
That you extol me thus ?

   Lucio. 'Faith, my lord, I fpoke it but according to the
trick : If you will hang me for it, you may, but I had
rather it would pleafe you, I might be whip'd.

   Duke. Whip'd firft, fir, and hang'd after.—
Proclaim it, provoft, round about the city ;
If any woman's wrong'd by this lewd fellow,
(As I have heard him fwear himfelf, there's one
Whom he begot with child,) let her appear,
And he fhall marry her : the nuptial finifh'd,
Let him be whip'd and hang'd.

   Lucio. I befeech your highnefs, do not marry me to a
whore! Your highnefs faid even now, I made you a duke ;
good my lord, do not recompence me, in making me a
cuckold.

   Duke. Upon mine honour, thou fhalt marry her.
Thy flanders I forgive ; and therewithal
Remit thy other forfeits :—Take him to prifon :
And fee our pleafure herein executed.

   Lucio. Marrying a punk, my lord, is preffing to death,
whipping, and hanging.

   Duke. Sland'ring a prince deferves it.—
She, Claudio, that you wrong'd, look you reftore.—

                     Joy

Joy to you, Mariana!—love her, Angelo ;
I have confefs'd her, and I know her virtue.—
Thanks, good friend Efcalus, for thy much goodnefs :
There's more behind, that is more gratulate.—
Thanks, Provoft, for thy care, and fecrecy ;
We fhall employ thee in a worthier place :—.
Forgive him, Angelo, that brought you home
The head of Ragozine for Claudio's ;
The offence pardons itfelf.—Dear Ifabel,
I have a motion much imports your good ;
Whereto if you'll a willing ear incline,
What's mine is yours, and what is yours is mine :—
So, bring us to our palace ; where we'll fhow
What's yet behind, that's meet you all fhould know.
                                      [*Exeunt.*

Thurston del.   H. Van den Berghe sc.

Much ado about Nothing

Page 57

Pub.d 1 Augst 1798 by Edwd. Harding 98 Pall Mall

Harding's Edition.

Much Ado about Nothing,

COMEDY,

BY

WILLIAM SHAKSPEARE.

ACCURATELY PRINTED

FROM THE TEXT OF

Mr. STEEVENS's LAST EDITION.

Ornamented with Plates.

London:

PUBLISHED BY E. HARDING, NO. 98, PALL-MALL;
J. WRIGHT, PICCADILLY; G. SAEL, STRAND;
AND VERNOR AND HOOD, POULTRY.

1798.

OBSERVATIONS.

TH E ſtory is taken from Arioſto, Orl. Fur. B. V.　PoƤ x.

It is true, as Mr. Pope has obſerved, that ſomewhat reſem‑ bling the ſtory of this play is to be found in the fifth book of the Orlando Furioſo.　In Spenſer's Faery Queen, B. II. c. iv. as remote an original may be traced.　A novel, however, of Belle‑ foreſt, copied from another of Bandello, ſeems to have furniſhed Shakſpeare with his fable, as it approaches nearer in all its parti‑ culars to the play before us, than any other performance known to be extant.　I have ſeen ſo many verſions from this once po‑ pular collection, that I entertain no doubt but that a great majo‑ rity of the tales it comprehends, have made their appearance in an Engliſh dreſs.　Of that particular ſtory which I have juſt mentioned, viz. the 18th hiſtory in the third volume, no tranſla‑ tion has hitherto been met with.

This play was entered at Stationers' Hall, Aug. 23, 1600.

STEEVENƧ.

Arioſto is continually quoted for the fable of *Much ado about Nothing*; but I ſuſpect our poet to have been ſatisfied with the *Geneura* of Turberville.　" The tale (ſays Harington) is a pretie comical matter, and hath bin written in *Engliſh* verſe ſome few years paſt, learnedly and with good grace, by M. George Tur‑ bervil."　*Arioſto*, fol. 1591, p. 39.　FARMER.

I ſuppoſe this comedy to have been written in 1600, in which year it was printed.　MALONƧ.

PERSONS REPRESENTED.

Don PEDRO, *Prince of* Arragon.

Don JOHN, *his baftard brother.*

CLAUDIO, *a young lord of* Florence, *favourite to Don*
        Pedro.

BENEDICK, *a young lord of* Padua, *favoured likewife by*
        Don Pedro.

LEONATO, *governor of* Meffina.

ANTONIO, *his brother.*

BALTHAZAR, *fervant to Don* Pedro.

BORACHIO, } *followers of Don* John.
CONRADE,

DOGBERRY, } *two foolifh officers.*
VERGES,

A Sexton.

A Friar.

A Boy.

HERO, *daughter to* Leonato.

BEATRICE, *niece to* Leonato.

MARGARET, } *gentlewomen attending on* Hero.
URSULA,

Meffengers, Watch, and Attendants.

SCENE, Meffina.

MUCH ADO ABOUT NOTHING.

ACT I. SCENE I.

Before LEONATO'S *Houfe*.

Enter LEONATO, HERO, BEATRICE, *and Others, with a*
Meffenger.

Leonato.

I LEARN in this letter, that Don Pedro of Arragon comes this night to Meffina.

Meff. He is very near by this; he was not three leagues off when I left him.

Leon. How many gentlemen have you loft in this action?

Meff. But few of any fort, and none of name.

Leon. A victory is twice itfelf, when the atchiever brings home full numbers. I find here, that Don Pedro hath beftowed much honour on a young Florentine, called Claudio.

Meff. Much deferved on his part, and equally remember'd by Don Pedro: He hath borne himfelf beyond the promife of his age; doing, in the figure of a lamb, the feats of a lion; he hath, indeed, better better'd expectation, than you muft expect of me to tell you how.

Leon. He hath an uncle here in Meffina will be very much glad of it.

B

Meff.

Mess. I have already delivered him letters, and there appears much joy in him ; even so much, that joy could not show itself modest enough, without a badge of bitterness.

Leon. Did he break out into tears ?

Mess. In great measure.

Leon. A kind overflow of kindness : There are no faces truer than those that are so washed. How much better is it to weep at joy, than to joy at weeping ?

Beat. I pray you, is signior Montanto returned from the wars, or no ?

Mess. I know none of that name, lady ; there was none such in the army of any sort.

Leon. What is he that you ask for, niece ?

Hero. My cousin means signior Benedick of Padua.

Mess. O, he is returned ; and as pleasant as ever he was.

Beat. He set up his bills here in Messina, and challenged Cupid at the flight : and my uncle's fool, reading the challenge, subscribed for Cupid, and challenged him at the bird-bolt.—I pray you, how many hath he killed and eaten in these wars ? But how many hath he killed ? for, indeed, I promised to eat all of his killing.

Leon. Faith, niece, you tax signior Benedick too much ; but he'll be meet with you, I doubt it not.

Mess. He hath done good service, lady, in these wars.

Beat. You had musty victual, and he hath holp to eat it : he is a very valiant trencher-man, he hath an excellent stomach.

Mess. And a good soldier too, lady.

Beat. And a good soldier to a lady ;—But what is he to a lord ?

Mess. A lord to a lord, a man to a man ; stuffed with all honourable virtues.

Beat.

Beat. It is fo, indeed ; he is no lefs than a ftuffed man : but for the ftuffing,—Well, we are all mortal.

Leon. You muft not, fir, miftake my niece ; there is a kind of merry war betwixt fignior Benedick and her : they never meet, but there is a fkirmifh of wit between them.

Beat. Alas, he gets nothing by that. In our laft conflict, four of his five wits went halting off, and now is the whole man governed with one : fo that if he have wit enough to keep himfelf warm, let him bear it for a difference between himfelf and his horfe ; for it is all the wealth that he hath left, to be known a reafonable creature.—Who is his companion now ? He hath every month a new fworn brother.

Meff. Is it poffible ?

Beat. Very eafily poffible : he wears his faith but as the fafhion of his hat, it ever changes with the next block.

Meff. I fee, lady, the gentleman is not in your books.

Beat. No : an he were, I would burn my ftudy. But, I pray you, who is his companion ? Is there no young fquarer now, that will make a voyage with him to the devil ?

Meff. He is moft in the company of the right noble Claudio.

Beat. O Lord ! he will hang upon him like a difeafe : he is fooner caught than the peftilence, and the taker runs prefently mad. God help the noble Claudio ! if he have caught the Benedick, it will coft him a thoufand pound ere he be cured.

Meff. I will hold friends with you, lady.

Beat. Do, good friend.

Leon. You will never run mad, niece.

Beat. No, not till a hot January.

Meff. Don Pedro is approach'd.

Enter Don PEDRO, *attended by* BALTHAZAR *and Others*;
Don JOHN, CLAUDIO, *and* BENEDICK.

D. Pedro. Good fignior Leonato, you are come to meet
your trouble: the fafhion of the world is to avoid coft,
and you encounter it.

Leon. Never came trouble to my houfe in the likenefs
of your grace: for trouble being gone, comfort fhould
remain; but, when you depart from me, forrow abides,
and happinefs takes his leave.

D. Pedro. You embrace your charge too willingly.—I
think, this is your daughter.

Leon. Her mother hath many times told me fo.

Bene. Were you in doubt, fir, that you afk'd her?

Leon. Signior Benedick, no; for then were you a child.

D. Pedro. You have it full, Benedick: we may guefs
by this what you are, being a man. Truly, the lady fathers herfelf:—Be happy, lady! for you are like an honourable father.

Bene. If fignior Leonato be her father, fhe would not
have his head on her fhoulders, for all Meffina, as like
him as fhe is.

Beat. I wonder, that you will ftill be talking, fignior
Benedick; no body marks you.

Bene. What, my dear lady Difdain! are you yet living?

Beat. Is it poffible, difdain fhould die, while fhe hath
fuch meet food to feed it, as fignior Benedick? Courtefy
itfelf muft convert to difdain, if you come in her prefence.

Bene. Then is courtefy a turn-coat:—But it is certain,
I am loved of all ladies, only you excepted: and I would
I could find in my heart that I had not a hard heart; for,
truly, I love none.

Beat. A dear happinefs to women; they would elfe
have.

have been troubled with a pernicious fuitor. I thank
God, and my cold blood, I am of your humour for that;
I had rather hear my dog bark at a crow, than a man
fwear he loves me.

Bene. God keep your ladyfhip ftill in that mind! fo
fome gentleman or other fhall 'fcape a predeftinate
fcratched face.

Beat. Scratching could not make it worfe, an 'twere
fuch a face as yours were.

Bene. Well, you are a rare parrot-teacher.

Beat. A bird of my tongue, is better than a beaft of
yours.

Bene. I would, my horfe had the fpeed of your tongue;
and fo good a continuer: But keep your way o' God's
name; I have done.

Beat. You always end with a jade's trick; I know you
of old.

D. Pedro. This is the fum of all: Leonato,—fignior
Claudio, and fignior Benedick,—my dear friend Leonato,
hath invited you all. I tell him, we fhall ftay here at the
leaft a month; and he heartily prays, fome occafion may
detain us longer: I dare fwear he is no hypocrite, but
prays from his heart.

Leon. If you fwear, my lord, you fhall not be forfworn.
—Let me bid you welcome, my lord: being reconciled to
the prince your brother, I owe you all duty.

D. John. I thank you: I am not of many words, but I
thank you.

Leon. Pleafe it your grace lead on?

D. Pedro. Your hand, Leonato; we will go together.

                [*Exeunt all but* BENEDICK *and* CLAUDIO.

Claud. Benedick, didft thou note the daughter of fignior Leonato?

Bene. I noted her not; but I looked on her.

Claud. Is she not a modest young lady?.

Bene. Do you question me, as an honest man should do, for my simple true judgement? or would you have me speak after my custom, as being a professed tyrant to their sex?

Claud. No, I pray thee, speak in sober judgement.

Bene. Why, i' faith, methinks she is too low for a high praise, too brown for a fair praise, and too little for a great praise: only this commendation I can afford her; that were she other than she is, she were unhandsome; and being no other but as she is, I do not like her.

Claud. Thou thinkest, I am in sport; I pray thee, tell me truly how thou likest her.

Bene. Would you buy her, that you inquire after her?

Claud. Can the world buy such a jewel?

Bene. Yea, and a case to put it into. But speak you this with a sad brow? or do you play the flouting Jack; to tell us Cupid is a good hare-finder, and Vulcan a rare carpenter? Come, in what key shall a man take you, to go in the song?

Claud. In mine eye, she is the sweetest lady that ever I looked on.

Bene. I can see yet without spectacles, and I see no such matter: there's her cousin, an she were not possessed with a fury, exceeds her as much in beauty, as the first of May doth the last of December. But I hope, you have no intent to turn husband; have you?

Claud. I would scarce trust myself, though I had sworn the contrary, if Hero would be my wife.

Bene. Is it come to this, i' faith? Hath not the world one man, but he will wear his cap with suspicion? Shall I never see a bachelor of threescore again? Go to, i' faith; an thou wilt needs thrust thy neck into a yoke, wear the

print

print of it, and figh away Sundays.   Look, Don Pedro is
returned to feek you.

Re-enter Don PEDRO.

D. Pedro. What fecret hath held you here, that you
followed not to Leonato's ?

Bene. I would, your grace would conftrain me to tell.

D. Pedro. I charge thee on thy allegiance.

Bene. You hear, Count Claudio: I can be fecret as a
dumb man, I would have you think fo; but on my allegiance,—mark you this, on my allegiance :—He is in love.
With who?—now that is your grace's part.—Mark, how
fhort his anfwer is :—With Hero, Leonato's fhort daughter.

Claud. If this were fo, fo were it uttered.

Bene. Like the old tale, my lord : it is not fo, nor 'twas
not fo; but, indeed, God forbid it fhould be fo.

Claud. If my paffion change not fhortly, God forbid it
fhould be otherwife.

D. Pedro. Amen, if you love her; for the lady is very
well worthy.

Claud. You fpeak this to fetch me in, my lord.

D. Pedro. By my troth, I fpeak my thought.

Claud. And, in faith, my lord, I fpoke mine.

Bene. And, by my two faiths and troths, my lord, I
fpoke mine.

Claud. That I love her, I feel.

D. Pedro. That fhe is worthy, I know.

Bene. That I neither feel how fhe fhould be loved, nor
know how fhe fhould be worthy, is the opinion that fire
cannot melt out of me; I will die in it at the ftake.

D. Pedro. Thou waft ever an obftinate heretick in the
defpite of beauty.

Claud.

Claud. And never could maintain his part, but in the force of his will.

Bene. That a woman conceived me, I thank her; that she brought me up, I likewise give her moſt humble thanks: but that I will have a recheat winded in my forehead, or hang my bugle in an inviſible baldrick, all women ſhall pardon me: Becauſe I will not do them the wrong to miſtruſt any, I will do myſelf the right to truſt none; and the fine is, (for the which I may go the finer,) I will live a bachelor.

D. Pedro. I ſhall ſee thee, ere I die, look pale with love.

Bene. With anger, with ſickneſs, or with hunger, my lord; not with love: prove, that ever I loſe more blood with love, than I will get again with drinking, pick out mine eyes with a ballad-maker's pen, and hang me up at the door of a brothel-houſe, for the ſign of blind Cupid.

D. Pedro. Well, if ever thou doſt fall from this faith, thou wilt prove a notable argument.

Bene. If I do, hang me in a bottle like a cat, and ſhoot at me; and he that hits me, let him be clapped on the ſhoulder, and call'd Adam.

D. Pedro. Well, as time ſhall try:
In time the ſavage bull doth bear the yoke.

Bene. The ſavage bull may; but if ever the ſenſible Benedick bear it, pluck off the bull's horns, and ſet them in my forehead: and let me be vilely painted; and in ſuch great letters as they write, *Here is good horſe to hire*, let them ſignify under my ſign,—*Here you may ſee Benedick the married man.*

Claud. If this ſhould ever happen, thou would'ſt be horn-mad.

D. Pedro. Nay, if Cupid have not ſpent all his quiver in Venice, thou wilt quake for this ſhortly.

Bene.

Bene. I look for an earthquake too then.

D. Pedro. Well, you will temporize with the hours. In the mean time, good fignior Benedick, repair to Leonato's; commend me to him, and tell him, I will not fail him at fupper; for, indeed, he hath made great preparation.

Bene. I have almoft matter enough in me for fuch an embaffage; and fo I commit you—

Claud. To the tuition of God: From my houfe, (if I had it,)—

D. Pedro. The fixth of July: Your loving friend, Benedick.

Bene. Nay, mock not, mock not: The body of your difcourfe is fometime guarded with fragments, and the guards are but flightly bafted on neither: ere you flout old ends any further, examine your confcience; and fo I leave you. [*Exit* BENEDICK.

Claud. My liege, your highnefs now may do me good.

D. Pedro. My love is thine to teach; teach it but how,
And thou fhalt fee how apt it is to learn
Any hard leffon that may do thee good.

Claud. Hath Leonato any fon, my lord?

D. Pedro. No child but Hero, fhe's his only heir:
Doft thou affect her, Claudio?

Claud. O my lord,
When you went onward on this ended action,
I look'd upon her with a foldier's eye,
That lik'd, but had a rougher tafk in hand
Than to drive liking to the name of love:
But now I am return'd, and that war-thoughts
Have left their places vacant, in their rooms
Come thronging foft and delicate defires,
All prompting me how fair young Hero is,
Saying, I lik'd her ere I went to wars.

D. Pedro

D. Pedro. Thou wilt be like a lover prefently,
And tire the hearer with a book of words :
If thou doft love fair Hero, cherifh it ;
And I will break with her, and with her father,
And thou fhalt have her : Was't not to this end,
That thou began'ft to twift fo fine a ftory ?

Claud. How fweetly do you minifter to love,
That know love's grief by his complexion !
But left my liking might too fudden feem,
I would have falv'd it with a longer treatife.

     D. Pedro. What need the bridge much broader than
         the flood ?
The faireft grant is the neceffity :
Look, what will ferve, is fit : 'tis once, thou lov'ft ;
And I will fit thee with the remedy.
I know, we fhall have revelling to-night ;
I will affume thy part in fome difguife,
And tell fair Hero I am Claudio ;
And in her bofom I'll unclafp my heart,
And take her hearing prifoner with the force
And ftrong encounter of my amorous tale :
Then, after, to her father will I break ;
And, the conclufion is, fhe fhall be thine :
In practice let us put it prefently.   [*Exeunt.*

SCENE II.

A Room in LEONATO'S *Houfe.*

Enter LEONATO *and* ANTONIO.

     Leon. How now, brother ? Where is my coufin, your
fon ? Hath he provided this mufick ?

     Ant. He is very bufy about it. But, brother, I can tell
you ftrange news that you yet dream'd not of.

Leon. Are they good?

Ant. As the event ftamps them; but they have a good cover, they fhow well outward. The prince and Count Claudio, walking in a thick-pleached alley in my orchard, were thus much overheard by a man of mine: The prince difcovered to Claudio, that he loved my niece your daughter, and meant to acknowledge it this night in a dance; and, if he found her accordant, he meant to take the prefent time by the top, and inftantly break with you of it.

Leon. Hath the fellow any wit, that told you this?

Ant. A good fharp fellow; I will fend for him, and queftion him yourfelf.

Leon. No, no; we will hold it as a dream, till it appear itfelf:—but I will acquaint my daughter withal, that fhe may be the better prepared for an anfwer, if peradventure this be true. Go you, and tell her of it. [*Several perfons crofs the ftage.*] Coufins, you know what you have to do. —O, I cry you mercy, friend; go you with me, and I will ufe your fkill:—Good coufins, have a care this bufy time. [*Exeunt.*

SCENE III.

Another Room in LEONATO'S *Houfe.*

Enter Don JOHN *and* CONRADE.

Con. What the goujere, my lord! why are you thus out of meafure fad?

D. John. There is no meafure in the occafion that breeds it, therefore the fadnefs is without limit.

Con. You fhould hear reafon.

D. John. And when I have heard it, what bleffing bringeth it?

Con

Con. If not a prefent remedy, yet a patient fufferance.

D. John. I wonder, that thou being (as thou fay'ſt thou art) born under Saturn, goeſt about to apply a moral medicine to a mortifying mifchief. I cannot hide what I am: I muſt be fad when I have caufe, and fmile at no man's jeſts; eat when I have ſtomach, and wait for no man's leifure; fleep when I am drowfy, and tend on no man's bufinefs; laugh when I am merry, and claw no man in his humour.

Con. Yea, but you muſt not make the full ſhow of this, till you may do it without controlment. You have of late ſtood out againſt your brother, and he hath ta'en you newly into his grace; where it is impoſſible you ſhould take true root, but by the fair weather that you make yourfelf; it is needful that you frame the feafon for your own harveſt.

D. John. I had rather be a canker in a hedge, than a rofe in his grace; and it better fits my blood to be difdain'd of all, than to faſhion a carriage to rob love from any: in this, though I cannot be faid to be a flattering honeſt man, it muſt not be denied but I am a plain-dealing villain. I am truſted with a muzzle, and enfranchifed with a clog; therefore I have decreed not to fing in my cage: If I had my mouth, I would bite; if I had my liberty, I would do my liking: in the mean time, let me be that I am, and feek not to alter me.

Con. Can you make no ufe of your difcontent?

D. John. I make all ufe of it, for I ufe it only. Who comes here? What news, Borachio?

Enter BORACHIO.

Bora. I came yonder from a great ſupper; the prince, your brother, is royally entertain'd by Leonato; and I can give you intelligence of an intended marriage.

D. John.

Thurston del   Hopwood sc

Much ado about Nothing

Page

Pub.d 1 Aug.t 1798 by Edward Harding 98 Pall Mall.

D. John. Will it ſerve for any model to build miſchief on ? What is he for a fool, that betroths himſelf to un-quietneſs ?

Bora. Marry, it is your brother's right hand.

D. John. Who ? the moſt exquiſite Claudio ?

Bora. Even he.

D. John. A proper ſquire ! And who, and who ? which way looks he ?

Bora. Marry, on Hero, the daughter and heir of Leo-nato.

D. John. A very forward March-chick ! How came you to this ?

Bora. Being entertain'd for a perfumer, as I was ſmok-ing a muſty room, comes me the prince and Claudio, hand in hand, in ſad conference : I whipt me behind the arras ; and there heard it agreed upon, that the prince ſhould woo Hero for himſelf, and having obtained her, give her to count Claudio.

D. John. Come, come, let us thither; this may prove food to my diſpleaſure ; that young ſtart-up hath all the glory of my overthrow; if I can croſs him any way, I bleſs myſelf every way : You are both ſure, and will aſſiſt me ?

Con. To the death, my lord.

D. John. Let us to the great ſupper; their cheer is the greater, that I am ſubdued : 'Would the cook were of my mind !—Shall we go prove what's to be done ?

Bora. We'll wait upon your lordſhip.   · [*Exeunt.*

ACT

ACT II.   SCENE I.

A Hall in Leonato's *House.*

Enter LEONATO, ANTONIO, HERO, BEATRICE, *and*
Others.

Leon. Was not count John here at fupper?

Ant. I faw him not.

Beat. How tartly that gentleman looks! I never can
fee him, but I am heart-burn'd an hour after.

Hero. He is of a very melancholy difpofition.

Beat. He were an excellent man, that were made juft in
the mid-way between him and Benedick: the one is too
like an image, and fays nothing; and the other, too like
my lady's eldeft fon, evermore tattling.

Leon. Then half fignior Benedick's tongue in Count
John's mouth, and half count John's melancholy in fignior Benedick's face,—

Beat. With a good leg, and a good foot, uncle, and
money enough in his purfe, fuch a man would win any
woman in the world,—if he could get her good will.

Leon. By my troth, niece, thou wilt never get thee a
hufband, if thou be fo fhrewd of thy tongue.

Ant. In faith, fhe is too curft.

Beat. Too curft is more than curft: I fhall leffen God's
fending that way: for it is faid, *God fends a curft cow fhort*
horns; but to a cow too curft he fends none.

Leon. So, by being too curft, God will fend you no
horns.

Beat. Juft, if he fend me no hufband; for the which
bleffing, I am at him upon my knees every morning and
evening:

evening: Lord, I could not endure a hufband with a beard on his face; I had rather lie in the woollen.

Leon. You may light upon a hufband, that hath no beard.

Beat. What fhould I do with him? drefs him in my apparel, and make him my waiting-gentlewoman? He that hath a beard, is more than a youth; and he that hath no beard, is lefs than a man: and he that is more than a youth, is not for me; and he that is lefs than a man, I am not for him: Therefore I will even take fix-pence in earneft of the bear-herd, and lead his apes into hell.

Leon. Well then, go you into hell?

Beat. No; but to the gate: and there will the devil meet me, like an old cuckold, with horns on his head, and fay, *Get you to heaven, Beatrice, get you to heaven; here's no place for you maids:* fo deliver I up my apes, and away to Saint Peter for the heavens; he fhows me where the bachelors fit, and there live we as merry as the day is long.

Ant. Well, niece, [*To* HERO.] I truft, you will be ruled by your father.

Beat. Yes, faith; it is my coufin's duty to make cour-tefy, and fay, *Father, as it pleafe you:*—but yet for all that, coufin, let him be a handfome fellow, or elfe make an-other courtefy, and fay, *Father, as it pleafe me.*

Leon. Well, niece, I hope to fee you one day fitted with a hufband.

Beat. Not till God make men of fome other metal than earth. Would it not grieve a woman to be over-mafter'd with a piece of valiant duft? to make an account of her life to a clod of wayward marl? No, uncle, I'll none: Adam's fons are my brethren; and truly, I hold it a fin match in my kindred.

Leon. Daughter, remember, what I told you: if the
prince

prince do folicit you in that kind, you know your anfwer.

Beat. The fault will be in the mufick, coufin, if you
be not woo'd in good time: if the prince be too important, tell him, there is meafure in every thing, and fo
dance out the anfwer. For hear me, Hero; Wooing,
wedding, and repenting, is as a Scotch jig, a meafure, and
a cinque-pace: the firft fuit is hot and hafty, like a Scotch
jig, and full as fantaftical; the wedding, mannerly-mo-
deft, as a meafure full of ftate and ancientry; and then
comes repentance, and, with his bad legs, falls into the
cinque-pace fafter and fafter, till he fink into his grave.

Leon. Coufin, you apprehend paffing fhrewdly.

Beat. I have a good eye, uncle; I can fee a church by
day-light.

Leon. The revellers are entering; brother, make good
room.

Enter Don PEDRO, CLAUDIO, BENEDICK, BALTHAZAR;
   Don JOHN, BORACHIO, MARGARET, URSULA, *and*
   Others, mafk'd.

D. Pedro. Lady, will you walk about with your friend?

Hero. So you walk foftly, and look fweetly, and fay
nothing, I am yours for the walk; and, efpecially, when
I walk away.

D. Pedro. With me in your company?

Hero. I may fay fo, when I pleafe.

D. Pedro. And when pleafe you to fay fo?

Hero. When I like your favour; for God defend, the
lute fhould be like the cafe!

D. Pedro. My vifor is Philemon's roof; within the
houfe is Jove.

Hero. Why, then your vifor fhould be thatch'd.

D. Pedro. Speak low, if you fpeak love. [*Takes her afide.*

    Bene.

Bene. Well, I would you did like me.

Marg. So would not I, for your own fake; for I have many ill qualities.

Bene. Which is one?

Marg. I fay my prayers aloud.

Bene. I love you the better; the hearers may cry, amen.

Marg. God match me with a good dancer!

Balth. Amen.

Marg. And God keep him out of my fight, when the dance is done!—Anfwer, clerk.

Balth. No more words; the clerk is anfwer'd.

Urf. I know you well enough; you are fignior Antonio.

Ant. At a word, I am not.

Urf. I know you by the waggling of your head.

Ant. To tell you true, I counterfeit him.

Urf. You could never do him fo ill-well, unlefs you were the very man: Here's his dry hand up and down; you are he, you are he.

Ant. At a word, I am not.

Urf. Come, come; do you think I do not know you by your excellent wit? Can virtue hide itfelf? Go to, mum, you are he: graces will appear, and there's an end.

Beat. Will you not tell me who told you fo?

Bene. No, you fhall pardon me.

Beat. Nor will you not tell me who you are?

Bene. Not now.

Beat. That I was difdainful,—and that I had my good wit out of the *Hundred merry Tales*;—Well, this was fignior Benedick that faid fo.

Bene. What's he?

Beat. I am fure, you know him well enough.

Bene. Not I, believe me.

C

Beat

Beat. Did he never make you laugh?

Bene. I pray you, what is he?

Beat. Why, he is the prince's jefter: a very dull fool; only his gift is in devifing impoffible flanders: none but libertines delight in him; and the commendation is not in his wit, but in his villainy; for he both pleafeth men, and angers them, and then they laugh at him, and beat him: I am fure, he is in the fleet; I would he had boarded me.

Bene. When I know the gentleman, I'll tell him what you fay.

Beat. Do, do: he'll but break a comparifon or two on me; which, peradventure, not mark'd, or not laugh'd at, ftrikes him into melancholy; and then there's a partridge wing faved, for the fool will eat no fupper that night. [*Mufick within.*] We muft follow the leaders.

Bene. In every good thing.

Beat. Nay, if they lead to any ill, I will leave them at the next turning. [*Dance. Then exeunt all but Don* JOHN, BORACHIO, *and* CLAUDIO.

D. John. Sure, my brother is amorous on Hero, and hath withdrawn her father to break with him about it: The ladies follow her, and but one vifor remains.

Bora. And that is Claudio: I know him by his bearing.

D. John. Are not you fignior Benedick?

Claud. You know me well; I am he.

D. John. Signior, you are very near my brother in his love: he is enamoured on Hero; I pray you, diffuade him from her, fhe is no equal for his birth: you may do the part of an honeft man in it.

Claud. How know you he loves her?

D. John. I heard him fwear his affection.

Bora. So did I too; and he fwore he would marry her to-night.

D. John.

D. John. Come, let us to the banquet.

[*Exeunt Don* JOHN *and* BORACHIO.

Claud. Thus answer I in name of Benedick,
But hear these ill news with the ears of Claudio.—
'Tis certain so ;—the prince wooes for himself.
Friendship is constant in all other things,
Save in the office and affairs of love :
Therefore, all hearts in love use their own tongues ;
Let every eye negociate for itself,
And trust no agent : for beauty is a witch,
Against whose charms faith melteth into blood.
This is an accident of hourly proof,
Which I mistrusted not : Farewell therefore, Hero!

Re-enter BENEDICK.

Bene. Count Claudio ?

Claud. Yea, the same.

Bene. Come, will you go with me ?

Claud. Whither ?

Bene. Even to the next willow, about your own busi-ness, count. What fashion will you wear the garland of? About your neck, like an usurer's chain ? or under your arm, like a lieutenant's scarf ? You must wear it one way, for the prince hath got your Hero.

Claud. I wish him joy of her.

Bene. Why, that's spoken like an honest drover; so they sell bullocks. But did you think, the prince would have served you thus ?

Claud. I pray you, leave me.

Bene. Ho! now you strike like the blind man ; 'twas the boy that stole your meat, and you'll beat the post.

Claud. If it will not be, I'll leave you. [*Exit.*

Bene. Alas, poor hurt fowl! Now will he creep into sedges.——But, that my lady Beatrice should know me

and not know me! The prince's fool!—Ha! it may be,
I go under that title, becaufe I am merry.—Yea; but fo;
I am apt to do myfelf wrong: I am not fo reputed: it is
the bafe, the bitter difpofition of Beatrice, that puts the
world into her perfon, and fo gives me out. Well, I'll
be revenged as I may.

Re-enter Don PEDRO, HERO, *and* LEONATO.

D. Pedro. Now, fignior, where's the count? Did you
fee him?

Bene. Troth, my lord, I have play'd the part of lady
Fame. I found him here as melancholy as a lodge in a
warren; I told him, and, I think, I told him true, that
your grace had got the good will of this young lady; and
I offered him my company to a willow tree, either to
make him a garland, as being forfaken, or to bind him
up a rod, as being worthy to be whipped.

D. Pedro. To be whipped! What's his fault?

Bene. The flat tranfgreffion of a fchool-boy; who, being overjoy'd with finding a bird's neft, fhows it his companion, and he fteals it.

D. Pedro. Wilt thou make a truft a tranfgreffion? The
tranfgreffion is in the ftealer.

Bene. Yet it had not been amifs, the rod had been
made, and the garland too; for the garland he might
have worn himfelf; and the rod he might have beftow'd
on you, who, as I take it, have ftol'n his bird's neft.

D. Pedro. I will but teach them to fing, and reftore
them to the owner.

Bene. If their finging anfwer your faying, by my faith,
you fay honeftly.

D. Pedro. The lady Beatrice hath a quarrel to you; the
gentleman, that danced with her, told her, fhe is much
wrong'd by you.

Bene.

Bene. O, she misused me past the endurance of a block; an oak, but with one green leaf on it, would have answer'd her; my very visor began to assume life, and scold with her: She told me, not thinking I had been myself, that I was the prince's jester; that I was duller than a great thaw; huddling jest upon jest, with such impossible conveyance, upon me, that I stood like a man at a mark, with a whole army shooting at me: She speaks poniards, and every word stabs: if her breath were as terrible as her terminations, there were no living near her, she would infect to the north star. I would not marry her, though she were endowed with all that Adam had left him before he transgress'd: she would have made Hercules have turn'd spit; yea, and have cleft his club to make the fire too. Come, talk not of her; you shall find her the infernal Até in good apparel. I would to God, some scholar would conjure her; for, certainly, while she is here, a man may live as quiet in hell, as in a sanctuary; and people sin upon purpose, because they would go thither; so, indeed, all disquiet, horror, and perturbation follows her.

Re-enter CLAUDIO, *and* BEATRICE.

D. Pedro. Look, here she comes.

Bene. Will your grace command me any service to the world's end? I will go on the slightest errand now to the Antipodes, that you can devise to send me on; I will fetch you a toothpicker now from the farthest inch of Asia; bring you the length of Prester John's foot; fetch you a hair off the great Cham's beard; do you any embassage to the Pigmies, rather than hold three words' conference with this harpy: You have no employment for me?

D. Pedro. None, but to desire your good company.

                        Bene.

Bene. O God, fir, here's a diſh I love not; I cannot endure my lady Tongue.   [*Exit.*

D. Pedro. Come, lady, come; you have loſt the heart of ſignior Benedick.

Beat. Indeed, my lord, he lent it me a while; and I gave him uſe for it, a double heart for his ſingle one: marry, once before, he won it of me with falſe dice, therefore your grace may well ſay, I have loſt it.

D. Pedro. You have put him down, lady, you have put him down.

Beat. So I would not he ſhould do me, my lord, left I ſhould prove the mother of fools. I have brought count Claudio, whom you ſent me to ſeek.

D. Pedro. Why, how now, count? wherefore are you ſad?

Claud. Not ſad, my lord.

D. Pedro. How then? Sick?

Claud. Neither, my lord.

Beat. The count is neither ſad, nor ſick, nor merry, nor well: but civil, count; civil as an orange, and ſome-thing of that jealous complexion.

D. Pedro. I' faith, lady, I think your blazon to be true; though, I'll be ſworn, if he be ſo, his conceit is falſe. Here, Claudio, I have wooed in thy name, and fair Hero is won; I have broke with her father, and his good will obtained: name the day of marriage, and God give thee joy!

Leon. Count, take of me my daughter, and with her my fortunes: his grace hath made the match, and all grace ſay Amen to it!

Beat. Speak, count, 'tis your cue.

Claud. Silence is the perfecteſt herald of joy: I were but little happy, if I could ſay how much.—Lady, as you

are

are mine, I am yours : I give away myſelf for you, and
dote upon the exchange.

Beat. Speak, couſin; or, if you cannot, ſtop his mouth
with a kiſs, and let not him ſpeak, neither.

D. Pedro. In faith, lady, you have a merry heart.

Beat. Yea, my lord; I thank it, poor fool, it keeps on
the windy ſide of care :—My couſin tells him in his ear,
that he is in her heart.

Claud. And ſo ſhe doth, couſin.

Beat. Good lord, for alliance!—Thus goes every one
to the world but I, and I am ſun-burn'd; I may ſit in a
corner, and cry, heigh ho! for a huſband.

D. Pedro. Lady Beatrice, I will get you one.

Beat. I would rather have one of your father's getting:
Hath your grace ne'er a brother like you? Your father
got excellent huſbands, if a maid could come by them.

D. Pedro. Will you have me, lady?

Beat. No, my lord, unleſs I might have another for
working-days; your grace is too coſtly to wear every day:
—But, I beſeech your grace, pardon me; I was born to
ſpeak all mirth, and no matter.

D. Pedro. Your ſilence moſt offends me, and to be
merry beſt becomes you; for, out of queſtion, you were
born in a merry hour.

Beat. No, ſure, my lord, my mother cry'd; but then
there was a ſtar danced, and under that was I born.—
Couſins, God give you joy!

Leon. Niece, will you look to thoſe things I told you
of?

Beat. I cry you mercy, uncle.—By your grace's pardon.   [*Exit* BEATRICE.

D. Pedro. By my troth, a pleaſant-ſpirited lady.

Leon. There's little of the melancholy element in her
my lord : ſhe is never ſad, but when ſhe ſleeps; and no

eve

ever fad then; for I have heard my daughter fay, fhe hath
often dream'd of unhappinefs, and waked herfelf with
laughing.

D. Pedro. She cannot endure to hear tell of a hufband.

Leon. O, by no means; fhe mocks all her wooers out of
fuit.

D. Pedro. She were an excellent wife for Benedick.

Leon. O Lord, my lord, if they were but a week married, they would talk themfelves mad.

D. Pedro. Count Claudio, when mean you to go to
church?

Claud. To-morrow, my lord: Time goes on crutches,
till love have all his rites.

Leon. Not till Monday, my dear fon, which is hence a
juft fevennight; and a time too brief too, to have all
things anfwer my mind.

D. Pedro. Come, you fhake the head at fo long a
breathing; but, I warrant thee, Claudio, the time fhall
not go dully by us; I will, in the interim, undertake one
of Hercules' labours; which is, to bring fignior Benedick,
and the lady Beatrice, into a mountain of affection, the
one with the other. I would fain have it a match; and I
doubt not but to fafhion it, if you three will but minifter
fuch affiftance as I fhall give you direction.

Leon. My lord, I am for you, though it coft me ten
nights' watchings.

Claud. And I, my lord.

D. Pedro. And you too, gentle Hero?

Hero. I will do any modeft office, my lord, to help my
coufin to a good hufband.

D. Pedro. And Benedick is not the unhopefulleft hufband that I know: thus far can I praife him; he is of a
noble ftrain, of approved valour, and confirm'd honefty.
I will teach you how to humour your coufin, that fhe
                                                            fhall

fhall fall in love with Benedick :—and I, with your two
helps, will fo practice on Benedick, that, in defpight of
his quick wit and his queafy ftomach, he fhall fall in love
with Beatrice. If we can do this, Cupid is no longer an
archer; his glory fhall be ours, for we are the only love-
gods. Go in with me, and I will tell you my drift.

                               [*Exeunt.*

SCENE II.

Another Room in LEONATO's *Houfe.*

Enter Don JOHN *and* BORACHIO.

D. John. It is fo; the count Claudio fhall marry the
daughter of Leonato.

Bora. Yea, my lord; but I can crofs it.

D. John. Any bar, any crofs, any impediment will be
medicinable to me : I am fick in difpleafure to him; and
whatfoever comes athwart his affection, ranges evenly
with mine. How canft thou crofs this marriage?

Bora. Not honeftly, my lord; but fo covertly that no
difhonefty fhall appear in me.

D. John. Show me briefly how.

Bora. I think, I told your lordfhip, a year fince, how
much I am in the favour of Margaret, the waiting-gentlewoman to Hero.

D. John. I remember.

Bora. I can, at any unfeafonable inftant of the night,
appoint her to look out at her lady's chamber-window.

D. John. What life is in that, to be the death of this
marriage?

Bora. The poifon of that lies in you to temper. Go
you to the prince your brother; fpare not to tell him,
that he hath wrong'd his honour in marrying the re-

                                            nowned

nowned Claudio (whofe eftimation do you mightily hold up) to a contaminated ftale, fuch a one as Hero.

D. John. What proof fhall I make of that?

Bora. Proof enough to mifufe the prince, to vex Claudio, to undo Hero, and kill Leonato: Look you for any other iffue?

D. John. Only to defpite them, I will endeavour any thing.

Bora. Go then, find me a meet hour to draw Don Pedro and the count Claudio, alone: tell them, that you know that Hero loves me; intend a kind of zeal both to the prince and Claudio, as—in love of your brother's honour who hath made this match; and his friend's reputation, who is thus like to be cozen'd with the femblance of a maid,—that you have difcover'd thus. They will fcarcely believe this without trial: offer them inftances; which fhall bear no lefs likelihood, than to fee me at her chamber-window; hear me call Margaret, Hero; hear Margaret term me Borachio; and bring them to fee this, the very night before the intended wedding: for, in the mean time, I will fo fafhion the matter, that Hero fhall be abfent; and there fhall appear fuch feeming truth of Hero's difloyalty, that jealoufy fhall be call'd affurance, and all the preparation overthrown.

D. John. Grow this to what adverfe iffue it can, I will put it in practice: Be cunning in the working this, and thy fee is a thoufand ducats.

Bora. Be you conftant in the accufation, and my cunning fhall not fhame me.

D. John. I will prefently go learn their day of marriage.
                                                          [*Exeunt.*

SCENE

SCENE III.

LEONATO's *Garden.*

Enter BENEDICK *and a* Boy.

Bene. Boy,—

Boy. Signior.

Bene. In my chamber-window lies a book; bring it hither to me in the orchard.

Boy. I am here already, sir.

Bene. I know that;—but I would have thee hence, and here again. [*Exit Boy.*]—I do much wonder, that one man, seeing how much another man is a fool when he dedicates his behaviours to love, will, after he hath laugh'd at such shallow follies in others, become the argument of his own scorn, by falling in love: And such a man is Claudio. I have known, when there was no musick with him but the drum and the fife; and now had he rather hear the tabor and the pipe: I have known, when he would have walk'd ten mile a-foot, to see a good armour; and now will he lie ten nights awake, carving the fashion of a new doublet. He was wont to speak plain, and to the purpose, like an honest man, and a soldier; and now is he turn'd orthographer; his words are a very fantastical banquet, just so many strange dishes. May I be so converted, and see with these eyes? I cannot tell; I think not: I will not be sworn, but love may transform me to an oyster; but I'll take my oath on it, till he have made an oyster of me, he shall never make me such a fool. One woman is fair; yet I am well: another is wise; yet I am well: another virtuous; yet I am well: but till all graces be in one woman, one woman shall not come in my grace. Rich she shall be, that's certain; wife, or I'll

none;

none; virtuous, or I'll never cheapen her; fair, or I'll
never look on her; mild, or come not near me; noble,
or not I for an angel; of good difcourfe, an excellent
mufician, and her hair fhall be of what colour it pleafe
God. Ha! the prince and monfieur Love! I will hide
me in the arbour.   [*Withdraws.*

Enter Don PEDRO, LEONATO, *and* CLAUDIO.

D. Pedro. Come, fhall we hear this mufick?
Claud. Yea, my good lord :—How ftill the evening is,
As hufh'd on purpofe to grace harmony!
D. Pedro. See you where Benedick hath hid himfelf?
Claud. O, very well, my lord: the mufick ended,
We'll fit the kid-fox with a penny-worth.

Enter BALTHAZAR, *with mufick.*

D. Pedro. Come, Balthazar, we'll hear that fong again.
Balth. O good my lord, tax not fo bad a voice
To flander mufick any more than once.
D. Pedro. It is the witnefs ftill of excellency,
To put a ftrange face on his own perfection :—
I pray thee, fing, and let me woo no more.
Balth. Becaufe you talk of wooing, I will fing;
Since many a wooer doth commence his fuit
To her he thinks not worthy; yet he wooes;
Yet will he fwear, he loves.
D. Pedro.   Nay, pray thee, come;
Or, if thou wilt hold longer argument,
Do it in notes.
Balth.   Note this before my notes,
There's not a note of mine that's worth the noting.
D. Pedro. Why thefe are very crotchets that he fpeaks;
Note, notes, forfooth, and noting!   [*Mufick.*
Bene. Now, *Divine air!* now is his foul ravifh'd!—Is
                                                    it

it not ftrange, that fheeps' guts fhould hale fouls out of men's bodies?—Well, a horn for my money, when all's done.

BALTHAZAR *fings.*

I.

Balth.　*Sigh no more, ladies, figh no more,*
　　　Men were deceivers ever;
　　One foot in fea, and one on fhore;
　　To one thing conftant never :
　　　　Then figh not fo,
　　　　But let them go,
　　And be you blith and bonny;
　Converting all your founds of woe
　Into, Hey nonny, nonny.

II.

　Sing no more ditties, fing no mo
　Of dumps fo dull and heavy;
　The fraud of men was ever fo,
　　Since fummer firft was leavy.
　　　Then figh not fo, &c.

D. Pedro. By my troth, a good fong.

Balth. And an ill finger, my lord.

D. Pedro. Ha? no; no, faith; thou fing'ft well enough for a fhift.

Bene. [*Afide.*] An he had been a dog, that fhould have howl'd thus, they would have hang'd him: and, I pray God, his bad voice bode no mifchief! I had as lief have heard the night raven, come what plague could have come after it.

D. Pedro. Yea, marry; [*To* CLAUDIO.]—Doft thou hear, Balthazar? I pray thee, get us fome excellent mufick; for to-morrow night we would have it at the lady Hero's chamber-window.

Balth.

Balth. The best I can, my lord.

D. Pedro. Do so: farewell. [*Exeunt* BALTHAZAR *and musick.*] Come hither, Leonato: What was it you told me of to-day? that your niece Beatrice was in love with signior Benedick?

Claud. O, ay:—Stalk on, stalk on; the fowl sits. [*Aside. to* PEDRO.] I did never think that lady would have loved any man.

Leon. No, nor I neither; but most wonderful, that she should so dote on signior Benedick, whom she hath in all outward behaviours seem'd ever to abhor.

Bene. Is't possible? Sits the wind in that corner? [*Aside.*

Leon. By my troth, my lord, I cannot tell what to think of it; but that she loves him with an enraged affection,—it is past the infinite of thought.

D. Pedro. May be, she doth but counterfeit.

Claud. 'Faith, like enough.

Leon. O God! counterfeit! There never was counterfeit of passion came so near the life of passion, as she discovers it.

D. Pedro. Why, what effects of passion shows she?

Claud. Bait the hook well; this fish will bite. [*Aside.*

Leon. What effects, my lord! She will sit you,—You heard my daughter tell you how.

Claud. She did, indeed.

D. Pedro. How, how, I pray you? You amaze me: I would have thought her spirit had been invincible against all assaults of affection.

Leon. I would have sworn it had, my lord; especially against Benedick.

Bene. [*Aside.*] I should think this a gull, but that the white-bearded fellow speaks it: knavery cannot, sure, hide himself in such reverence.

Claud. He hath ta'en the infection; hold it up. [*Aside.*

D. Pedro.

D. Pedro. Hath she made her affection known to Benedick ?

Leon. No; and fwears she never will: that's her torment.

Claud. 'Tis true, indeed; fo your daughter fays: *Shall
I,* fays she, *that have fo oft encounter'd him with fcorn, write
to him that I love him?*

Leon. This fays she now when she is beginning to write
to him: for she'll be up twenty tim s a night; and there
will she fit in her fmock, till she have writ a sheet of paper:—my daughter tells us all.

Claud. Now you talk of a sheet of paper, I remember a
pretty jeft your daughter told us of.

Leon. O!—When she had writ it, and was reading it
over, she found Benedick and Beatrice between the
sheet ?—

Claud. That.

Leon. O! she tore the letter into a thoufand halfpence;
rail'd at herfelf, that she should be fo immodeft to write
to one that she knew would flout her: *I meafure him,* fays
she, *by my own spirit; for I should flout him, if he writ to me;
yea, though I love him, I should.*

Claud. Then down upon her knees she falls, weeps,
fobs, beats her heart, tears her hair, prays, curfes;—*O
fweet Benedick! God give me patience!*

Leon. She doth indeed; my daughter fays fo: and the
ecftafy hath fo much overborne her, that my daughter is
fometime afraid she will do a defperate outrage to herfelf;.
It is very true.

D. Pedro. It were good, that Benedick knew of it by
fome other, if she will not difcover it.

Claud. To what end? He would but make a fport of
it, and torment the poor lady worfe.

D. Pedro. An he should, it were an alms to hang him:

　Q 2　　　　　　　　　　　　　　　　She's

She's an excellent fweet lady; and, out of all fufpicion, fhe is virtuous.

Claud. And fhe is exceeding wife.

D. Pedro. In every thing, but in loving Benedick.

Leon. O my lord, wifdom and blood combating in fo tender a body, we have ten proofs to one, that blood hath the victory. I am forry for her, as I have juft caufe, being her uncle and her guardian.

D. Pedro. I would, fhe had beftowed this dotage on me; I would have daff'd all other refpects, and made her half myfelf: I pray you, tell Benedick of it, and hear what he will fay.

Leon. Were it good, think you?

Claud. Hero thinks furely, fhe will die: for fhe fays, fhe will die if he love her not; and fhe will die ere fhe make her love known; and fhe will die if he woo her, ra-ther than fhe will 'bate one breath of her accuftom'd croffnefs.

D. Pedro. She doth well: if fhe fhould make tender of her love, 'tis very poffible he'll fcorn it; for the man, as you know all, hath a contemptible fpirit.

Claud. He is a very proper man.

D. Pedro. He hath, indeed, a good outward happinefs.

Claud. 'Fore God, and in my mind, very wife.

D. Pedro. He doth, indeed, fhow fome fparks that are like wit.

Leon. And I take him to be valiant.

D. Pedro. As Hector, I affure you: and in the manag-ing of quarrels you may fay he is wife; for either he avoids them with great difcretion, or undertakes them with a moft chriftian-like fear.

Leon. If he do fear God, he muft neceffarily keep peace; if he break the peace, he ought to enter into a quarrel with fear and trembling.

D. Pedro.

Much ado about Nothing

Page 33

Pub.d Aug.t 1796 by Edw.d Harding 98 Pall

D. Pedro. And fo will he do; for the man doth fear God, howfoever it feems not in him, by fome large jefts he will make. Well, I am forry for your niece: Shall we go feek Benedick, and tell him of her love?

Claud. Never tell him, my lord; let her wear it out with good counfel.

Leon. Nay, that's impoffible; fhe may wear her heart out fir——

D. Pedro. Well, we'll hear farther of it by your daughter ——— the while. I love Benedick well; and I could wifh he would modeftly examine himfelf, to fee how much he is unworthy fo good a lady.

Leon. My lord, will you walk? dinner is ready.

Claud. If he do not dote on her upon this, I will never truft my expectation. [*Afide.*

D. Pedro. Let there be the fame net fpread for her; and that muft your daughter and her gentlewomen carry. The fport will be, when they hold one an opinion of another's dotage, and no fuch matter; that's the fcene that I would fee, which will be merely a dumb fhow. Let us fend her to call him in to dinner. [*Afide.*

Exeunt D. PEDRO, CLAUDIO, *and* LEONATO.

BENEDICK advances from the Arbour.

Bene. This can be no trick: The conference was fadly borne.—They have the truth of this from Hero. They feem to pity the lady; it feems, her affections have their full bent. Love me! why, it muft be requited. I hear how I am cenfured: they fay, I will bear myfelf proudly, if I perceive the love come from her; they fay too, that fhe will rather die than give any fign of affection.—I did never think to marry:—I muft not feem proud:—Happy are they that hear their detractions, and can put them to mending. They fay, the lady is fair; 'tis a truth, I can

              D   bear

bear them witnefs : and virtuous ;—'tis fo, I cannot reprove it : and wife, but for loving me :—By my troth, it
is no addition to her wit ;—nor no great argument of her
folly, for I will be horribly in love with her.—I may
chance have fome odd quirks and remnants of wit broken
on me, becaufe I have rail'd fo long againft marriage :
But doth not the appetite alter ? A man loves the meat in
his youth, that he cannot endure in his age : Shall quips,
and fentences, and thefe paper bullets of the brain, awe a
man from the career of his humour ? No : The world muft
be peopled.   When I faid, I would die a bachelor, I did
not think I fhould live till I were married.—Here comes
Beatrice : By this day, fhe's a fair lady : I do fpy fome
marks of love in her.

Enter BEATRICE.

Beat. Againft my will, I am fent to bid you come in
to dinner.

Bene. Fair Beatrice, I thank you for your pains.

Beat. I took no more pains for thofe thanks, than you
take pains to thank me ; if it had been painful, I would
no: have come.

Bene. You take pleafure then in the meffage ?

Beat. Yea, juft fo much as you may take upon a knife's
point, and choke a daw withal :—You have no ftomach,
fignior ; fare you well.   [*Exit.*

Bene. Ha ! *Againft my will I am fent to bid you come in to
dinner*—there's a double meaning in that. *I took no more
pains for thofe thanks, than you took pains to thank me*—that's
as much as to fay, Any pains that I take for you is as
eafy as thanks :—If I do not take pity of her, I am a
villain ; if I do not love her, I am a Jew : I will go get
her picture.   [*Exit.*

ACT

Thurston del   H. Van den Berghe Sculp.t 1798

Much ado about Nothing

Page 33

Pub.d Aug.t 1798 by Edw.d Harding 98 Pall Mall.

ACT III. SCENE I.

LEONATO's *Garden.*

Enter HERO, MARGARET, *and* URSULA.

Hero. Good Margaret, run thee into the parlour;
There fhalt thou find my coufin Beatrice
Propofing with the Prince and Claudio:
Whifper her ear, and tell her, I and Urfula
Walk in the orchard, and our whole difcourfe
Is all of her; fay, that thou overheard'ft us;
And bid her fteal into the pleached bower,
Where honey-fuckles, ripen'd by the fun,
Forbid the fun to enter;—like favourites,
Made proud by princes, that advance their pride,
Againft that power that bred it:—there will fhe hide her,
To liften our propofe: This is thy office,
Bear thee well in it, and leave us alone.
 Marg. I'll make her come, I warrant you, prefently.
             [*Exit.*

 Hero. Now, Urfula, when Beatrice doth come,
As we do trace this alley up and down,
Our talk muft only be of Benedick;
When I do name him, let it be thy part
To praife him more than ever man did merit:
My talk to thee muft be, how Benedick
Is fick in love with Beatrice: Of this matter
Is little Cupid's crafty arrow made,
That only wounds by hearfay. Now begin;

Enter BEATRICE, *behind.*

For look where Beatrice, like a lapwing, runs
Clofe by the ground, to hear our conference.
       D 2   *Urf.*

Urf. The pleasant'st angling is to see the fish
Cut with her golden oars the silver stream,
And greedily devour the treacherous bait :
So angle we for Beatrice ; who even now
Is couched in the woodbine coverture :
Fear you not my part of the dialogue.

Hero. Then go we near her, that her ear lose nothing
Of the false sweet bait that we lay for it.——

[*They advance to the bower.*

No, truly, Ursula, she is too disdainful ;
I know, her spirits are as coy and wild
As haggards of the rock.

Urf.   But are you sure,
That Benedick loves Beatrice so entirely ?

Hero. So says the prince, and my new-trothed lord.

Urf. And did they bid you tell her of it, madam ?

Hero. They did intreat me to acquaint her of it :
But I persuaded them, if they lov'd Benedick,
To wish him wrestle with affection,
And never to let Beatrice know of it.

Urf. Why did you so ? Doth not the gentleman
Deserve as full, as fortunate a bed,
As ever Beatrice shall couch upon ?

Hero. O God of love ! I know, he doth deserve
As much as may be yielded to a man :
But nature never fram'd a woman's heart
Of prouder stuff than that of Beatrice :
Disdain and scorn ride sparkling in her eyes,
Misprising what they look on ; and her wit
Values itself so highly, that to her
All matter else seems weak : she cannot love,
Nor take no shape nor project of affection,
She is so self-endeared.

Urf.   Sure, I think so ;

And

And therefore, certainly, it were not good
She knew his love, left she make sport at it.

　Hero. Why, you speak truth : I never yet saw man,
How wise, how noble, young, how rarely featur'd,
But she would spell him backward : if fair-faced,
She'd swear, the gentleman should be her sister;
If black, why, nature, drawing of an antick,
Made a foul blot : if tall, a lance ill-headed ;
If low, an agate very vilely cut :
If speaking, why, a vane blown with all winds ;
If silent, why, a block moved with none.
So turns she every man the wrong side out;
And never gives to truth and virtue, that
Which simpleness and merit purchaseth.

　Urs. Sure, sure, such carping is not commendable.

　Hero. No : not to be so odd, and from all fashions,.
As Beatrice is, cannot be commendable :
But who dare tell her so ? If I should speak,
.She'd mock me into air; O, she would laugh me
Out of myself, press me to death with wit.
Therefore let Benedick, like cover'd fire,
Consume away in sighs, waste inwardly :
It were a better death than die with mocks ;
Which is as bad as die with tickling.

　Urs. Yet tell her of it ; hear what she will say.

　Hero. No; rather I will go to Benedick,
And counsel him to fight against his passion :
And, truly, I'll devise some honest slanders
To stain my cousin with : One doth not know
How much an ill word may empoison liking.

　Urs. O, do not do your cousin such a wrong.
She cannot be so much without true judgement,
(Having so swift and excellent a wit,

As fhe is priz'd to have,) as to refufe
So rare a gentleman as fignior Benedick.

Hero. He is the only man of Italy,
Always excepted my dear Claudio.

Urf. I pray you, be not angry with me, madam,
Speaking my fancy; fignior Benedick,
For fhape, for bearing, argument, and valour,
Goes foremoft in report through Italy.

Hero. Indeed, he hath an excellent good name.

Urf. His excellence did earn it, ere he had it.—
When are you married, madam?

Hero. Why, every day;—to-morrow: Come, go in;
I'll fhow thee fome attires; and have thy counfel,
Which is the beft to furnifh me to-morrow.

Urf. She's lim'd I warrant you; we have caught her,
     madam.

Hero. If it prove fo, then loving goes by haps:
Some Cupid kills with arrows, fome with traps.

             [*Exeunt* HERO *and* URSULA.

       BEATRICE *advances.*

Beat. What fire is in mine ears? Can this be true?
     Stand I condemn'd for pride and fcorn fo much?
Contempt, farewell! and maiden pride, adieu!
     No glory lives behind the back of fuch.
And, Benedick, love on, I will requite thee;
     Taming my wild heart to thy loving hand;
If thou doft love, my kindnefs fhall incite thee
     To bind our loves up in a holy band:
For others fay, thou doft deferve; and I
Believe it better than reportingly.   [*Exit.*

                 SCENE

SCENE II.

A Room in LEONATO's *House.*

Enter Don PEDRO, CLAUDIO, BENEDICK, *and* LEONATO.

D. Pedro. I do but ftay till your marriage be confummate, and then go I toward Arragon.

Claud. I'll bring you thither, my lord, if you'll vouchfafe me.

D. Pedro. Nay, that would be as great a foil in the new glofs of your marriage, as to fhew a child his new coat, and forbid him to wear it. I will only be bold with Benedick for his company; for, from the crown of his head to the fole of his foot, he is all mirth; he hath twice or thrice cut Cupid's bow-ftring, and the little hangman dare not fhoot at him: he hath a heart as found as a bell, and his tongue is the clapper; for what his heart thinks his tongue fpeaks.

Bene. Gallants, I am not as I have been.

Leon. So fay I; methinks, you are fadder.

Claud. I hope, he be in love.

D. Pedro. Hang him, truant; there's no true drop of blood in him, to be truly touch'd with love: if he be fad, he wants money.

Bene. I have the tooth-ach.

D. Pedro. Draw it.

Bene. Hang it!

Claud. You muft hang it firft, and draw it afterwards.

D. Pedro. What? figh for the tooth-ach?

Leon. Where is but a humour, or a worm?

Bene. Well, Every one can mafter a grief, but he that has it.

Claud.

Claud. Yet fay I, he is in love.

D. Pedro. There is no appearance of fancy in him, unlefs it be a fancy that he hath to ftrange difguifes ; as, to
be a Dutch-man to-day ; a French-man to-morrow ; or in
the fhape of two countries at once, as, a German from
the waift downward, all flops ; and a Spaniard from the
hip upward, no doublet : Unlefs he have a fancy to this
foolery, as it appears he hath, he is no fool for fancy, as
you would have it appear he is.

Claud. If he be not in love with fome woman, there is
no believing old figns : he brufhes his hat o' mornings;
What fhould that bode?

D. Pedro. Hath any man feen him at the barber's?

Claud. No, but the barber's man hath been feen with
him ; and the old ornament of his cheek hath already
ftuffed tennis-balls.

Leon. Indeed, he looks younger than he did, by the
lofs of a beard.

D. Pedro. Nay, he rubs himfelf with civet : Can you
fmell him out by that ?

Claud. That's as much as to fay, The fweet youth's in
love.

D. Pedro. The greateft note of it is his melancholy.

Claud. And when was he wont to wafh his face ?

D. Pedro. Yea, or to paint himfelf ? for the which, I
hear what they fay of him.

Claud. Nay, but his jefting fpirit ; which is now crept
into a luteftring, and now governed by ftops.

D. Pedro. Indeed, that tells a heavy tale for him : Conclude, conclude, he is in love.

Claud. Nay, but I know who loves him.

D. Pedro. That would I know too ; I warrant, one that
knows him not.

Claud.

Claud. Yes, and his ill conditions; and, in defpite of all, dies for him.

D. Pedro. She fhall be buried with her face upwards.

Bene. Yet is this no charm for the tooth-ach.—Old fignior, walk afide with me; I have ftudied eight or nine wife words to fpeak to you, which thefe hobby-horfes muft not hear.   [*Exeunt* BENEDICK *and* LEONATO.

D. Pedro. For my life, to break with him about Beatrice.

Claud. 'Tis even fo: Hero and Margaret have by this play'd their parts with Beatrice; and then the two bears will not bite one another when they meet.

Enter Don JOHN.

D. John. My lord and brother, God fave you.

D. Pedro. Good den, brother.

D. John. If your leifure ferv'd, I would fpeak with you.

D. Pedro. In private?

D. John. If it pleafe you;—yet count Claudio may hear; for what I would fpeak of, concerns him.

D. Pedro. What's the matter?

D. John. Means your lordfhip to be married to-morrow?   [*To* CLAUDIO.

D. Pedro. You know, he does.

D. John. I know not that, when he knows what I know.

Claud. If there be any impediment, I pray you, difcover it.

D. John. You may think, I love you not; let that appear hereafter, and aim better at me by that I now will manifeft: For my brother, I think, he holds you well; and in dearnefs of heart hath holp to effect your enfuing marriage: furely, fuit ill fpent, and labour ill beftowed!

D. Pedro.

D. Pedro. Why, what's the matter?

D. John. I came hither to tell you; and, circumstances shorten'd, (for she hath been too long a talking of,) the lady is disloyal.

Claud. Who? Hero?

D. John. Even she; Leonato's Hero, your Hero, every man's Hero.

Claud. Disloyal?

D. John. The word is too good to paint out her wickedness; I could say, she were worse; think you of a worse title, and I will fit her to it. Wonder not till further warrant: go but with me to-night, you shall see her chamber-window enter'd; even the night before her wedding day: if you love her then, to-morrow wed her; but it would better fit your honour to change your mind.

Claud. May this be so?

D. Pedro. I will not think it.

D. John. If you dare not trust that you see, confess not that you know: if you will follow me, I will show you enough; and when you have seen more, and heard more, proceed accordingly.

Claud. If I see any thing to-night why I should not marry her to-morrow; in the congregation, where I should wed, there will I shame her.

D. Pedro. And, as I wooed for thee to obtain her, I will join with thee to disgrace her.

D. John. I will disparage her no farther, till you are my witnesses: bear it coldly but till midnight, and let the issue show itself.

D. Pedro. O day untowardly turned!

Claud. O mischief strangely thwarting!

D. John. O plague right well prevented!

So will you say, when you have seen the sequel. [*Exeunt.*

SCENE

SCENE III.

A Street.

Enter DOGBERRY *and* VERGES, *with the* Watch.

Dogb. Are you good men and true ?

Verg. Yea, or elfe it were pity but they fhould fuffer falvation, body and foul.

Dogb. Nay, that were a punifhment too good for them, if they fhould have any allegiance in them, being chofen for the prince's watch.

Verg. Well, give them their charge, neighbour Dog-berry.

Dogb. Firft, who think you the moft defartlefs man to be conftable ?

1. Watch. Hugh Oatcake, fir, or George Seacoal; for they can write and read.

Dogb. Come hither, neighbour Seacoal: God hath bleffed you with a good name: to be a well-favoured man is the gift of fortune; but to write and read comes by nature.

2. Watch. Both which, mafter conftable,——

Dogb. You have; I knew it would be your anfwer. Well, for your favour, fir, why, give God thanks, and make no boaft of it; and for your writing and reading, let that appear when there is no need of fuch vanity. You are thought here to be the moft fenfelefs and fit man for the conftable of the watch; therefore bear you the lantern: This is your charge; You fhall comprehend all vagrom men; you are to bid any man ftand, in the prince's name.

2. Watch. How if he will not ftand ?

Dogb. Why then, take no note of him, but let him go;

4 and

and prefently call the reft of the watch together, and thank God you are rid of a knave.

Verg. If he will not ftand when he is bidden, he is none of the prince's fubjects.

Dogb. True, and they are to meddle with none but the prince's fubjects :—You fhall alfo make no noife in the ftreets; for, for the watch to babble and to talk, is moft tolerable and not to be endured.

2. *Watch.* We will rather fleep than talk; we know what belongs to a watch.

· *Dogb.* Why, you fpeak like an ancient and moft quiet watchman; for I cannot fee how fleeping fhould offend: only, have a care that your bills be not ftolen :—Well, you are to call at all the ale-houfes, and bid thofe that are drunk get them to bed.

2. *Watch.* How if they will not?

Dogb. Why then, let them alone till they are fober; if they make you not then the better anfwer, you may fay, they are not the men you took them for.

2. *Watch.* Well, fir.

Dogb. If you meet a thief, you may fufpect him, by virtue of your office, to be no true man : and, for fuch kind of men, the lefs you meddle or make with them, why, the more is for your honefty.

2. *Watch.* If we know him to be a thief, fhall we not lay hands on him?

Dogb. Truly, by your office, you may; but, I think, they that touch pitch will be defiled : the moft peaceable way for you, if you do take a thief, is, to let him fhow himfelf what he is, and fteal out of your company.

Verg. You have been always called a merciful man, partner.

Dogb. Truly, I would not hang a dog by my will; much more a man who hath any honefty in him.

5   *Verg.*

Verg. If you hear a child cry in the night, you muſt call to the nurſe, and bid her ſtill it.

2. *Watch.* How if the nurſe be aſleep, and will not hear us?

Dogb. Why then, depart in peace, and let the child wake her with crying : for the ewe that will not hear her lamb when it baes, will never anſwer a calf when he bleats.

Verg. 'Tis very true.

Dogb. This is the end of the charge. You, conſtable, are to preſent the prince's own perſon; if you meet the prince in the night, you may ſtay him.

Verg. Nay by'r lady, that, I think, he cannot.

Dogb. Five ſhillings to one on't, with any man that knows the ſtatues, he may ſtay him : marry, not without the prince be willing : for, indeed, the watch ought to offend no man ; and it is an offence to ſtay a man againſt his will.

Verg. By'r lady, I think, it be ſo.

Dogb. Ha, ha, ha! Well, maſters, good night : an there be any matter of weight chances, call up me : keep your fellows' counſels and your own, and good night.—Come, neighbour.

2. *Watch.* Well, maſters, we hear our charge : let us go ſit here upon the church-bench till two, and then all to-bed.

Dogb. One word more, honeſt neighbours: I pray you, watch about ſignior Leonato's door ; for the wedding being there to-morrow, there is a great coil to-night : Adieu, be vigitant, I beſeech you.

[*Exeunt* DOGBERRY *and* VERGES.

Enter BORACHIO *and* CONRADE.

Bora. What! Conrade,—

Watch.

Watch. Peace, ftir not.   [*Afide.*

Bora. Conrade, I fay!

Con. Here, man, I am at thy elbow.

Bora. Mafs, and my elbow itch'd; I thought, there would a fcab follow.

Con. I will owe thee an anfwer for that; and now forward with thy tale.   *

Bora. Stand thee clofe then under this penthoufe, for it drizzles rain; and I will, like a true drunkard, utter all to thee.

Watch. [*Afide.*] Some treafon, mafters; yet ftand clofe.

Bora. Therefore know, I have earned of Don John a thoufand ducats.

Con. Is it poffible that any villainy fhould be fo dear?

Bora. Thou fhould'ft rather afk, if it were poffible any villainy fhould be fo rich; for when rich villains have need of poor ones, poor ones may make what price they will.

Con. I wonder at it.

Bora. That fhows, thou art unconfirm'd: Thou knoweft, that the fafhion of a doublet, or a hat, or a cloak, is nothing to a man.

Con. Yes, it is apparel.

Bora. I mean, the fafhion.

Con. Yes, the fafhion is the fafhion.

Bora. Tufh! I may as well fay, the fool's the fool. But fee'ft thou not what a deformed thief this fafhion is?

Watch. I know that Deformed; he has been a vile thief this feven year; he goes up and down like a gentleman: I remember his name.

Bora. Didft thou not hear fomebody?

Con. No; 'twas the vane on the houfe.

Bora. See'ft thou not, I fay, what a deformed thief this fafhion is? how giddily he turns about all the hot bloods,

between

between fourteen and five and thirty? fometime, fafhion-
ing them like Pharaoh's foldiers in the reechy painting;
fometime, like god Bel's priefts in the old church window; fometime, like the fhave ı Hercules in the fmirch'd
wormeaten tapeftry, where his codpiece feems as maffy as
his club?

Con. All this I fee; and fee, that the fafhion wears out
more apparel than the man: But art not thou thyfelf
giddy with the fafhion too, that thou haft fhifted out of
thy tale into telling me of the fafhion?

Bora. Not fo neither: but know, that I have to-night
wooed Margaret, the lady Hero's gentlewoman, by the
name of Hero; fhe leans me out at her miftrefs' chamber-
window, bids me a thoufand times good night,—I tell
this tale vilely:—I fhould firft tell thee, how the prince,
Claudio, and my mafter, planted, and placed, and poffeffed by my mafter Don John, faw afar off in the orchard
this amiable encounter.

Con. And thought they, Margaret was Hero?

Bora. Two of them did, the prince and Claudio; but
the devil my mafter knew fhe was Margaret; and partly
by his oaths, which firft poffeffed them, partly by the dark
night, which did deceive them, but chiefly by my villainy, which did confirm any flander that Don John had
made, away went Claudio enraged; fwore he would meet
her as he was appointed, next morning at the temple, and
there, before the whole congregation, fhame her with
what he faw over-night, and fend her home again without
a hufband.

1.*Watch.* We charge you in the prince's name, ftand.

2.*Watch.* Call up the right mafter conftable: We have
here recovered the moft dangerous piece of lechery that
ever was known in the commonwealth.

1.*Watch.*

1.*Watch.* And one Deformed is one of them; I know him, he wears a lock.

Con. Mafters, mafters,—

2.*Watch.* You'll be made bring Deformed forth, I warrant you.

Con. Mafters,—

1.*Watch.* Never fpeak; we charge you, let us obey you to go with us.

Bora. We are like to prove a goodly commodity, being taken up of thefe men's bills.

Con. A commodity in queftion, I warrant you. Come, we'll obey you.   [*Exeunt.*

SCENE IV.

A Room in LEONATO'S *Houfe.*

Enter HERO, MARGARET, *and* URSULA.

Hero. Good Urfula, wake my coufin Beatrice, and defire her to rife.

Urf. I will, lady.

Hero. And bid her come hither.

Urf. Well.   [*Exit* URSULA.

Marg. Troth, I think, your other rabato were better.

Hero. No, pray thee, good Meg, I'll wear this.

Marg. By my troth, it's not fo good; and I warrant, your coufin will fay fo.

Hero. My coufin's a fool, and thou art another; I'll wear none but this.

Marg. I like the new tire within excellently, if the hair were a thought browner: and your gown's a moft rare fafhion, i' faith. I faw the duchefs of Milan's gown, that they praife fo.

Hero. O, that exceeds, they fay.

                                                  Marg.

Marg. By my troth it's but a night-gown in respect of ours: Cloth of gold, and cuts, and laced with silver; set with pearls, down sleeves, side sleeves, and skirts round, underborne with a bluish tinsel: but for a fine, quaint, graceful, and excellent fashion, yours is worth ten on't.

Hero. God give me joy to wear it, for my heart is exceeding heavy!

Marg. 'Twill be heavier soon, by the weight of a man.

Hero. Fie upon thee! art not ashamed?

Marg. Of what, lady? of speaking honourably? Is not marriage honourable in a beggar? Is not your lord honourable without marriage? I think, you would have me say, saving your reverence,—*a husband:* an bad thinking do not wrest true speaking, I'll offend no body: Is there any harm in—*the heavier for a husband?* None, I think, an it be the right husband, and the right wife; otherwise 'tis light, and not heavy: Ask my lady Beatrice else, here she comes.

Enter BEATRICE.

Hero. Good morrow, coz.

Beat. Good morrow, sweet Hero.

Hero. Why, how now! do you speak in the sick tune?

Beat. I am out of all other tune, methinks.

Marg. Clap us into—*Light o' love;* that goes without a burden; do you sing it, and I'll dance it.

Beat. Yea, *Light o' love,* with your heels!—then if your husband have stables enough, you'll see he shall lack no barns.

Marg. O illegitimate construction! I scorn that with my heels.

Beat. 'Tis almost five o'clock, cousin; 'tis time you were ready. By my troth I am exceeding ill:—hey ho!

Marg. For a hawk, a horse, or a husband.

E   *Beat.*

Beat. For the letter that begins them all, H.

Marg. Well, an you be not turn'd Turk, there's no more failing by the ftar.

Beat. What means the fool, trow?

Marg. Nothing I; but God fend every one their heart's defire!

Hero. Thefe gloves the count fent me, they are an excellent perfume.

Beat. I am ftuff'd, coufin, I cannot fmell.

Marg. A maid, and ftuff'd! there's goodly catching of cold.

Beat. O, God help me! God help me! how long have you profefs'd apprehenfion?

Marg. Ever fince you left it: Doth not my wit become me rarely?

Beat. It is not feen enough, you fhould wear it in your cap:—By my troth, I am fick.

Marg. Get you fome of this diftill'd Carduus Benedictus, and lay it to your heart; it is the only thing for a qualm.

Hero. There thou prick'ft her with a thiftle.

Beat. Benedictus! why Benedictus? you have fome moral in this Benedictus.

Marg. Moral? no, by my troth, I have no moral meaning; I meant, plain holy-thiftle. You may think, perchance, that I think you are in love: nay, by'r lady, I am not fuch a fool to think what I lift; nor I lift not to think what I can; nor, indeed, I cannot think, if I would think my heart out of thinking, that you are in love, or that you will be in love, or that you can be in love: yet Benedick was fuch another, and now is he become a man: he fwore he would never marry; and yet now, in defpite of his heart, he eats his meat without grudging: and how you may be converted, I know not;

but

but methinks you look with your eyes as other women
do.

Beat. What pace is that thy tongue keeps?

Marg. Not a falfe gallop.

Re-enter URSULA.

Urf. Madam, withdraw; the prince, the count, fignior
Benedick, Don John, and all the gallants of the town, are
come to fetch you to church.

Hero. Help to drefs me, good cos, good Meg, good
Urfula.　　　　　　　　　　　　　　　　[*Exeunt.*

SCENE V.

Another Room in LEONATO'S *Houfe.*

Enter LEONATO, *with* DOGBERRY *and* VERGES.

Leon. What would you with me, honeft neighbour?

Dogb. Marry, fir, I would have fome confidence with
you, that decerns you nearly.

Leon. Brief, I pray you; for you fee, 'tis a bufy time
with me.

Dogb. Marry, this it is, fir.

Verg. Yes, in truth it is, fir.

Leon. What is it, my good friends?

Dogb. Goodman Verges, fir, fpeaks a little of the matter: an old man, fir, and his wits are not fo blunt, as, God
help, I would defire they were; but, in faith, honeft, as
the fkin between his brows.

Verg. Yes, I thank God, I am as honeft as any man
living, that is an old man, and no honefter than I.

Dogb. Comparifons are odorous: *palabras*, neighbour
Verges.

Leon. Neighbours, you are tedious.

Dogb.

Dogb. It pleafes your worfhip to fay fo, but we are the poor duke's officers; but, truly, for mine own part, if I were as tedious as a king, I could find in my heart to be-ftow it all of your worfhip.

Leon. All thy tedioufnefs on me! ha!

Dogb. Yea, and 'twere a thoufand times more than 'tis: for I hear as good exclamation on your worfhip, as of any man in the city; and though I be but a poor man, I am glad to hear it.

Verg. And fo am I.

Leon. I would fain know what you have to fay.

Verg. Marry, fir, our watch to-night, excepting your worfhip's prefence, have ta'en a couple of as arrant knaves as any in Meffina.

Dogb. A good old man, fir; he will be talking; as they fay, When the age is in, the wit is out; God help us! it is a world to fee!—Well faid, i' faith, neighbour Verges: —well, God's a good man; An two men ride of a horfe, one muft ride behind :—An honeft foul, i' faith, fir; by my troth he is, as ever broke bread : but, God is to be worfhipp'd : All men are not alike; alas, good neigh-bour!

Leon. Indeed, neighbour, he comes too fhort of you.

Dogb. Gifts, that God gives.

Leon. I muft leave you.

Dogb. One word, fir : our watch, fir, have, indeed, comprehended two afpicious perfons, and we would have them this morning examined before your worfhip.

Leon. Take their examination yourfelf, and bring it me; I am now in great hafte, as it may appear unto you.

Dog. It fhall be fuffigance.

Leon. Drink fome wine ere you go : fare you well.

Enter

Enter a Meſſenger.

Meſſ. My lord, they ſtay for you to give your daughter
to her huſband.

Leon. I will wait upon them ; I am ready.

[*Exeunt* LEONATO *and* Meſſenger.

Dogb. Go, good partner, go, get you to Francis Seacoal, bid him bring his pen and inkhorn to the gaol ; we
are now to examination theſe men.

Verg. And we muſt do it wiſely.

Dogb. We will ſpare for no wit, I warrant you ; here's
that [*Touching his forehead.*] ſhall drive ſome of them to a
non com: only get the learned writer to ſet down our
excommunication, and meet me at the gaol.   [*Exeunt.*

ACT IV.   SCENE I.

The Infide of a Church.

Enter Don PEDRO, *Don* JOHN, LEONATO, Friar, CLAU-
DIO, BENEDICK, HERO, *and* BEATRICE, *&c.*

Leon. Come, friar Francis, be brief; only to the plain
form of marriage, and you fhall recount their particular
duties afterwards.

Friar. You come hither, my lord, to marry this lady?

Claud. No.

Leon. To be married to her, friar; you come to marry
her.

Friar. Lady, you come hither to be married to this
count?

Hero. I do.

Friar. If either of you know any inward impediment
why you fhould not be conjoined, I charge you, on your
fouls, to utter it.

Claud. Know you any, Hero?

Hero. None, my lord.

Friar. Know you any, count?

Leon. I dare make his anfwer, none.

Claud. O, what men dare do! what men may do! what
men daily do! not knowing what they do!

Bene. How now! Interjections? Why, then fome be of
laughing, as, ha! ha! he!

Claud. Stand thee by, friar:—Father, by your leave;
Will you with free and unconftrained foul
Give me this maid, your daughter?

Leon. As freely, fon, as God did give her me.

Claud.

Claud. And what have I to give you back, whose worth
May counterpoise this rich and precious gift?

D. Pedro. Nothing, unless you render her again.

Claud. Sweet prince, you learn me noble thankfulness.—
There, Leonato, take her back again;
Give not this rotten orange to your friend;
She's but the sign and semblance of her honour:—
Behold, how like a maid she blushes here:
O, what authority and show of truth
Can cunning sin cover itself withal!
Comes not that blood as modest evidence,
To witness simple virtue? Would you not swear,
All you that see her, that she were a maid,
By these exterior shows? But she is none:
She knows the heat of a luxurious bed:
Her blush is guiltiness, not modesty.

Leon. What do you mean, my lord?

Claud.   Not to be married,
Not knit my soul to an approved wanton.

Leon. Dear my lord, if you, in your own proof
Have vanquish'd the resistance of her youth,
And made defeat of her virginity,——

Claud. I know what you would say; If I have known her,
You'll say, she did embrace me as a husband,
And so extenuate the 'forehand sin:
No, Leonato,
I never tempted her with word too large;
But, as a brother to his sister, show'd
Bashful sincerity, and comely love.

Hero. And seem'd I ever otherwise to you?

Claud. Out on thy seeming! I will write against it:
You seem to me as Dian in her orb;
As chaste as is the bud ere it be blown;
But you are more intemperate in your blood

           Than

Than Venus, or thofe pamper'd animals
That rage in favage fenfuality.

    Hero. Is my lord well, that he doth fpeak fo wide?

    Leon. Sweet prince, why fpeak not you?

    D. Pedro.   What fhould I fpeak?
I ftand difhonour'd; that have gone about
To link my dear friend to a common ftale.

    Leon. Are thefe things fpoken? or do I but dream?

    D. John. Sir, they are fpoken, and thefe things are true.

    Bene. This looks not like a nuptial.

    Hero.   True, O God!

    Claud. Leonato, ftand I here?
Is this the prince? Is this the prince's brother?
Is this face Hero's? Are our eyes our own?

    Leon. All this is fo; But what of this, my lord?

    Claud. Let me but move one queftion to your daughter;
And, by that fatherly and kindly power
That you have in her, bid her anfwer truly.

    Leon. I charge thee do fo, as thou art my child.

    Hero. O God defend me! how am I befet!—
What kind of catechizing call you this?

    Claud. To make you anfwer truly to your name.

    Hero. Is it not Hero? Who can blot that name
With any juft reproach?

    Claud.   Marry, that can Hero;
Hero itfelf can blot out Hero's virtue.
What man was he talk'd with you yefternight
Out at your window, betwixt twelve and one?
Now, if you are a maid, anfwer to this.

    Hero. I talk'd with no man at that hour, my lord.

    D. Pedro. Why, then are you no maiden.—Leonato,
I am forry you muft hear; Upon mine honour,
Myfelf, my brother, and this grieved count,
Did fee her, hear her, at that hour laft night,

                          Talk

Talk with a ruffian at her chamber-window;
Who hath,, indeed, moft like a liberal villain,
Confefs'd the vile encounters they have had
A thoufand times in fecret.

 D. John.   Fie, fie! they are
Not to be nam'd, my lord, not to be fpoke of;
There is not chaftity enough in language,
Without offence, to utter them: Thus, pretty lady,
I am forry for thy much mifgovernment.

 Claud. O Hero! what a Hero hadft thou been,
If half thy outward graces had been placed ,
About thy thoughts, and counfels of thy heart!
But, fare thee well, moft foul, moft fair! farewell,
Thou pure impiety, and impious purity!
For thee I'll lock up all the gates of love,
And on my eye-lids fhall conjecture hang,
To turn all beauty into thoughts of harm,
And never fhall it more be gracious.

 Leon. Hath no man's dagger here a point for me?

            [HERO *fwoons.*
 Beat. Why, how now, coufin? wherefore fink you down?
 D. John. Come, let us go: thefe things, come thus to light,
Smother her fpirits up.

    [*Exeunt Don* PEDRO, *Don* JOHN, *and* CLAUDIO.
 Bene. How doth the lady?
 Beat.   Dead, I think;—Help, uncle;—
Hero! why, Hero!—Uncle!—Signior Benedick!—friar!
 Leon. O fate, take not away thy heavy hand!
Death is the faireft cover for her fhame,
That may be wifh'd for.
 Beat.   How now, coufin Hero?
 Friar. Have comfort, lady.
 Leon.   Doft thou look up?
 Friar.   Yea; Wherefore fhould fhe not?

              Leon

                3

Leon. Wherefore? Why, doth not every earthly thing
Cry shame upon her? Could she here deny
The story that is printed in her blood?—
Do not live, Hero; do not ope thine eyes:
For did I think thou would'st not quickly die,
Thought I thy spirits were stronger than thy shames,
Myself would, on the rearward of reproaches,
Strike at thy life. Griev'd I, I had but one?
Chid I for that at frugal nature's frame?
O, one too much by thee! Why had I one?
Why ever waft thou lovely in my eyes?
Why had I not, with charitable hand,
Took up a beggar's issue at my gates;
Who smirched thus, and mired with infamy,
I might have said, *No part of it is mine,*
This shame derives itself from unknown loins?
But mine, and mine I lov'd, and mine I prais'd,
And mine that I was proud on; mine so much,
That I myself was to myself not mine,
Valuing of her; why, she—O, she is fallen
Into a pit of ink! that the wide sea
Hath drops too few to wash her clean again;
And salt too little, which may season give
To her foul tainted flesh!

    Bene.   Sir, sir, be patient:
For my part, I am so attir'd in wonder,
I know not what to say.

    Beat. O, on my soul, my cousin is belied!

    Bene. Lady, were you her bedfellow last night?

    Beat. No, truly, not; although, until last night,
I have this twelvemonth been her bedfellow.

    Leon. Confirm'd, confirm'd! O, that is stronger made
Which was before barr'd up with ribs of iron!
Would the two princes lie? and Claudio lie?

Who lov'd her so, that, speaking of her foulness,
Wash'd it with tears? Hence from her; let her die.

 Friar. Hear me a little;
For I have only been silent so long,
And given way unto this course of fortune,
By noting of the lady: I have mark'd
A thousand blushing apparitions start
Into her face; a thousand innocent shames
In angel whiteness bear away those blushes;
And in her eye there hath appear'd a fire,
To burn the errors that these princes hold
Against her maiden truth:—Call me a fool;
Trust not my reading, nor my observations,
Which with experimental seal doth warrant
The tenour of my book; trust not my age,
My reverence, calling, nor divinity,
If this sweet lady lie not guiltless here
Under some biting error.

 Leon.   Friar, it cannot be:
Thou seest, that all the grace that she hath left,
Is, that she will not add to her damnation
A sin of perjury; she not denies it:
Why seek'st thou then to cover with excuse
That which appears in proper nakedness?

 Friar. Lady, what man is he you are accus'd of?

 Hero. They know, that do accuse me; I know none:
If I know more of any man alive,
Than that which maiden modesty doth warrant,
Let all my sins lack mercy!—O my father,
Prove you that any man with me convers'd
At hours unmeet, or that I yesternight
Maintain'd the change of words with any creature,
Refuse me, hate me, torture me to death.

 Friar. There is some strange misprision in the princes.

              Bene.

Bene. Two of them have the very bent of honour;
And if their wifdoms be mifled in this,
The practice of it lives in John the baftard,
Whofe fpirits toil in frame of villainies.

    Leon. I know not; If they fpeak but truth of her,
Thefe hands fhall tear her; if they wrong her honour,
The proudeft of them fhall well hear of it.
Time hath not yet fo dried this blood of mine,
Nor age fo eat up my invention,
Nor fortune made fuch havock of my means,
Nor my bad life reft me fo much of friends,
But they fhall find, awak'd in fuch a kind,
Both ftrength of fimb, and policy of mind,
Ability in means, and choice of friends,
To quit me of them throughly.

    Friar.   Paufe a while,
And let my counfel fway you in this cafe.
Your daughter here the princes left for dead;
Let her awhile be fecretly kept in,
And publifh it, that fhe is dead indeed:
Maintain a mourning oftentation;
And on your family's old monument
Hang mournful epitaphs, and do all rites
That appertain unto a burial.

    Leon. What fhall become of this? What will this do?

    Friar. Marry, this, well carried, fhall on her behalf
Change flander to remorfe; that is fome good:
But not for that, dream I on this ftrange courfe,
But on this travail look for greater birth.
She dying, as it muft be fo maintain'd,
Upon the inftant that fhe was accus'd,
Shall be lamented, pitied and excus'd,
Of every hearer: For it fo falls out,
That what we have we prize not to the worth,

                            Whiles

Whiles we enjoy it ; but being lack'd and loft,
Why, then we rack the value ; then we find
The virtue, that poffeffion would not fhow us
Whiles it was ours :—So will it fare with Claudio :
When he fhall hear fhe died upon his words,
The idea of her life fhall fweetly creep
Into his ftudy of imagination ;
And every lovely organ of her life
Shall come apparel'd in more precious habit,
More moving-delicate, and full of life,
Into the eye and profpect of his foul,
Than when fhe liv'd indeed :—then fhall he mourn,
(If ever love had intereft in his liver,)
And wifh he had not fo accufed her ;
No, though he thought his accufation true.
Let this be fo, and doubt not but fuccefs
Will fafhion the event in better fhape
Than I can lay it down in likelihood.
But if all aim but this be levell'd falfe,
The fuppofition of the lady's death
Will quench the wonder of her infamy :
And, if it fort not well, you may conceal her
(As beft befits her wounded reputation,)
In fome reclufive and religious life,
Out of all eyes, tongues, minds, and injuries.

   Bene. Signior Leonato, let the friar advife you :
And though, you know, my inwardnefs and love
Is very much unto the prince and Claudio,
Yet, by mine honour, I will deal in this
As fecretly, and juftly, as your foul
Should with your body.

   Leon.   Being that I flow in grief,
The fmalleft twine may lead me.

   Friar. 'Tis well confented ; prefently away ;

For

For to ftrange fores ftrangely they ftrain the cure.—
Come, lady, die to live: this wedding day,
  Perhaps, is but prolong'd; have patience, and endure.
          ·   [*Exeunt* FRIAR, HERO, *and* LEONATO.

Bene. Lady Beatrice, have you wept all this while?

Beat. Yea, and I will weep a while longer.

Bene. I will not defire that.

Beat. You have no reafon, I do it freely.

Bene. Surely, I do believe your fair coufin is wrong'd.

Beat. Ah, how much might the man deferve of me,
that would right her!

Bene. Is there any way to fhow fuch friendfhip?

Beat. A very even way, but no fuch friend.

Bene. May a man do it?

Beat. It is a man's office, but not yours.

Bene. I do love nothing in the world fo well as you; Is
not that ftrange?

Beat. As ftrange as the thing I know not: It were as
poffible for me to fay, I loved nothing fo well as you: but
believe me not; and yet I lie not; I confefs nothing, nor
I deny nothing:—I am forry for my coufin.

Bene. By my fword, Beatrice, thou loveft me.

Beat. Do not fwear by it, and eat it.

Bene. I will fwear by it, that you love me; and I will
make him eat it, that fays, I love not you.

Beat. Will you not eat your word?

Bene. With no fauce that can be devifed to it: I proteft, I love thee.

Beat. Why then, God forgive me!

Bene. What offence, fweet Beatrice?

Beat. You have ftaid me in a happy hour; I was about
to proteft, I loved you.

Bene. And do it with all thy heart.

                                        ' *Beat.*

Beat. I love you with so much of my heart, that none
is left to protest.

Bene. Come, bid me do any thing for thee.

Beat. Kill Claudio.

Bene. Ha! not for the wide world.

Beat. You kill me to deny it: Farewell.

Bene. Tarry, sweet Beatrice.

Beat. I am gone, though I am here;—There is no love
in you :—Nay, I pray you, let me go.

Bene. Beatrice,—

Beat. In faith, I will go.

Bene. We'll be friends first.

Beat. You dare easier be friends with me, than fight
with mine enemy.

Bene. Is Claudio thine enemy?

Beat. Is he not approved in the height a villain, that
hath slander'd, scorn'd, dishonour'd my kinswoman?—O,
that I were a man!—What! bear her in hand until they
come to take hands; and then with public accusation,
uncovered slander, unmitigated rancour,—O God, that I
were a man! I would eat his heart in the market-place.

Bene. Hear me, Beatrice.

Beat. Talk with a man out at a window?—a proper
saying!

Bene. Nay but, Beatrice;—

Beat. Sweet Hero!—she is wrong'd, she is slander'd,
she is undone.

Bene. Beat—

Beat. Princes, and counties! Surely, a princely testi-
mony, a goodly count-confect; a sweet gallant, surely!
O that I were a man for his sake! or that I had any friend
would be a man for my sake! But manhood is melted into
courtesies, valour into compliment, and men are only
turned into tongue, and trim ones too; he is now as va-

liant

liant as Hercules, that only tells a lie, and fwears it:—I
cannot be a man with wifhing, therefore I will die a woman with grieving.

Bene. Tarry, good Beatrice: By this hand, I love
thee.

Beat. Ufe it for my love fome other way than fwearing
by it.

Bene. Think you in your foul, the count Claudio hath
wrong'd Hero?

Beat. Yea, as fure as I have a thought, or a foul.

Bene. Enough, I am engaged, I will challenge him; I
will kifs your hand, and fo leave you: By this hand,
Claudio fhall render me a dear account: As you hear of
me, fo think of me. Go, comfort your coufin: I muft
fay, fhe is dead; and fo, farewell.   [*Exeunt.*

SCENE II.

A Prifon.

Enter DOGBERRY, VERGES, *and* Sexton, *in gowns; and*
the Watch, *with* CONRADE, *and* BORACHIO.

Dogb. Is our whole diffembly appear'd?

Verg. O, a ftool and a cufhion for the fexton!

Sexton. Which be the malefactors?

Dogb. Marry, that am I and my partner.

Verg. Nay, that's certain; we have the exhibition to
examine.

Sexton. But which are the offenders that are to be examined? let them come before mafter conftable.

Dogb. Yea, marry, let them come before me.—What is
your name, friend?

Bora. Borachio.

Dogb. Pray write down—Borachio.——Yours, firrah?
                                              Con.

Con. I am a gentleman, fir, and my name is Conrade.

Dogb. Write down—mafter gentleman Conrade.—Mafters, do you ferve God?

Con. Bora. Yea, fir, we hope.

Dogb. Write down—that they hope they ferve God:—and write God firft; for God defend but God fhould go before fuch villains!—Mafters, it is proved already that you are little better than falfe knaves; and it will go near to be thought fo fhortly. How anfwer you for yourfelves?

Con. Marry, fir, we fay we are none.

Dogb. A marvellous witty fellow, I affure you; but I will go about with him.—Come you hither, firrah; a word in your ear, fir; I fay to you, it is thought, you are falfe knaves.

Bora. Sir, I fay to you, we are none.

Dogb. Well, ftand afide.—'Fore God, they are both in a tale: Have you writ down—that they are none?

Sexton. Mafter conftable, you go not the way to examine; you muft call forth the watch that are their accufers.

Dogb. Yea, marry, that's the efteft way:—Let the watch come forth:—Mafters, I charge you, in the prince's name, accufe thefe men.

1. *Watch.* This man faid, fir, that Don John, the prince's brother, was a villain.

Dogb. Write down—prince John a villain:—Why this is flat perjury, to call a prince's brother—villain.

Bora. Mafter conftable,—

Dogb. Pray thee, fellow, peace; I do not like thy look, I promife thee.

Sexton. What heard you him fay elfe?

2. *Watch.* Marry, that he had received a thoufand ducats

F

eats of Don John, for accuſing the lady Hero wrongfully.

Dogb. Flat burglary, as ever was committed.

Verg. Yea, by the maſs, that it is.

Sexton. What elſe, fellow?

1. *Watch.* And that count Claudio did mean, upon his
words, to diſgrace Hero before the whole aſſembly, and
not marry her.

Dogb. O villain! thou wilt be condemned into everlaſt-
ing redemption for this.

Sexton. What elſe?

2. *Watch.* This is all.

Sexton. And this is more, maſters, than you can deny.
Prince John is this morning ſecretly ſtolen away; Hero
was in this manner accuſed, in this very manner refuſed,
and upon the grief of this, ſuddenly died.—Maſter conſtable, let theſe men be bound, and brought to Leonato's; I
will go before, and ſhow him their examination. [*Exit.*

Dogb. Come, let them be opinion'd.

Verg. Let them be in band.

Con. Off, coxcomb!

Dogb. God's my life! where's the ſexton? let him write
down—the prince's officer, coxcomb.—Come, bind them:
——Thou naughty varlet!

Con. Away! you are an aſs, you are an aſs.

Dogb. Doſt thou not ſuſpect my place? Doſt thou not
ſuſpect my years?—O that he were here to write me down
—an aſs!—but, maſters, remember, that I am an aſs;
though it be not written down, yet forget not that I am
an aſs:—No, thou villain, thou art full of piety, as ſhall
be proved upon thee by good witneſs. I am a wiſe fellow; and, which is more, an officer; and, which is more,
a houſholder; and, which is more, as pretty a piece of fleſh

as any is in Meffina; and one that knows the law, go to;
and a rich fellow enough, go to; and a fellow that hath
had loffes; and one that hath two gowns, and every thing
handfome about him :—Bring him away.   O, that I had
been writ down—an afs !   [*Exeunt.*

ACT V.   SCENE I.

Before LEONATO's *Houſe.*

Enter LEONATO *and* ANTONIO.

Ant. If you go on thus, you will kill yourſelf;
And 'tis not wiſdom, thus to ſecond grief
Againſt yourſelf. .

    Leon. I pray thee, ceaſe thy counſel,
Which falls into mine ears as profitleſs
As water in a ſieve : give not me counſel ;
Nor let no comforter delight mine ear,
But ſuch a one whoſe wrongs do ſuit with mine.
Bring me a father, that ſo lov'd his child,
Whoſe joy of her is overwhelm'd like mine,
And bid him ſpeak of patience ;
Meaſure his woe the length and breadth of mine,
And let it anſwer every ſtrain for ſtrain ;
As thus for thus, and ſuch a grief for ſuch,
In every lineament, branch, ſhape, and form :
If ſuch a one will ſmile, and ſtroke his beard ;
Cry—ſorrow, wag ! and hem, when he ſhould groan ;
Patch grief with proverbs ; make misfortune drunk
With candle-waſters ; bring him yet to me,
And I of him will gather patience.
But there is no ſuch man : For, brother, men
Can counſel, and ſpeak comfort to that grief
Which they themſelves not feel ; but, taſting it,
Their counſel turns to paſſion, which before
Would give preceptial medicine to rage,
Fetter ſtrong madneſs in a ſilken thread,
Charm ach with air, and agony with words :

                                No,

Much ado about Nothing

Page 68

Pub.ᵈ 1 Aug 1793 by Edwᵈ Harding 98 Pall Mall

No, no; 'tis all men's office to fpeak patience
To thofe that wring under the load of forrow;
But no man's virtue, nor fufficiency,
To be fo moral, when he fhall endure
The like himfelf: therefore give me no counfel:
My griefs cry louder than advertifement.

Ant. Therein do men from children nothing differ.

Leon. I pray thee, peace; I will be flefh and blood;
For there was never yet philofopher, `
That could endure the tooth-ach patiently;
However they have writ the ftyle of gods,
And made a pifh at chance and fufferance.

Ant. Yet bend not all the harm upon yourfelf;
Make thofe, that do offend you, fuffer too.

Leon. There thou fpeak'ft reafon: nay, I will do fo:
My foul doth tell me, Hero is bely'd;
And that fhall Claudio know, fo fhall the prince,
And all of them, that thus difhonour her.

Enter Don PEDRO *and* CLAUDIO.

Ant. Here comes the prince, and Claudio, haftily.

D. Pedro. Good den, good den.

Claud. Good day to both of you.

Leon. Hear you, my lords,—

D. Pedro. We have fome hafte, Leonato.

Leon. Some hafte, my lord!—well, fare you well, my
lord:—
Are you fo hafty now?—well, all is one.

D. Pedro. Nay, do not quarrel with us, good old man.

Ant. If he could right himfelf with quarreling,
Some of us would lie low.

Claud. Who wrongs him?

Leon. Marry,
Thou, thou doft wrong me; thou diffembler, thou:—

F 3

Nay,

Nay, never lay thy hand upon thy fword,
I fear thee not.

   Claud.   Marry, befhrew my hand,
If it fhould give your age fuch caufe of fear :
In faith, my hand meant nothing to my fword.

   Leon. Tufh, tufh, man, never fleer and jeft at me :
I fpeak not like a dotard, nor a fool ;
As, under privilege of age, to brag
What I have done being young, or what would do,
Were I not old : Know, Claudio, to thy head,
Thou haft fo wrong'd mine innocent child and me,
That I am forc'd to lay my reverence by ;
And, with grey hairs, and bruife of many days,
Do challenge thee to trial of a man.
I fay, thou haft bely'd mine innocent child ;
Thy flander hath gone through and through her heart,
And fhe lyes buried with her anceftors :
O ! in a tomb where never fcandal flept,
Save this of her's, fram'd by thy villainy.

   Claud. My villainy!

   Leon.   Thine, Claudio; thine I fay.

   D. Pedro. You fay not right, old man.

   Leon.   '   My lord, my lord,
I'll prove it on his body, if he dare ;
Defpite his nice fence, and his active practice,
His May of youth, and bloom of luftyhood.

   Claud. Away, I will not have to do with you.

   Leon. Canft thou fo daff me ? Thou haft kill'd my child;
If thou kill'ft me, boy, thou fhalt kill a man.

   Ant. He fhall kill two of us, and men indeed :
But that's no matter; let him kill one firft ;—
Win me and wear me,—let him anfwer me :—
Come, follow me, boy; come, boy, follow me :

      7

Sir boy, I'll whip you from your foining fence;
Nay, as I am a gentleman, I will.

 Leon. Brother,—

 Ant. Content yourself: God knows, I lov'd my niece;
And she is dead, slander'd to death by villains;
That dare as well answer a man, indeed,
As I dare take a serpent by the tongue:
Boys, apes, braggarts, Jacks, milksops!—

 Leon.   Brother Antony,—

 Ant. Hold you content; What, man! I know them, yea,
And what they weigh, even to the utmost scruple:
Scambling, out-facing, fashion-mong'ring boys,
That lie, and cog, and flout, deprave and slander,
Go antickly, and show outward hideousness,
And speak off half a dozen dangerous words,
How they might hurt their enemies, if they durst,
And this is all.

 Leon. But, brother Antony,—

 Ant.   Come, 'tis no matter;
Do not you meddle, let me deal in this.

 D. Pedro. Gentlemen both, we will not wake your patience.
My heart is sorry for your daughter's death;
But, on my honour, she was charg'd with nothing
But what was true, and very full of proof.

 Leon. My lord, my lord,—

 D. Pedro.   I will not hear you.

 Leon.   No?

Brother, away:—I will be heard;—

 Ant.   And shall,
Or some of us will smart for it.

     [*Exeunt* LEONATO *and* ANTONIO.

   Enter BENEDICK.

 D. Pedro. See, see; here comes the man we went to seek,

      F 4   *Claud.*

Claud. Now, fignior! what news!

Bene. Good day, my lord.

D. Pedro. Welcome, fignior: You are almoft come to part almoft a fray.

Claud. We had like to have had our two nofes fnapped off with two old men without teeth.

D. Pedro. Leonato and his brother: What think'ft thou? Had we fought, I doubt, we fhould have been too young for them.

Bene. In a falfe quarrel there is no true valour. I came to feek you both.

Claud. We have been up and down to feek thee; for we are high-proof melancholy, and would fain have it beaten away: Wilt thou ufe thy wit?

Bene. It is in my fcabbard; Shall I draw it?

D. Pedro. Doft thou wear thy wit by thy fide?

Claud. Never any did fo, though very many have been befide their wit.—I will bid thee draw, as we do the min-ftrels; draw, to pleafure us.

D. Pedro. As I am an honeft man, he looks pale:—Art thou fick, or angry?

Claud. What! courage, man! What though care kill'd a cat, thou haft mettle enough in thee to kill care.

Bene. Sir, I fhall meet your wit in the career, an you charge it againft me:—I pray you, choofe another fubject.

Claud. Nay, then give him another ftaff; this laft was broke crofs.

D. Pedro. By this light, he changes more and more; I think, he be angry indeed.

Claud. If he be, he knows how to turn his girdle.

Bene. Shall I fpeak a word in your ear?

Claud. God blefs me from a challenge!

Bene. You are a villain;—I jeft not:—I will make it good how you dare, with what you dare, and when you

dare;—

dare :—Do me right, or I will proteſt your cowardice. You have kill'd a ſweet lady, and her death ſhall fall heavy on you : Let me hear from you.

Claud. Well, I will meet you, ſo I may have good cheer.

D. Pedro. What, a feaſt ? a feaſt ?

Claud. I' faith, I thank him ; he hath bid me to a calf's-head and a capon ; the which if I do not carve moſt curiouſly, ſay, my knife's naught.—Shall I not find a woodcock too ?

Bene. Sir, your wit ambles well ; it goes eaſily.

D. Pedro. I'll tell thee how Beatrice prais'd thy wit the other day : I ſaid, thou hadſt a fine wit ; *True, ſays ſhe, a fine little one : No,* ſaid I, *a great wit ; Right, ſays ſhe, a great groſs one : Nay,* ſaid I, *a good wit ; Juſt,* ſaid ſhe, *it hurts no body : Nay,* ſaid I, *the gentleman is wiſe ; Certain,* ſaid ſhe, *a wiſe gentleman : Nay,* ſaid I, *he hath the tongues ; That I believe,* ſaid ſhe, *for he ſwore a thing to me on Monday night, which he forſwore on Tueſday morning ; there's a double tongue, there's two tongues.* Thus did ſhe, an hour together, tranſ-ſhape thy particular virtues ; yet, at laſt, ſhe concluded with a ſigh, thou waſt the propereſt man in Italy.

Claud. For the which ſhe wept heartily, and ſaid, ſhe cared not.

D. Pedro. Yea, that ſhe did ; but yet, for all that, an if ſhe did not hate him deadly, ſhe would love him dearly : the old man's daughter told us all.

Claud. All, all ; and moreover, *God ſaw him when he was hid in the garden.*

D. Pedro. But when ſhall we ſet the ſavage bull's horns on the ſenſible Benedick's head ?

Claud. Yea, and text underneath, *Here dwells Benedick the married man ?*

Bene. Fare you well, boy ; you know my mind ; I will
leave

leave you now to your goffip-like humour: you break
jefts as braggarts do their blades, which, God be thanked,
hurt not.—My lord, for your many courtefies I thank
you: I muft difcontinue your company: your brother,
the baftard, is fled from Meffina: you have, among you,
kill'd a fweet and innocent lady: For my lord Lack-beard,
there, he and I fhall meet; and till then, peace be with
him.   [*Exit* BENEDICK.

D. Pedro. He is in earneft.

Claud. In moft profound earneft; and, I'll warrant
you, for the love of Beatrice.

D. Pedro. And hath challeng'd thee?

Claud. Moft fincerely.

D. Pedro. What a pretty thing man is, when he goes in
his doublet and hofe, and leaves off his wit!

Enter DOGBERRY, VERGES, *and the Watch, with* CON-
RADE *and* BORACHIO.

Claud. He is then a giant to an ape: but then is an ape
a doctor to fuch a man.

D. Pedro. But, foft you, let be; pluck up, my heart,
and be fad! Did he not fay, my brother was fled?

Dogb. Come, you, fir; if juftice cannot tame you, fhe
fhall ne'er weigh more reafons in her balance: nay, an
you be a curfing hypocrite once, you muft be look'd to.

D. Pedro. How now, two of my brother's men bound!
Borachio, one!

Claud. Hearken after their offence, my lord!

D. Pedro. Officers, what offence have thefe men done?

Dogb. Marry, fir, they have committed falfe report;
moreover, they have fpoken untruths; fecondarily, they
are flanders; fixth and laftly, they have bely'd a lady;
thirdly, they have verified unjuft things: and, to conclude, they are lying knaves.

                                        D. Pedro.

D. Pedro. Firſt, I aſk thee what they have done ; thirdly,
I aſk thee what's their offence ; ſixth and laſtly, why they
are committed ; and, to conclude, what you lay to their
charge.

Claud. Rightly reaſoned, and in his own diviſion ; and,
by my troth, there's one meaning well ſuited.

D. Pedro. Who have you offended, maſters, that you
are thus bound to your anſwer ? this learned conſtable is
too cunning to be underſtood : What's your offence ?

Bora. Sweet prince, let me go no further to mine anſwer ; do you hear me, and let this count kill me. I have
deceived even your very eyes : what your wiſdoms could
not diſcover, theſe ſhallow fools have brought to light ;
who, in the night, overheard me confeſſing to this man,
how Don John your brother incenſed me to ſlander the
lady Hero ; how you were brought into the orchard, and
ſaw me court Margaret in Hero's garments ; how you diſ-
graced her, when you ſhould marry her : my villainy they
have upon record ; which I had rather ſeal with my death,
than repeat over to my ſhame : the lady is dead upon mine
and my maſter's falſe accuſation ; and, briefly, I deſire
nothing but the reward of a villain.

D. Pedro. Runs not this ſpeech like iron through your
blood ?

Claud. I have drunk poiſon, whiles he utter'd it.

D. Pedro. But did my brother ſet thee on to this ?

Bora. Yea, and paid me richly for the practice of it.

D. Pedro. He is compos'd and fram'd of treachery :—
And fled he is upon this villainy.

Claud. Sweet Hero ! now thy image doth appear
In the rare ſemblance that I lov'd at firſt.

Dogb. Come, bring away the plaintiffs ; by this time
our Sexton hath reform'd ſignior Leonato of the matter :

And

And maſters, do not forget to ſpecify, when time and
place ſhall ſerve, that I am an aſs.

Verg. Here, here comes maſter ſignior Leonato, and the
Sexton too.

Re-enter LEONATO *and* ANTONIO, *with the* Sexton.

Leon. Which is the villain? Let me ſee his eyes;
That when I note another man like him,
I may avoid him: Which of theſe is he?

Bora. If you would know your wronger, look on me.

Leon. Art thou the ſlave, that with thy breath haſt kill'd
Mine innocent child?

Bora.   Yea, even I alone.

Leon. No, not ſo, villain; thou bely'ſt thyſelf;
Here ſtand a pair of honourable men,
A third is fled, that had a hand in it :—
I thank you, princes, for my daughter's death;
Record it with your high and worthy deeds;
'Twas bravely done, if you bethink you of it.

Claud. I know not how to pray your patience,
Yet I muſt ſpeak: Chooſe your revenge yourſelf;
Impoſe me to what penance your invention
Can lay upon my ſin: yet ſinn'd I not,
But in miſtaking.

D. Pedro.   By my ſoul, nor I;
And yet, to ſatisfy this good old man,
I would bend under any heavy weight
That he'll enjoin me to.

Leon. I cannot bid you bid my daughter live,
That were impoſſible; but, I pray you both,
Poſſeſs the people in Meſſina here
How innocent ſhe died: and, if your love
Can labour aught in ſad invention,
Hang her an epitaph upon her tomb,

                                        And

And fing it to her bones ; fing it to-night :—
To-morrow morning come you to my houfe ;
And fince you could not be my fon-in-law,
Be yet my nephew : my brother hath a daughter,
Almoft the copy of my child that's dead,
And fhe alone is heir to both of us ;
Give her the right you fhould have given her coufin,
And fo dies my revenge.

   Claud.　　　　　　　　O, noble fir,
Your over-kindnefs doth wring tears from me !
I do embrace your offer ; and difpofe
For henceforth of poor Claudio.

   Leon. To-morrow then I will expect your coming ;
To-night I take my leave.—This naughty man
Shall face to face be brought to Margaret,
Who, I believe, was pack'd in all this wrong,
Hir'd to it by your brother.

   Bora.　　　　　　　No, by my foul, fhe was not ;
Nor knew not what fhe did, when fhe fpoke to me ;
But always hath been juft and virtuous,
In any thing that I do know by her.

   Dogb. Moreover, fir, (which, indeed, is not under white and black,) this plaintiff here, the offender, did call me afs : I befeech you, let it be remembered in his punifh-ment : And alfo, the watch heard them talk of one De-formed : they fay, he wears a key in his ear, and a lock hanging by it ; and borrows money in God's name ; the which he hath ufed fo long, and never paid, that now men grow hard-hearted, and will lend nothing for God's fake : Pray you, examine him upon that point.

   Leon. I thank thee for thy care and honeft pains.

   Dogb. Your worfhip fpeaks like a moft thankful and reverend youth ; and I praife God for you.

   Leon. There's for thy pains.

                                     Dogb,

Dogb. God fave the foundation!

Leon. Go, I difcharge thee of thy prifoner, and I thank thee.

Dogb. I leave an arrant knave with your worſhip; which, I befeech your worſhip, to correɛ̃ yourſelf, for the example of others. God keep your worſhip; I wiſh your worſhip well; God reſtore you to health : I humbly give you leave to depart; and if a merry meeting may be wiſh'd, God prohibit it.—Come, neighbour.

       . [*Exeunt* DOGBERRY, VERGES, *and* Watch.

Leon. Until to-morrow morning, lords, farewell.

Ant. Farewell, my lords; we look for you to-morrow.

D. Pedro. We will not fail.

Claud.   · To-night I'll mourn with Hero.

       [*Exeunt* D. PEDRO *and* CLAUDIO.

Leon. Bring you theſe fellows on; we'll talk with Margaret,

How her acquaintance grew with this lewd fellow.

                              [*Exeunt.*

SCENE II.

LEONATO'S *Garden.*

Enter BENEDICK *and* MARGARET, *meeting.*

Bene. Pray thee, ſweet miſtreſs Margaret, deſerve well at my hands, by helping me to the ſpeech of Beatrice.

· *Marg.* Will you then write me a ſonnet in praiſe of my beauty?

Bene. In ſo high a ſtyle, Margaret, that no man living ſhall come over it; for, in moſt comely truth, thou de-ſerveſt it.

Marg. To have no man come over me? why, ſhall I always keep below ſtairs?

                                 Bene.

Bene. Thy wit is as quick as the greyhound's mouth, it catches.

Marg. And your's as blunt as the fencer's foils, which hit, but hurt not.

Bene. A moft manly wit, Margaret, it will not hurt a woman; and fo, I pray thee, call Beatrice: I give thee the bucklers.

Marg. Give us the fwords, we have bucklers of our own.

Bene. If you ufe them, Margaret, you muft put in the pikes with a vice; and they are dangerous weapons for maids.

Marg. Well, I will call Beatrice to you, who, I think, hath legs.   [*Exit* MARGARET.

Bene. And therefore will come.

   The god of love,   [Singing.]
   That fits above,
  And knows me, and knows me,
   How pitiful I deferve,—

I mean, in finging; but in loving,—Leander the good fwimmer, Troilus the firft employer of pandars, and a whole book full of thefe quondam carpet-mongers, whofe names yet run fmoothly in the even road of a blank verfe, why, they were never fo truly turn'd over and over as my poor felf, in love: Marry, I cannot fhow it in rhyme; I have try'd; I can find out no rhyme to *lady* but *baby,* an innocent rhyme; for *fcorn, born,* a hard rhyme; for *fchool, fool,* a babbling rhyme; very ominous endings: No, I was not born under a rhyming planet, nor I cannot woo in feftival terms.—

Enter BEATRICE.

Sweet Beatrice, would'ft thou come when I called thee?

Beat. Yea, fignior, and depart when you bid me.

             Bene.

Bene. O, stay but till then!

Beat. Then, is spoken; fare you well now:—and yet, ere I go, let me go with that I came for, which is, with knowing what hath passed between you and Claudio.

Bene. Only foul words; and thereupon I will kiss thee.

Beat. Foul words is but foul wind, and foul wind is but foul breath, and foul breath is noisome; therefore I will depart unkiss'd.

Bene. Thou hast frighted the word out of his right sense, so forcible is thy wit: But, I must tell thee plainly, Claudio undergoes my challenge; and either I must shortly hear from him, or I will subscribe him a coward. And, I pray thee now, tell me, for which of my bad parts didst thou first fall in love with me?

Beat. For them all together; which maintain'd so politick a state of evil, that they will not admit any good part to intermingle with them. But for which of my good parts did you first suffer love for me?

Bene. *Suffer love*; a good epithet! I do suffer love, indeed, for I love thee against my will.

Beat. In spite of your heart, I think; alas! poor heart! If you spite it for my sake, I will spite it for yours; for I will never love that which my friend hates.

Bene. Thou and I are too wise to woo peaceably.

Beat. It appears not in this confession: there's not one wise man among twenty, that will praise himself.

Bene. An old, an old instance, Beatrice, that lived in the time of good neighbours: if a man do not erect in this age his own tomb ere he dies, he shall live no longer in monument, than the bell rings, and the widow weeps.

Beat. And how long is that, think you?

Bene. Question?—Why, an hour in clamour, and a quarter in rheum: Therefore it is most expedient for the wife, (if Don Worm, his conscience, find no impediment

to

to the contrary,) to be the trumpet of his own virtues,
as I am to myſelf: So much for praiſing myſelf, (who, I
myſelf will bear witneſs, is praiſe-worthy,) and now tell
me, How doth your couſin ?

Beat. Very ill.

Bene. And how do you ?

Beat. Very ill too.

Bene. Serve God, love me, and mend : there will I leave
you too, for here comes one in haſte.

Enter URSULA.

Urſ. Madam, you muſt come to your uncle ; yonder's
old coil at home : it is proved, my lady Hero hath been
falſely accuſed, the prince and Claudio mightily abuſed ;
and Don John is the author of all, who is fled and gone :
Will you come preſently?

Beat. Will you go hear this news, ſignior ?

Bene. I will live in thy heart, die in thy lap, and be
buried in thy eyes; and, moreover, I will go with thee to
thy uncle's. [*Exeunt.*

SCENE III.

The Inſide of a Church.

Enter Don PEDRO, CLAUDIO, *and Attendants with muſick
and tapers.*

Claud. Is this the monument of Leonato ?

Atten. It is, my lord.

Claud. [*Reads from a ſcroll.*]

> *Done to death by ſlanderous tongues*
>   *Was the Hero that here lies:*
> *Death, in guerdon of her wrongs,*
>   *Gives her fame which never dies:*

So the life, that died with shame,
Lives in death with glorious fame.

Hang thou there upon the tomb,   [affixing it.
Praising her when I am dumb.—

Now, mufick, found, and fing your folemn hymn.

SONG.

Pardon, Goddefs of the night,
Thofe that flew thy virgin knight;
For the which, with fongs of woe,
Round about her tomb they go.
Midnight, affift our moan;
Help us to figh and groan,
Heavily, heavily:
Graves, yawn, and yield your dead,
Till death be uttered,
Heavily, heavily.

Claud. Now, unto thy bones good night!
        Yearly will I do this rite.
D. Pedro. Good morrow, mafters; put your torches out:
    The wolves have prey'd; and look, the gentle day,
Before the wheels of Phœbus, round about
    Dapples the drowfy eaft with fpots of grey:
Thanks to you all, and leave us; fare you well.
Claud. Good morrow, mafters; each his feveral way.
    D. Pedro. Come, let us hence, and put on other weeds;
And then to Leonato's we will go.
    Claud. And, Hymen, now with luckier iffue fpeed's,
Than this, for whom we render'd up this woe! [*Exeunt.*

SCENE

SCENE IV.

A Room in LEONATO's *Houſe.*

Enter LEONATO, ANTONIO, BENEDICK, BEATRICE, URSULA, Friar, *and* HERO.

Friar. Did I not tell you ſhe was innocent ?

Leon. So are the prince and Claudio, who accus'd her,
Upon the error that you heard debated :
But Margaret was in ſome fault for this ;
Although againſt her will, as it appears
In the true courſe of all the queſtion.

Ant. Well, I am glad that all things ſort ſo well.

Bene. And ſo am I, being elſe by faith enforc'd
To call young Claudio to a reckoning for it.

Leon. Well, daughter, and you gentlewomen all,
Withdraw into a chamber by yourſelves ;
And, when I ſend for you, come hither maſk'd :
The prince and Claudio promis'd by this hour
To viſit me :—You know your office, brother ;
You muſt be father to your brother's daughter,
And give her to young Claudio.   [*Exeunt Ladies.*

Ant. Which I will do with confirm'd countenance.

Bene. Friar, I muſt entreat your pains, I think.

Friar. To do what, ſignior ?

Bene. To bind me, or undo me, one of them.—
Signior Leonato, truth it is, good ſignior,
Your niece regards me with an eye of favour.

Leon. That eye my daughter lent her; 'Tis moſt true.

Bene. And I do with an eye of love requite her.

Leon. The ſight whereof, I think, you had from me,
From Claudio, and the prince ; But what's your will ?

Bene. Your anſwer, ſir, is enigmatical :

G 2   But,

But, for my will, my will is, your good will
May ftand with ours, this day to be conjoin'd
I ı the ftate of honourable marriage ;—
In which, good friar, I fhall defire your help.
   Leon. My heart is with your liking.
   Friar.   And my help.
Here comes the prince, and Claudio.

   Enter Don PEDRO, *and* CLAUDIO, *with Attendants.*

   D. Pedro. Good morrow to this fair affembly.
   Leon. Good morrow, prince; good morrow, Claudio;
We here attend you; Are you yet determin'd
To-day to marry with my brother's daughter?
   Claud. I'll hold my mind, were fhe an Ethiop.
   Leon. Call her forth, brother, here's the friar ready.
                                 [*Exit* ANTONIO.
   D. Pedro. Good morrow, Benedick: Why, what's the
      matter,
That you have fuch a February face,
So full of froft, of ftorm, and cloudinefs?
   Claud. I think, he thinks upon the favage bull :—
Tufh, fear not, man, we'll tip thy horns with gold,
And all Europa fhall rejoice at thee;
As once Europa did at lufty Jove,
When he would play the noble beaft in love.
   Bene. Bull Jove, fir, had an amiable low;
And fome fuch ftrange bull leap'd your father's cow,
And got a calf in that fame noble feat,
Much like to you, for you have juft his bleat.

   Re-enter ANTONIO, *with the Ladies mafk'd.*

   Claud. For this I owe you: here come other reckonings.
Which is the lady I muft feize upon?
   Ant. This fame is fhe, and I do give you her,
                                   Claud.

Claud. Why, then she's mine : Sweet, let me see your face.

Leon. No, that you shall not, till you take her hand
Before this friar, and swear to marry her.

Claud. Give me your hand before this holy friar;
I am your husband, if you like of me.

Hero. And when I liv'd, I was your other wife :
          [*Unmasking.*
And when you lov'd, you were my other husband.

Claud. Another Hero?

Hero.   Nothing certainer :
One Hero died defil'd; but I do live,
And, surely as I live, I am a maid.

D. Pedro. The former Hero! Hero that is dead!

Leon. She died, my lord, but whiles her slander liv'd.

Friar. All this amazement can I qualify;
When, after that the holy rites are ended,
I'll tell you largely of fair Hero's death :
Mean time, let wonder seem familiar,
And to the chapel let us presently.

Bene. Soft and fair, friar.—Which is Beatrice?

Beat. I answer to that name; [*Unmasking.*] What is
  your will?

Bene. Do not you love me?

Beat.   No, no more than reason.

Bene. Why, then your uncle, and the prince, and Claudio,
Have been deceived; for they swore you did.

Beat. Do not you love me?

Bene.   No, no more than reason.

Beat. Why, then my cousin, Margaret, and Ursula,
Are much deceiv'd; for they did swear, you did.

Bene. They swore that you were almost sick for me.

Beat. They swore that you were well-nigh dead for me.

Bene. 'Tis no such matter :—Then, you do not love me?

Beat. No, truly, but in friendly recompence.

            Leon.

Leon. Come, coufin, I am fure you love the gentleman.

Claud. And I'll be fworn upon't, that he loves her;
For here's a paper, written in his hand,
A halting fonnet of his own pure brain,
Fashion'd to Beatrice.

Hero. And here's another,
Writ in my coufin's hand, ftolen from her pocket,
Containing her affection unto Benedick.

Bene. A miracle! here's our own hands againft our
hearts!—Come, I will have thee; but, by this light, I
take thee for pity.

Beat. I would not deny you;—but, by this good day,
I yield upon great perfuafion; and, partly, to fave your
life, for I was told you were in a confumption.

Bene. Peace, I will ftop your mouth.— [*Kiffing her.*

D. Pedro. How doft thou, Benedick the married man?

Bene. I'll tell thee what, prince; a college of wit-
crackers cannot flout me out of my humour: Doft thou
think, I care for a fatire, or an epigram? No: if a man
will be beaten with brains, he fhall wear nothing handfome about him: In brief, fince I do purpofe to marry, I
will think nothing to any purpofe that the world can fay
againft it; and therefore never flout at me for what I have
faid againft it; for man is a giddy thing, and this is my
conclufion.—For thy part, Claudio, I did think to have
beaten thee; but in that thou art like to be my kinfman,
live unbruis'd, and love my coufin.

Claud. I had well hoped, thou would'ft have denied
Beatrice, that I might have cudgell'd thee out of thy fingle
life, to make thee a double dealer; which, out of queftion, thou wilt be, if my coufin do not look exceeding
narrowly to thee.

Bene. Come, come, we are friends:—let's have a dance

ere

ere we are married, that we may lighten our own hearts, and our wives' heels.

Leon. We'll have dancing afterwards.

Bene. Firſt, o' my word; therefore, play, muſick.— Prince, thou art ſad; get thee a wife, get thee a wife: there is no ſtaff more reverend than one tipp'd with horn.

Enter a Meſſenger.

Meſſ. My lord, your brother John is ta'en in flight, And brought with armed men back to Meſſina.

Bene. Think not on him till to-morrow; I'll deviſe thee brave puniſhments for him.—Strike up, pipers.

                              [*Dance. Exeunt.*

Lightning Source UK Ltd.
Milton Keynes UK
UKHW012358020119
334667UK00008B/1004/P